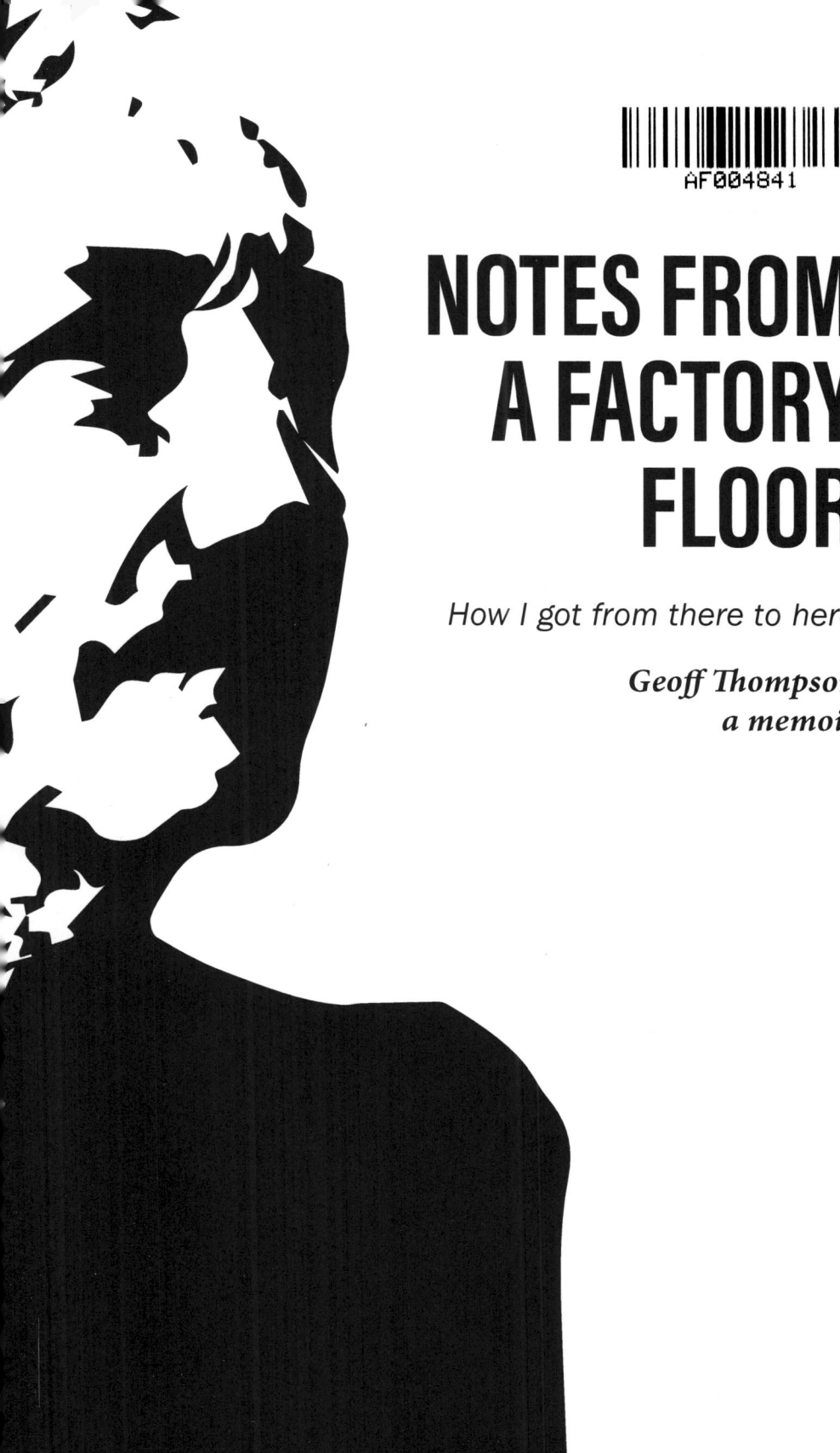

NOTES FROM A FACTORY FLOOR

How I got from there to here

Geoff Thompson
a memoir

NOTES FROM A FACTORY FLOOR

How I got from there to here

Geoff Thompson
a memoir

Geoff Thompson Ltd.

First published in Great Britain in 2020 by Urbane Publications Ltd
Unit E3 The Premier Centre Abbey Park Romsey SO51 9DG

Copyright © Geoff Thompson, 2020

The moral right of Geoff Thompson to be identified as the author of this work has been asserted in accordance with the Copyright, Designs and Patents Act of 1988.

All rights reserved. No part of this publication may be reproduced, stored in a retrieval system, or transmitted in any form or by any means, electronic, mechanical, photocopying, recording or otherwise, without the prior permission of both the copyright owner and the above publisher of this book.

A CIP catalogue record for this book is available from the British Library.

ISBN 978-1-916499-82-9
MOBI 978-1-912666-72-0

Design and Typeset by Michelle Morgan

Cover by Paul Shammasian and Michelle Morgan

Printed and bound by 4edge Limited,UK

Find Geoff on Instagram
#geoff_thompson_official

CONTENTS

PREFACE	p.1
INTRODUCTION	p.3
CHAPTER ONE. The End and the Beginning	p.10
CHAPTER TWO. The Depression	p.14
CHAPTER THREE. Climbing the Fear Pyramid	p.24
CHAPTER FOUR. Changes	p.34
CHAPTER FIVE. The Door Years	p.40
CHAPTER SIX. Watch My Back	p.62
CHAPTER SEVEN. About Sharon	p.78
CHAPTER EIGHT. Getting Published	p.88
CHAPTER NINE. Martial Arts, Metaphysics and a Chuck Norris	p.108
CHAPTER TEN. Post Vegas Epiphany	p.145
CHAPTER ELEVEN. The Writing	p.163
CHAPTER TWELVE. Invitation to The Royal Court Theatre	p.186
CHAPTER THIRTEEN. A Thirty-Two City Book Tour	p.193
CHAPTER FOURTEEN. Bouncer: My First Short Film	p.201
CHAPTER FIFTEEN. The Atonement Years	p.215
CHAPTER SIXTEEN. Clubbed.	p.237
CHAPTER SEVENTEEN. The National Theatre Studio	p.298
AFTERWORD	p.324

To God, my eternal Father and benefactor.

To Sharon, my love, my counsel.

Preface

People are forever bumping into me in the street - old friends, associates, folk from my past - and I can tell within seconds of our encounter, from their dissonant bearing, and the redundant enquiries, that the character they are talking to is not the man they remember from before. The Geoff Thompson they expect to engage can vary wildly, depending on what they know me for, where they know me from and what they know me as: Geoff the council-estate kid, Geoff the factory worker, Geoff the hod carrier, Geoff the bricklayer, Geoff the heavyset, knuckle-dragging bouncer (a lot of people come looking for the bouncer; they always leave disappointed). They look for Geoff the karate man, Geoff the guru and more recently, but less frequently they come searching for Geoff the writer.

It is not surprising that the man they seek is not the man they find. I have changed my reality more times than most people change their cars. It would seem however that not everyone got the memo, and of those that did, only a rare few have taken heed. Many of my friends have either not changed, or they have changed, but not in line with me; certainly their rise has been out of step with mine.

I have changed so radically over the years that when people come looking for the character I used to be, they can't find him; the me of old is no longer there. They scan me quizzically, these kindly folks, searching for the personality they remember, the identity that corresponds with their recollection of me in time and space. Then they initiate a conversation with the ghost of an old incarnation about a subject that was buried with the cadaver of my past. People I meet are stuck at various stations of my life that were pertinent to them but are no longer relevant to me. They always have that same, strange searching expression on their face, as though I look vaguely like the Geoff Thompson they remember but I am patently not the Geoff Thompson they knew.

It happened again only the other day when I was in Leamington, a delightful spa town, just down the road from where I live. Whilst queuing for a cup of tea I was approached by a genial man who tried to converse with *Geoff the self-defence teacher*. After fencing off a couple of naive questions about personal security, hardcore combatives and 'what techniques work on the street', I politely informed him that Geoff Thompson the self-defence guru was gone ('that parrot is dead!'), he is no more, but, FYI, he has left the crumbs of his path in books and videos and podcasts and articles and interviews that will comprehensively answer any questions he might like answered; questions that I had no interest in fielding in a café where I'd hoped to be anonymous.

No complaints and no judgment. It is absolutely usual for us to trek the same mountain as our friends and peers, but from a different aspect, and at varying rates of ascent. That is why I have written this book. I wanted to bring people up to date with where I am now, and with who I am at this moment in time.

It is probable that you may not know me at all, and that this is your first experience of the world of Geoff Thompson.

Perhaps you have never read a book written by me, or watched a film that came from my pen, or sat through a stage play that I poured years into producing. For those of you who are not familiar with me, who do not know my life, there are many other worthy reasons for regarding this book. I am sure you are already aware of what these might be otherwise why would you be holding this tome?

Hopefully this new telling will bring anyone interested in my path up to date with the ever-evolving status of my identity. Although, by the time you read this book, and percolate on the stories I am about to share, I can't guarantee that I will not have reduced again. The Geoff you find in these pages will likely be an entirely different man to the one you bump into in the street.

Introduction

I am often asked, at book signings, at screenings of my films, performances of my plays, at public speaking events, even in anonymous cafés where people find me at a table savouring a coffee and reading a book, how did I manoeuvre myself from a shitty room in a Coventry bedsit to the hallowed halls of BAFTA Piccadilly? How did I transcend my designated class and matriculate into, if not a higher class or a different class, certainly a world where class holds no relevance? Not that it no longer exists in the world, only that it no longer lives in the world of me. How did I negotiate the terrain and what happened along the way to that snotty comprehensive kid, brought up on a council estate, herded by conditioning, shackled by the prevailing culture, denied his potentials, tethered at the ankle to the ball-and-chain of social mores, the crippling encumbrance of my station? What was the trajectory, who did I meet along the way (the angels and demons of my destiny), what monsters did I encounter and what of the saints?

What are my field notes, the essential lessons of my pilgrimage, the essence of my 'hero's journey'?

Or more succinctly, and in the words of William Morris; now that I have made it this far, 'what do I actually know?'

Mirroring Chinese literature, I'd like to start by presenting a brief overview that will be accurate in its chronology. Once I've outlined the arc of my story, I will endeavour to articulate my notes, my experiences and my learning (what I know) in a more spontaneous and random manner.

This may not be what a conventional book needs, but it will be what I want to write. It'll provide a general outline to my story, a narrative-skeleton that I can flesh out and sculpt and dress with the muscle and skin of experiential detail.

Also, it will give me – and you - an idea of where I'm heading.

The mass of my words will be about what the book wants…which may not be what I want, but it will be what I need.

When I say *need*, I do mean that in the literal sense; what I need to remember, what I need to write, what I need to hear, what I need to understand or expose or clarify or articulate.

Ultimately it will be what I need to re-experience and atone.

I have left some damage along my path.

I have hurt people.

This needs to be addressed if my book is to be worth the ink and paper that you hold in your hand, if it is to be deemed worthy of your investment of money and time.

I have atoned some in the last 20 years of personal cleansing. Much of it not pretty to look at - certainly the detail would be unfit for a keynote speech or a Ted talk or dinner party repartee.

I guess that's why beginning this book is filling me with trepidation. I'm worried that some of the bodies I reveal in this historical dig might still have some life in them. The dead (as Jung said) will have their say; we can never truly get away from the fact that we will always be dealing with the dead, our ancestors, and the unpaid Karma left on our debit sheet.

So, overall, the order of events may be mixed up. Stories will be recalled as they present themselves. Lessons will be shared when the landscape demands it.

Beginning and end - the arc of my story - will probably meet, hopefully in a pleasing finale, but I can't guarantee it. All I can promise is that I will tell the truth, the whole truth and nothing but the truth.

This book is biographical. I will only relate and retell what I have experienced personally and what I know to be true. Certainly, it will be categorical to what I know to be true right now.

All truths are intermediary and those that are not can never be articulated, let alone written down in a book.

Chronologically, this latest book starts where my first book *Watch My Back* (the anecdotal tales of my life as a bouncer) left off. But I'd like to begin if I may, one step removed from that, before I even contemplated manning a nightclub door, let alone writing a memoir about it.

I'd like to begin with depression.

This story really starts where my last episode of manic depression ended. It was unequivocally the major turning point of my life.

Society tends to view the arrival of depression as a harbinger, announcing the end of life as we know it. We suspect, but rarely announce, that once the black crow of mental illness has us in its beak, she will never let us go, and our only hiding place will be under the chemical blanket of drink, drugs or the *rock-and-roll* of excessive human consumption. Whether our narcotic of choice is found on the print of a doctor's prescription, in the bottom of a whisky glass or at the sharp end of a dirty needle the resulting numbness is the same.

Let me tell you what most of us fear when depression calls. Certainly this was my designated blackmailer, the internal voice that assailed me in those darker times: *you can never escape me.*

The *black dog* of melancholy hounds its victims with the menace of a scriptural demon. We live in terror of its promised perpetuity; now that it has found us once surely it will know how to find us again and again ad infinitum.

As convincing as its rhetoric is - and many suffer lives of quiet desperation because they believe its lie - it is not true, and I am the living proof.

Up until this time, I had suffered many depressions, each deeper and each darker than the last. They just seemed to appear, these black forces, these ravaging vandals, uninvited, and out of the blue. They would arrive with much noise and tumult and without any prior notice: no introduction, no kiss-my-arse, nothing. They just turned up, kicked down the mind-door and took my mental fortitude by storm. They would steal into my mind like enemy crusaders, colonising my body and soul, they wreaked havoc, they raped and they pillaged, they bled my vital resources until I was spent, a dry human husk, a staggering extra in my very own version of *The Walking Dead*. Then, when they were good and ready - and not a moment before - they would swagger away again, those arrogant bastards, temporarily sated, but always with the smug assurance that they would come back again, if not sooner definitely later, and there would be nothing I could do to stop it.

On this final visit something in me changed.

I did something spontaneous, something brave and radical; instead of turning away from the adverse forces that pilloried me, I turned into them instead. Rather than trying to blanket them mute with the usual suspects of prescribed medication, self-medication and a cocktail of temporary balm-fixes - sex, self-elected seclusion and the suspension of all normal living - I went cold turkey and met this gunslinger-enemy at my own personal O.K. Corral for a Tombstone style showdown. In other words, instead of looking away, I looked deeply into my own feelings and anxieties and fears. Instead of running away from fear, I ran towards it. Rather than recoil from *my wonderful creation* I embraced it. Instead of closing my eyes I started to live with my eyes wide open. I had tried to close my ears many times before to the caterwaul of depressive sirens, all to no avail. In fact, the attempted evasion only added volume to my fears. This time I opened my ears and sharpened the acoustic, I leaned in instead of leaning out, I listened, and for the first time in my whole life I embraced this dark angel and said *OK, you are here again. You are here. Come in. Sit down. Let me take care of you. What have you got to say to me, what do you want me to see? Deliver your message, show me your wares.*

I was shocked to realise that the moment I confronted my fears head-on, they diminished substantially.

Perhaps depression was not the mythical harbinger of doom after all; maybe it was a projection from my own mind, seeking desperately to speak with me, trying hard to find a common language in order to impart an uncommon truth.

I don't know exactly, all I am sure of is this: the leper of my fear turned into the Christ of my potential the moment I embraced it.

Intuitively - and it was definitely an intuitive gift, I had never consciously thought of doing anything remotely like this before - I wrote down all my fears on a piece of paper and I confronted them systematically, one by one, gaining desensitisation and courage and developing technique and confidence, and awareness along the way, until I reached my ultimate fear: violent confrontation.

To overcome this final dread I took a job as a nightclub bouncer and spent a decade going toe-to-toe with the multi-faceted manifestations of my mind-projected monsters. This led me to telling my story *The Hero's Journey* to my peers over breakfast in the factory canteen. I also perfected my storytelling on the growing army of martial arts students that had gathered around me looking for meaningful instruction, searching for truthful, useful and potent modalities. Eventually my experiences matriculated to the printed page: I wrote a book about my adventures called *Watch My Back: A Bouncer's Story*. It was written on three cheap reporters' pads using a Bic pen. I wrote it whilst working in an engineering factory that paid me to clean around oily lathes, and labour for hardy drillers who spent 10 hours of every day making precise manifolds for smart cars that they would never be able to afford, unless the lottery finger pointed in their direction. In fact, that was it …the factory or the lottery. My office was a locked cubicle, my desk a piece of discarded cardboard, balanced on clenched knees, and my seat was a throne, no less, cast from the very best white porcelain, and provided by (my sponsor) Armitage Shanks.

I wrote my first book on a factory toilet!

It took me several months to complete that first, handwritten draft.

It was written in 1988 and published four years later in 1992. It is an early biography about the battle with depression, and my adventures in the world of nightclub bouncing. At the time I wrote it I was still in my first marriage. I was working in the factory by day and standing on club doors by night.

My children were at school, not yet teenagers. I was thirty-two years old when I left the factories, when I left the doors and (unfortunately) when I left my first marriage.

A lot has happened since then...

I became a published author, a hard man of repute, a leading martial arts teacher, an entrepreneur and business owner, a journalist, a publisher, a playwright, a screenwriter, a blogger, a self-help guru and all round buccaneer. I have been a good guy for brief ecstatic moments. For ten long years I was the bad guy, up to my neck in the boiling rivers of blood and fire of Dante's seventh circle. I corresponded with the notorious gangster Reggie Kray by letter and telephone, and shared a dangerous repartee with Ronnie Biggs and Mad Frankie Fraser in a Talk Radio sound booth. I have made real fast money and lost the same money real fast (I started with nothing, and I still have most of it left). I have won some virtue, and sold my integrity to the highest bidder, loved people half to death, and hated the same people with equal fervour and killed everything good we shared.

I studied Judo full time for two years under the greatest occidental judoka of his generation (Neil Adams): I won a black belt and two cauliflower ears.

I had tea in Las Vegas with Chuck Norris.

I experienced an epiphany that set me on a path of spiritual redemption and painful atonement.

I was invited into the Royal Court Young Writers Group in London.

The legendary actor Pete Postlethwaite recited lines to me from my first stage play (*Doorman*) in a London pub. I choreographed Ray Winstone in a fight scene on a beer-sticky pub carpet and wrestled outside the same bar with Paddy Considine (shooting my first film *Bouncer*). I went to the BAFTAs (twice) had a West End launch for my first movie (*Clubbed*) and visited Paris for the premier of the same film. I published forty-five books, made ten films, penned numerous stage plays and toured them nationally, acted in a pop video with the rapper Kano, wrote an acclaimed musical (just to prove I could), and choreographed a West End play (just because I was asked). I wrote an award-winning feature length monologue for actor James Cosmo, filmed in one location, shot in black and white. I worked with Orlando Bloom on my third feature film about the metaphysical power of forgiveness... there's a lot I haven't written about yet.

There is a lot still to say.

That is the basic arc of this book.

Along the way the learning, ah man the learning! The learning has been immense. It has been exciting and it has expanded me beyond measure.

In the rest of the book I will cover this arc in more detail and expand and expound on the essentials of my own personal odyssey. This is as much for my benefit as it is for you, the reader.

I want to understand what happened to me, the how and the why; if I can articulate it for you I can crystallise it within myself.

For the new journey to begin the old story has to end.

What better way of ending the old story than with a new book, a book of truth, my notes. My notes from a factory toilet.

The End and the Beginning

I hesitate to sit down. I err in preparation of peeling away the cellophane around my very posh notepads (Moleskin - a gift, a prompt, from a friend, a little nudge 'write...for fuck's sake write') revealing the virgin pages, unsheathing my quality pen (a gift from my mum, 'write!') and creating a connection between the ink and the page, the hand and the mind, and the mind with my God. It is always a delicious agony when the force of Nature uses me as a force for good.

I was going to delay the writing. I was planning to wait until the conditions were right, and the muse was present and the lighting perfect and the wind was blowing in the right direction, and the mood settled, when all of those spurious jobs (the delicious distractions) were completed; later today, tomorrow morning, next week, next year. But I already knew that delay would not serve my cause, it would only add the unnecessary weight of anticipation to the heavy workload I am being called to undertake. I am too wizened and too seasoned and too savvy to be rustled like cattle by the cowboy of procrastination. I have lost too many hours, and more than one golden opportunity, when hesitation led to cancellation and the muse alighted in the pen of a more alert scribe, a more courageous writer.

The timing for creativity is rarely right, I have found; certainly the conditions are never quite how I would like them to be. Perhaps I am not waiting for the muse at all, rather the muse is waiting for me and my lower community of lazy postponements to get in line and stay in line. I quietly suspect that my rag-tag of old perceptions, fears, outdated beliefs and ancient conditioning has probably invented the muse as a literary scapegoat, an outer-force that I can blame when my inner-will is too slack to do the work, and too scared to admit it.

I kidded myself that the weather was too warm to sit down today and write, the sun in my garden was calling me to leisure not labour; a cup of tea with one of those healthy vegan snacks that my daughter Kerry keeps making for me was the order of the day. And anyway, there was no point (was there?) in starting a new project today, when I knew I'd have to break my rhythm as soon as tomorrow. I was mentoring a friend in London. It had been in the diary for a month. No need to start today, I told myself, I could start tomorrow. I could stop off at Waterstones in Piccadilly while I was in town, pick up (another) one of those vacuum packs of new Moleskins, and start writing on the train journey home. If I booked first class, off-peak, Branson often proffered me four seats for the price of one - sometimes I'd get a whole carriage to myself. All that room to spread out, all that time to pontificate. Surely this represented the perfect conditions to start a book that I had been putting off and hiding from for years.

Ah, tomorrow, tomorrow, if only I was so easy to deceive.

Experience has shown me that *tomorrow* is an arrogant conceit.

I have seen enough young friends expire decades before their due date - because of accidental illness or wild folly - to know that tomorrow is guaranteed to no creature. How urgently they would re-order their schedule of priorities, I am certain, if tragedy had not intervened, and yanked them soul from coil whilst they were busy making plans and busier still not carrying them out. Any of us could be ripped out of the corner of our kitchen this very afternoon and thrust into the room of scales with no prior warning, of that I am sure. And I already know from my study into the esoteric that the room of scales is also the room of queues: two queues to be specific.

In the bardo, the very long queue is designated for *excuse makers*.

We should never be excuse makers.

Procrastination is one of the weapons used by God's master swordsmen - the adverse forces - and they use it to defeat us or teach us how to perfect our own weapons.

I kid myself that I need the right conditions, the right equipment, the right atmosphere before I can place pen to pad. If my life has taught me one thing it is this: if there are conditions at all, those conditions are created by me, the tools can be obtained for next to nothing at any local stationers, and if there is a favouring atmosphere, I am the one who creates it, I am the one who brings it; everything else is just weak rationalisation, weak will and lack of personal sovereignty.

All I needed to write my first book was a purpose that was strong enough to overpower the prevailing mores; when the purpose was in place, the rest came to me as easy as breathing.

So, I fill the first lines on an empty pad that just happened to be lying on my desk, with a lovely pen my mum bought me (to tell our stories) and I begin, writing a book I am very afraid to write. No adjournments or postponements or re-scheduling, no 'putting off 'til tomorrow' because that would be an insult to every conscious cell that resides in me and every single body that resides without.

I am afraid of this book because even in its contemplation I know that I am going 'once more unto the breach'. I know I will have to tell the truth, no fibs, no half-truths; certainly no blood-red lies.

Already I can feel an invisible queue forming inside me, outside of me and all around. I can hear the lauding compliments and a caterwaul of complaints. My inner community, some of whom are cheering (this book offers them a way out, redemption), others are screaming (to the adverse forces in me, revelation equals desolation), and more than one voice is packing its bags ready to go into hiding, hoping that my *urge to purge* somehow misses them this time around and they get to live another day.

In this outing I'd like to fill the gaps between my first book three decades ago and my life now, forty published books on, and many reinventions later.

A lot has happened to me in the last thirty years.

Part of the intimidation with this undertaking is not so much in knowing what I should say. I like to speak and I speak often. I know what I should say, I just don't know where I should start. There have been so many happenings, so many experiences, so many incarnations, even within my short six decades, that remembering them all, and putting them in to the right order seems a gargantuan task.

So, I've decided not to worry too much about chronology and concentrate instead on essence; the essential learning that my eventful life has offered. It will help me to disseminate and panhandle and sort my experiences in order to separate the gravel from the silt and sift out those nuggets of gold. I hope too, that this writing will help my children and my grandchildren, who may at some point, during my lifetime or after my death, come to this writing, pore over the words presented here and take some nourishment from them. Others too, now and in the future, might benefit from the words on the page. More than anything I pray that, if nothing else, my honest confessions might atone for some of the many crimes I committed. Certainly I hope that it will help refine and perfect me, and perhaps transport me one step closer to the Omega Point, my Home.

If there is one thing I have learned from my life this time around, it is that Home is the ultimate destination for all wayfaring souls.

2

The Depression

I have changed bodies many times over the last six decades, my physicality transfiguring and shapeshifting according to the shifting sands of my ever-evolving perceptions. Whilst my body has changed as often as the weather, my aspiration to be someone and do something vital with my life has remained a steady constant, a sleeping backboard to the ever-changing wardrobe of my first thirty years.

As a young damaged kid, I was skinny and bony with long hair and a middle parting that I combed and shampooed and coiffed to distraction. I had a pretty face; people often mistook me for a girl. Even at the working men's club where I was taught how to drink pints and throw darts and chalk scores and bang snooker balls around a green baize, older men would stagger over to me on or near the dance floor, spastic drunk and ask me for a dance. A dance! Me! I was a boy. My dad always looked embarrassed when grown men mistook me for a young girl; 'he's a boy' he'd say apologetically. And when the message didn't penetrate the layers of inebriation he'd re-iterate 'no, honestly he *is* a boy'. He'd repeat it until the drunk staggered off, bumping into tables, looking for a real girl.

Later I became athletic - still skinny, still scared, but fitter and more muscular, with disproportionate chest muscles, the result of thousands of reps on a makeshift bench press in our garage. My mum had bought me a Weider weight training kit for Christmas and the only exercise I knew was the bench.

Later still, barely sixteen, I met Nina at The Red Lion pub. By seventeen she was pregnant with our first child, Kerry, and by eighteen we were married, living with my parents and dreaming of one day getting our own council flat; we were on the housing list. My aspirations for worldly success completely outweighed any ability I had to deliver them. As a consequence, my grand ambitions to be someone - a martial arts champion, a self-employed *something*, a writer - went into hibernation. The black dog of depression - my perennial bully- was the natural consequence of allowing my wild and untrammelled imagination to write cheques that this young father and dissatisfied factory worker was unable to cash.

At this point, I feel compelled to interject and let you know that success in life, whatever that means to you, is possible. It is possible, even if it's not probable. What you want, what you aspire to, your dreams and ambitions, those aspirations that keep you awake at night, they are definitely and unequivocally available. The fact that most people do not fully or even partially realise their goals is no refutation of potential. If you doubt the possibility of all things, you need only look out of your window at the vast and beautiful universe, filled to the brim and over, with *all* things.

The proof is there for everyone to see.

More on this later...

For now, my later incarnation and re-incarnation into the many changing faces of Geoff Thompson was temporarily stalled. Instead I played at being a husband, and tried at being a dad, and took a responsible job, just as I'd been schooled to. I was a bony teenage husband and father, transported occasionally out of my distracted mind by the dreams and ambitions of youth and then hounded back into domesticity and normality, by the dreads and fears of conditioning. This was the shape I made at the time, and it was the same shape as all my peers, the one we'd been trained into from birth. But I always felt misshapen. My naturally sharp edges, the burrs and nicks and quirks of who I really was, were filed flat by the prevailing mores, just so that I could be squeezed into the wrong hole of the wrong jigsaw in the wrong life.

It is discomforting for me to see these words written on the page.

They make me sound disingenuous and selfish and ungrateful for the blessings of a beautiful wife, and my wonderful children. When I was first married, I loved my wife very much, I was smitten. She was seventeen when we married, and I was eighteen. By the time we reached twenty, we were two very different people. Any allure, any desire and respect she might have held for me at seventeen had been lost in the rush of those few years, and I spent most of my time wondering where it had all gone and what I might have done to discredit myself in her eyes. Naively, I concluded that my situation was probably normal, everyone I knew was quietly discontented, and as far as I could see, all men had to beg for sex, and all men felt humiliated and emasculated and full of self-hatred post coitus. It was normal. Looking back of course I can see that it was not normal in any sense of the word. I think my young wife was probably suffering with post-natal depression at the time, and I didn't know how to recognise the signs, let alone help her through it. My requests for the great sex we used to share must have been vexing for her. Why was I pushing her for intercourse, couldn't I see how unhappy she was? At the age of twenty one, I did not have the maturity to read this, and I don't think she hated me exactly, but I do think that her depression made her feel as though she did. Either way, she told me that I made her skin crawl, so for me her repulsion was a reality. But my kids, ah man, they were (they are) such beautiful souls. They were and they remain my life. I was never ungrateful, or disingenuous, but I was confused, and I was selfish. I was little more than a child myself at the time; I don't think I knew how to be anything else. Later I learned that selfishness - *proper selfishness*, as Charles Handy might say - is not such a bad thing. In fact when it is directed towards Truth it leads us to an authentic life.

Behind the veil of humdrum normality I always felt a powerful life force. I have always felt it and I have always been afraid of its might. It was urging me, prompting me, pushing me towards something bigger, something better, a supernormal or supernatural form of existence that lay just beyond the pale of my working life. But every time it peeped its head above the parapet of my sleepy consciousness to remind me of potential, it was hammered back into darkness by the culling mallet of conditioning, the voice of fear that told me to *Get your head out of your arse: be grateful for what you've got: don't get above your station: and who the fuck do you think you are anyway?*

So conditioned domesticity acted as a temporary freezing agent to my growth. My potential was put into suspended animation, and I remained the same stalled shape until another black dog of depression woke me with a start and took me to the darkest place in my life so far. It visited me when I was working shifts at a chemical factory in the suburbs of Coventry, where the smells and sounds of big industry forced local property prices into the ground and general stress levels through the firmament. As is the way with depression, it turned up out of the blue, when I least expected it, and took over my life. Despite being the darkest depression I had experienced thus far in my young life, and irrespective of the abject terror that raced through my veins like fire, I still went to work, I still trained in martial arts and I still turned up every day for my wife and for my kids and for my family, even though my days and weeks were minute to minute, hour to hour misery. I can remember doing everything possible to try and rid myself of this squatting, blackmailing miserable bastard of a visitor, crouched permanently at the doorway of my heart. I can remember scrubbing my skin red-raw in the shower in the hope that it might magically, miraculously cure my sadness and end my despair. It did not. It stayed. It bullied. It visited at all hours, this demon, this Dementor. It stayed in my body and mind rent free for as long as it wanted. And my defilement, this sullied thing within me, it had a voice, its own voice, and it would whisper its threats, its predictions, its opinions. It told me that I was a waste of life, that I was useless and dirty and disgusting. It promised me that if people knew the depth of my personal depravities, what I got up to privately, what I thought about in moments of sexual arousal, my mother would abandon me, my friends would despise me, my wife would disown me, she'd divorce me, dump me for someone else, anyone else, and I would become a leper in my own life, the man with no name, the untouchable that I already secretly believed I was.

My first, accidental victory over depression had occurred some years before this latest episode, when I was on holiday in exotic Skegness, with my wife and young daughters. I'd no sooner arrived at the cheap, anonymous caravan site on a tumbleweed seaside resort in the East of England, when the whisperer turned up. Just as I was settling into the rest and recuperation of our yearly holiday, I felt the ever so familiar tingle of melancholy, a drop of adrenalin, which was followed immediately by the inner voice of doom that informed me *I'm back*. Depression. The shade got to work quickly. As usual it promised me that it was going to stick around forever, it assured me that the assault would be severe, so acute in fact that it would devastate my holiday. In turn this would ruin the holiday for my wife (who didn't understand depression, it scared her, which made things feel worse) and it would spoil any chance of my kids enjoying themselves. It predicted that I would crumble under the weight of its attack, as I always did, I would be in agony (I always was), and two weeks would feel like *ten fucking years*. I'd be forced to abandon the holiday and go home - wife and kids in tow - beg the doctor for medication, swallow the chemically induced blanket and hide, hide, hide from the world.

I remember vividly that initial flush and rush of melancholy followed by the assault of hopelessness; dread was on its tail and the belief that, once I was netted by the force of depression, I would be hauled over the coals of a never-ending realm of sadness. Then I felt terror, terror, terror, real terror, terror that the world was inhospitable, terror that society was hostile, that its creatures were cruel and violent and inhuman; threat was lurking around every corner and it was specifically waiting for me.

Then I felt a new feeling.

It arose in me fast, out of nowhere. A flash, a fiery spike, a sentinel angel. It was an energy that I had not felt before in relation to depression. Anger. Actually, I felt rage! *How fucking dare you threaten the happiness of my wife and my children.* I turned on this whispering entity and I promised it that no matter what it said, no matter what it threatened or how bad I felt I would not, under any circumstances, spoil my family's holiday. In fact, I would not even mention to them that I felt depressed; I would not even allow it a voice in my world.

Boom! It went.

In a miraculous instant the depression, every last trace of it was gone, banished by a single unconscious act of selflessness, one single solitary stand of courage.

This was my first metaphysical encounter with an enemy that had always dominated me absolutely. This was when I first fought back, when I discovered a technique that actually worked against it. This would become part of my armoury, a weapon I'd hone, finesse and sharpen, a tool to call on in later encounters when my enemies were manifest and their threats real.

More on this later…

This was my first minor expansion in consciousness, in relation to dealing with the forces in me and the energies around me. My first *major* shapeshift or reincarnation happened, as I mentioned, when I was working shifts at the chemical factory. It was almost immediately after I won my first black belt in the art of Japanese Shotokan karate. I'd been dabbling in martial arts on and off since I was eleven years old. First I studied Aikido, then Shotokan, then Chinese Gung Fu and later I went back to Karate. I trained seriously and constantly and after three years of dedicated practice, I won my first senior belt in a demanding test under the legendary teacher Enoeda Sensei. I'd arrived (or at least I felt as though I'd arrived). I was a black belt; you don't get them from Sainsbury's, let me tell you. Not only was I a black belt but I was a black belt in an art and in an association (the KUGB) that was famous for its high standards and infamous for its intolerance of chancers. A Dan grade in Shotokan carried a guarantee of excellence. Nobody questioned it.

If, however, I thought my new silk belt and my teacher's certificate would act as a battle flag to ward off those adverse forces, I was in for a shock. They did not. If anything, the opposite was true. Before winning my black belt I was just scared; now I was a black belt who was scared. It mentally confused me. I was perplexed. I wasn't supposed to be afraid anymore. I was a qualified expert. I could kill with my bare hands. Milk curdled under my gaze. I was formidable. A warrior. The fear should have gone, that was the implicit deal, right? You win a black belt, you lose your fear, job done, move on, next challenge please. But, like the perennial weed that evades every effort to remove it, fear was ever there, just waiting to creep through the cracks. The dissonance exhausted me. It was so tiring, living a lie. Everyone thinking that you are a force to be reckoned with and you secretly knowing that the slightest breeze could still blow you over. I may have won some acclaim with my new grade, but I was still only a beginner in the greater jihad, the inner fight. I had no permanent centre yet, just a fancy exterior without foundation.

That was all to come. Later, when I learned the real secrets of fear, and developed an eye wall that could withstand the force of any storm, inner or outer.

But for now I was spent, and confused, questioning why my outer self and my inner self were so incongruent. Also, the massive over-training I'd undertaken to win my black belt had left me burnt out, and without guard. I was physically, emotionally and spiritually on my knees and once more depression entered through the cracks and spread through my bones like fire.

I was there again.

In that place.

Despair was my absolute bedfellow. Anonymity was the only thing that called me. Like the frightened Prince of Vedanta, Arjuna Pandava, I did not want my earthly kingdom, or any other. I wanted to run away, become a mendicant, a social outcast, roam the desert lands of despair, if needs be beg for my supper. I wanted a place to hide. Responsibility felt excruciatingly fearful. Work, family, friends, even taking a full breath was physically exhausting. Getting out of bed in the morning took superhuman effort; all I wanted to do was crawl under a rock, and disappear.

But I had things to do and places to go, ambitions, there was a whole life out there that needed living, I should not be feeling like this again.

I was a black belt for fuck's sake!

I felt like the biggest coward in the world.

When my brother Ray died at the tender age of forty-two, his death certificate said that he died from alcoholism, but I know he did not. I was with him when he left this mortal coil, and amongst the many truths he shared with me as he vacated his body was that he did not die from the drink, he died from the fear. Alcohol was the symptom; fear was the cause.

At the bottom of my pit of despair, bullied by my own body chemistry, taunted by the voices of my inner opponents and convinced that I was shit under the shoe of humanity, I found anger once again. Through anger came hope and hope brought with it, if not a specific destination, certainly a general direction. My anger may have had its origins in the carnal, but it was highly potent and pragmatically effective when taking on my nemesis, Depression. When I was at my lowest ebb, when I felt that all was lost, and life was a meaningless folly, all I remember thinking was, 'I'm not fucking having this anymore' (expletives used because expletives were present). Man, I was so angry, I can still feel it now as I write these words. It burned in me, it bubbled over, it spat out in every direction. I had a wife, I had kids, I had a job, I had a life and I was not prepared to give it all up because depression insisted or certainly implied that I should. Depression (I told myself) could go and fuck itself. I was not going to be subjugated by it any longer.

Anger was followed by a plan. Very basic at first, but obvious; if I had tried everything to get rid of depression – to wrap a black belt around it, smother it in tablets from the doctor, drown it with beer from the off licence, or escape it with the oily porn that was passed around the factory canteen - if I'd already tried to run from it and hide from it, and cower and beg and barter and bargain with it, if I had already done everything to avoid the feelings of this dark harbinger and it hadn't worked, what was left? What else could I do? What was the one thing that, until now, I had not even considered, because even the consideration was anathema?

An image flashed into my mind. It was prompting me to remember something important. An imperative. A secret that I'd learned long ago and forgotten, one that needed remembering again today, and every day for the rest of my life. I was standing in the playground at school. Cardinal Wiseman comprehensive in Coventry. It was a large expanse of tarmac, nestled between the classrooms and school buildings, an impromptu soccer pitch that twenty of us kicked a tennis ball around, scuffing our toes and dreaming of being George Best; possible, but not probable. Working class kids were schooled to leave education at sixteen and go straight to the prison of menial employment - do not pass Go, do not collect £200.

I'm in the playground, my first few weeks in the big school. I am overwhelmed by the volume, size, colours and hustle of this juvenile metropolis. I have only just left the familiar puddle of primary school and feel as though I am sinking in an ocean without landmarks. In common vernacular, I am shitting my shorts. I've arrived here from a small catholic primary where I had accidentally become the school god. I was goalkeeper for the first squad football team and not afraid to make a full body dive on the playground concrete; the girls loved me. I had a pretty face. I had a dark shining mane and I was blissfully happy in my small world.

At the big school I was not happy. I was invisible. Anonymous amongst the gods of every other primary in the district, who had all alighted in senior school at the same time on the same day. We shared a common playground with the second and third year students, right up to the sixth formers who were practically grown men compared to us pubeless plebs. Some of them sported beards; we didn't even have hair on our nuts yet. Many of them didn't even bother to wear school uniform. There were no girls in this forsaken apocalypse. Ours was a boy's only education. I was no god in this new kingdom, or a demigod, I was not even a serf. I was a spit of a boy, lost in an ocean of otherness.

This new world was all otherness.

New buildings, new teachers, new subjects, new clothes, new pen and pencil and ruler and rubber, new books to read, new exercise books with nothing yet written on the pages. I was separated from all of my old school friends, the boys and girls of my year who knew I was a god, *they knew*. This was the first time I ever remember not being the top boy.

This was my very first, undiagnosed experience with depression.

I wouldn't have called it that at eleven. I might have called it fear or sadness. If I'd had the lexicon, the mature articulation, I might have labelled myself lonely. Even though my two older brothers were at the same school, and even though my mum worked as the head cleaner at Wiseman, even though the playground was wall-to-wall adolescence, I was alone.

One of the other boys picked on me - this is the gist of my vision, the lesson I was prompted to recall. Obviously, no one had yet informed this lad of my god-like status in primary school so he judged as he found, and he found me lacking. I was fair game. A friend from my old junior school (who did know I was *someone*) noticed the bully and spotted my angst. He pulled me to one side: 'come with me,' he said 'let me show you something'. I followed him, weaving through the busy playground. He walked right over to the bully who was stood in a cluster of other eleven year olds. He poked the boy in the back, and when he turned around my erstwhile saviour said, 'Geoff wants a fight with you'.

I felt my lower apertures loosen, as my adrenalin did a lap of honour around my veins and through my lower intestines. I heard my internal dialogue scream, 'what!' But I didn't say a word. The bully looked at me; his face glowed in a blush of rude-red and he shook his head - he did not want to fight with me. As he walked away, my friend winked at me and said, 'I know him. He's a wanker. He always bottles it.'

I smiled.

My first lesson in what Victor Frankle would later call 'paradoxical intention'. If you stood before the thing or person you feared most, if you invited the fear in, rather than turning it away, fear would cease to exist. It would have no life because the oxygen that feeds fear comes from our own fearful and emotional engagement with it.

So this is where I found myself, in a corner, hemmed in on all sides by fears, shrunk by the terror of my own shadow. I felt like Reinhold Messner, the legendary climber when he got stuck on the side of the inhospitable mountain Nanga Parbat. Half frozen by the savage cold, battered by hostile winds, cowed by his physical and mental exhaustion, he sat in his tent and cried for his wife. He was too scared to go up the mountain, he was too scared to go down, and he was too scared to stay where he was. At that moment in time he said he was afraid to live. Afraid to live!

That was me. That's how I felt in my tiny Coventry terrace, waking up in a cold sweat, my wife lying next to me asleep, my kids in the next room also asleep. A house full of people and yet completely alone. Waking into the stillness of a 4am day, sleep a million miles away and my biggest fear, my greatest terror at that ungodly hour was *how the fuck am I going to get through another long day?*

Anger. I mentioned anger. And an unfamiliar voice. Coming from me, or perhaps coming through me. A voice that I did not recognise as my own declaring bravely *I am not having this anymore.* This voice was a phoenix, and it rose from the ashes of my burning depression. From out of somewhere, from out of nowhere, something, someone inside me said 'enough!' - and this someone, this new self, was speaking not to the bedroom ceiling or to a specific person or the image in the mirror or any particular fear; it was talking to fear in general.

I was speaking to my demon.

A dragon had been stalking me for as long as I could remember, attacking my body, invading my mind, pillaging all of my seminal energies. And now a knight had appeared and was ready to fight. And this I, this new I, born not despite the depression rather birthed out of and because of it had a cunning plan. 'I will write down every single thing I am afraid of and, one by one, systematically face those fears in order to either dispel them or develop some kind of desensitisation.'

So that is what I did. And the doing, even the contemplation of the doing, shot a bolt of light through my darkness. Hope was born. Instead of believing, as I had always unquestioningly believed, that depression was *my lot*, the ancestral curse (I'd inherited my mum's nerves, as she liked to say) and that there was no fighting this devil, I decided to challenge it and go nose-to-nose with my terror; I determined to face it and wrestle out my own truth.

3

Climbing the Fear Pyramid

I have detailed the process of building a fear pyramid in my book *Fear the Friend of Exceptional People*, so I won't insult you by telling you again what was better told first time around, but I'll give you the overview of a process that changed and transformed my life. It took me from a young man frightened of spiders in the bath, to a nightclub bouncer who stood on the doors of drinking establishments in a city that was polled as the most violent in Europe for its size and population.

I drew a pyramid on a piece of paper.

That was the first step.

I called it a fear pyramid.

The idea was not one I had read about. I was not taught this as a technique in a classroom or on an internet tutorial; it came to me direct, from the teacher-less teaching of intuition. It was a gift from God.

On each step of the pyramid I wrote down one of my fears, the lesser fear on the bottom step and worst fear on the top step. Then I set about systematically confronting and overcoming those fears until I reached the top. Each fear confronted and overcome brought me an exponential injection of new strength, renewed courage and expanded knowing. *Knowing* is mined gold. It is the reward for working at the coal face of fear. I am not talking about learned knowing, the intellectual accumulation that comes from reading books or from attending lectures or listening to *another* podcast or even from talking to heroes or touching the cloak of greats or imbibing the learnings of rishis and gurus and Oprah guests (I love Oprah) or even standing on the carpet with someone who is standing on the carpet of proximity. I'm talking about the knowing that is earned, not learned. Life will not release its essence unless we squeeze it out with our bare hands.

An interesting thing happened as I climbed my pyramid of fears. As I overcame the mundane and obvious anxieties, other more subtle and unconscious dreads appeared and wrote themselves large on the steps of my mountain. I was able to recognise things that had been right in front of me for decades, but I had just not been able to see them before. I realised (for instance) that I was afraid of my (first) wife. I know. It's embarrassing. But I was afraid of her. She was a lovely woman but she was dominant. She was an amazing mum, but she was very fond of telling people that, 'when I say jump, Geoff asks *how high*'. I should have stood up for myself, and I could have stood up for myself but I didn't. I was afraid of marital confrontation, or any kind of confrontation for that matter. I hated the disquiet it triggered in me. I did not want the discomfort. So to avoid feeling uneasy, I failed to stand up for myself. This of course created an imbalance in the marriage that would eventually split us apart. This was not my wife's fault. It was me that was in error. She unconsciously rebalanced what was lacking in our relationship. I kidded myself that I was not afraid of confrontation, I was certainly not afraid of her, but back then I regularly lied to myself and just as readily believed my lies; it was easier than confronting the truth. 'Anything for a quiet life,' I told myself. This is how I rationalised my weakness of character. The truth, the knowing I earned from defeating and removing the demigods of my surface fears told me that, yes, I *was* scared of her, I was afraid of a familial conflict, plain and simple.

As soon as I was able to see this and admit it, if only to myself, my wife went on the pyramid with all the other scary monsters.

I was also afraid of my mum (I can feel a pattern forming). She too was a dominant matriarch who, even as an adult, I dared not confront. She loved me, she loved my brothers and sister and she would take a bat to anyone in our defence. But the fact remains that I was always terrified of my mother. Specifically, I was afraid of her withdrawing her love. The fear I felt even in the contemplation of her withdrawing from me, was completely disproportionate and highly irrational but nevertheless it was there.

So, my lovely mum took residence on her own step of the mountain.

What I realised too, as the removal of a weed reveals the presence of a root, was that I was afraid of change. Actually, everyone I knew seemed to be afraid of change, even though change was the only constant. The fear of change was what kept me in a small city, doing menial work, driving a crap car, glued in an unhappy marriage, tethered to a heavy rock in the deep pool of mediocrity.

Later of course - much later - this seminal exercise in confrontation-desensitisation would lead to an exponential level of growth. I would stretch my inner and outer geography and take myself body and soul to all sorts of exciting and exotic places for meetings with book publishers, film production companies and theatres, in London and beyond.

For now, though, my world did not extend outside my terraced house, in a small Coventry suburb.

Fear of change went on my ever-growing fear pyramid.

Change of course is only mastered when you start to court change rather than place your every effort into resisting it.

I was afraid of success. I was not even sure what success was or what it could be, other than the vague idea of being somewhere better than I was right then, being anywhere better than I was right now.

As far as I could see, success was something that everyone was hunting for, but nobody seemed able to definitively articulate. In my world people worked in day jobs that they despised and they took employment that they were unlikely to change for an entire career. This was the *job for life* that we chased with all our might and dreaded with all our heart. We chased it because it promised security. We dreaded it because we quietly knew that security was a prison. If we chased success at all, it was only ever after a pint at the club, where we regaled wild, random and rare success stories that we'd heard tell of, and that might one day happen to us. These stories were often contrived, usually exotic and beautiful but nearly always unlikely successes that seemed irresistibly within our reach but offensively beyond our grasp. Under-educated boys like us would masturbate over these tales of unearned riches, but they were beauties that we could never bed in the flesh. They were half-stories, or unqualified rumours, or part truths or blood-red lies, successes that we'd read about in the newspapers, seen on the TV or heard about from a friend who knew a man, who knew a man… Most of us chased success with a cross predicting an invisible football on a pools coupon, and later still, when the gamble became pandemic you could spend a weeks' wage and a wasted life on a clutch of lottery cards and newspaper and magazine and TV competitions and postcode lotteries that dangled a carrot of hope, and postponed the effort to strive. Baited by the wriggling worm of winners' stories, those small few that won big, the masses staked their future on the random chance of becoming an instant millionaire.

It is an easier sell for the conditioned imagination than success in any conventional sense.

The odds of changing your reality and earning 'real' money were so stacked against the man on the street that a forty-five million-to-one chance of winning freedom by guessing six random numbers and a bonus ball felt more realistic, more achievable. How powerful conditioning is when we believe our only chance to escape the minimum wage is to predict a series of lottery numbers in a specific sequence, a chance that is rarer than being hit on the head by a falling satellite.

I was afraid of success so, just like everyone else, I fed my ambition on massively unlikely anomalies like a lottery win, writing a one-hit-wonder pop song (even though I was no lyricist) that pay your mortgage for the next forty years, or being offered a seven figure, three-book deal for a tome that only existed in the wildest corners of my imagination.

Success is so often talked about but rarely ever truly investigated.

No one does the rigour on success.

What is it?

No-one seems to know; only that it involves a lot of money, a great deal of fame and celebrity and lots of accolades.

I was afraid of success.

I was afraid for many reasons not least because the moment you start seriously looking below the surface at what it really is, success (in all its potential) develops its own voice and it asks questions of you, it demands specifics, it calls you out: 'what is your plan? Show me your schematic!'

It starts a Socratic dialectic that scares the living shit out of people because it exposes vanity (why do you want success?) laziness (are you doing the work?) ignorance (what does success look like to you?) weak rationalisation (your failure cannot be blamed on anyone other than yourself) lies (you say you are doing the work, where's your proof?) weak character (why haven't you started? Why have you given up?). The moment you start to seriously look at success, what it is and what it means reveals itself. It shows you what success demands and the character and insight and courage it takes to destroy old beliefs and the worlds that those beliefs maintain. It demands that you tool new beliefs which, in turn, can do nothing other than create new worlds.

I was afraid of success because success meant personal change, as in, *I would have to change. Me personally.*

This triggered all sorts of new fears.

How would my wife feel if I suddenly went from being Geoff the factory worker to Geoff the published author appearing on live TV with Holly and Phil, or Desert Island Discs with Lauren Laverne? How would my friends feel, how would my peers react when their under-educated friend starts quoting ancient Hindu scriptures or Plato or Socrates or Jesus of Nazareth or Mohammed from the Koran. And what of my mum and dad? How will they cope when their son picks up the pen and airs their dirty laundry? Even a small world change can have big world effects. If you drop a pebble anywhere in the water, the ripples will be received by the whole pool.

One of the very early items on my pyramid of fear was spiders. I was afraid of a very small, harmless eight-legged creature that could do little more than tickle my arm if it was let loose. My fear might appear, on paper, like a cartoon anxiety, but in those days, a spider on the ceiling of my bedroom would be enough to stop me from sleeping at night. It was not so much the spider but my flaccid mind-attention and my very feral imagination that would allow a harmless insect to run around my psyche like a totem and create havoc.

You may see very little connection between confronting my fear of spiders (I literally kept picking up spiders and putting them down again until the fear dissipated) and my ability to negotiate change and eventually hold my nerve in life or death encounters as a nightclub bouncer, but they are directly related; they are separated only by degree.

What I learned in the process of facing my fear of spiders was directly transferable to overcoming every other fear in my bank vault of perceptual terror. If I can recognise the rise of fear: if I can understand the chemical components and the natural process of fight or flight: if I can develop the hardiness to stay in that fear and resist the urge to freeze or lash out or run away: if I can hold my centre and not emotionally engage the biological urge to permission its autonomy over me: if I can manually take over the process and make myself move when I want to freeze, and make myself stay when I want to run: if I can command restraint when my survival system instructs attack: if I can recognise the chemical release of the autonomic nervous system as natural but outdated, then I can start to retrain myself into a new kind of man.

So what I learned in overcoming the least fear on the lowest step of my pyramid (spiders), I took with me to the next step, and my second strongest fear (dentists) and what I learned on step two I took with me to step three and step four and so on. The automatic and unconscious effect of this process was exponential. I naturally started to be more outgoing with my new bravery. I instinctively sought to improve my skills. The vacuum left by the removal of a spent fear demanded occupancy and that space was taken up by consciousness, awareness, more knowledge, new experiences and fresh adventures that, in turn, furnished me with bespoke and unique maps.

It goes without saying I hope that fear of success had to have its own step. It was added to the growing list, but I would make sure not to underestimate how threatening personal change can be both to the lower ego, and to the world at large. I have seen many lives interrupted, distorted beyond recognition and beaten to death by the natives when people courted change, but failed to anticipate its effects. I once corresponded briefly with a young Australian lad, who was so afraid of the consequence of a seemingly simply change of employment that he became suicidal. I have also known many young men and women become desperately sad and depressed because family specifically, friends peripherally, and society in general would not validate or understand and support their individual life choices.

When we enact change in our lives, we have to be prepared to go it alone, we have to anticipate that others might not understand our decisions or agree with our direction. We have to accept that they might even hate us for the way in which we take our inherited story and edit it in a style that better suits us.

My own bout of depression, and the subsequent exercise in desensitisation, forced me to look inwards, and start a dialectic with myself. It insisted that I be brutally, even savagely, honest about who I was and why I was unhappy, and what it was that I was really afraid of and what I could do to lessen that fear and allow joy into my life.

The mundane fears in our lives often act as house ghosts, self-imposed ghouls that we place at the exit of our conditioned borderlands of limitation and at the entrance to our esoteric kingdom of potential. When we dismiss and dissolve the mundane by facing it down, we will uncover the real fears, beyond the veils that cover our truth.

As I systematically climbed the pyramid, and continued to smite the surface fears, more and more subtle underlying fears presented themselves for processing: blame was one of them. You might not see blame as a fear. Most people don't. Blame is the common bat we swing, to slug the uncommon ball of personal culpability for six. Blame is a way of diverting or projecting or covering our fear of responsibility.

In our own lives, in our own world, we are responsible for everything.

Few of us want to take responsibility for anything, let alone everything; taking responsibility is painful. It is much easier and more convenient to project it onto others. But when we blindly pass on responsibility, we immediately lose autonomy; they sit at opposing ends of the same stick, to let go of one end, is to automatically let go of the other. Blame is the narcotic of the masses, and once it starts there is no end to it. Blame is addictive, it is delicious, and so easily available: we can blame the wife, we can blame the husband, the father, the brother, that bloke who abused us as a kid, the teacher at school who treated us badly, local councillors who don't keep their promises, violent terrorists, invading immigrants, greedy bankers, the corrupt government - collectively known to the masses as *the powers that be* - even God gets our opprobrium when we run out of mortals to blame. He takes a lot of the flack when lives fall apart and people don't want to accept responsibility. He even gets the rap from people who don't believe in Him.

When I was stuck in the factory working soul-destroying shifts I blamed my first wife. I told anyone who'd listen that it was her fault: if it wasn't for her I'd be gone from that job in a heartbeat. I was so convincing in my rhetoric that even I believed it. One day, tired of my bullshit, she challenged me: 'If you really want to leave the factory, leave. I give you permission, stop blaming me!'

The scales fell from my eyes, and like the unveiling of a hideous statue, I was left standing before my own raw unadulterated fear.

Once I stopped blaming my wife for my sorry lot, once I realised that I was my only enemy, I was forced to look at blame and projection, and I was called to identify what it was that I was really afraid of.

Blame, in its rawest form is synonymous with the fear of change.

To me, at that point in my development, on that particular step of my pyramid, change meant doing the work; change meant study; it was challenging, it demanded courage, it meant going it alone, improving my intellect, expanding my consciousness, losing old friends - even family members - who I knew would not venture with me to a new job, let alone to new worlds. Success was frightening because it didn't just mean a change of job or car, or house number or post code or city or even a change of country; it meant an absolute and unequivocal change of reality. You literally change who you are.

Climbing the ascending steps revealed something vital to me, something seminal: by removing the mundane fears, I located who I really was, my true self. This higher 'I' was not difficult to find; *he was the one who was doing all the removing.* He was the one who took captaincy, the one who exposed the fears and wrote the fears down on paper and set out on a Maslovian quest to reach the top of his hierarchy of needs. He was the one that orchestrated and observed the whole metamorphosis.

I also discovered another vital truth: we are not really afraid of *things*, of occurrences, we do not fear the 'this-and-that' of corporeal existence, rather we are afraid of the feeling of being afraid. We are afraid of the massive discomfort that the adrenal cocktail evokes in us. It is hugely uncomfortable, of course, but it is supposed to be, it is unlikely that we would ever be spurred into action without the fierce jolt, and sharp encouragement of adrenalin.

I'd always hoped that fear might be something I could eschew on my way to success. I realised much later that not only could it not be avoided; it was a necessary part of expansion.

Fear is the first house ghost we must overcome in order to go to a deeper level. Whilst we are afraid of the physical discomfort associated with adrenalin we are never going to progress beyond the usual reptilian response.

By confronting and dissolving the surface fears, I was able to reveal the deeper fears below; then, through the same process of confronting, disproving and dissolving my fear, I was able to go to the next fear, and so on until I uncovered the cause of my fear, the cause of all fears…the frightened false ego.

Some of the fears I encountered on the pyramid were cleverly disguised and configured by the ego to make tracing their source difficult. I discovered that they may be referred fears, a decoy locating itself in the opposite location to its true nature. Or, it may be triangulated, like an anonymous phone call that is patched through several disparate lines in order to hide the original location of the caller.

My fears only existed whilst I believed in them, and, whilst I had faith in them my fears fed on the seminal energy of my emotional engagement.

The very moment I noticed this, the recognition and the liberation were instant and simultaneous.

I often had to go through this elaborate sequence of events with fear - locating the symptom, tracing the fear back to root etc. - before I was able to finally remove it. Once I saw the illusion of fear, it disappeared. Each time I took victory over a particular fear its nature was liberated and the energy it contained was automatically released and I expanded my conscious net. My courage expanded too, as did my wisdom and subsequently my reality.

Every fear I overcame set a new precedent. It acted as a reference point for the next challenge, offered an expansion of true knowing, and I earned a certainty that enabled me to negotiate the next fear and the next fear. Eventually I reached, what was then, the penultimate step. I was able to see the one particular fear that stood sentinel at the peak of my pyramid; the fear of violent confrontation.

My bid to overcome this debilitating fear led me to making a radical decision. One that irreversibly changed my life. Actually, it almost ended my life.

I will detail this decision imminently.

Before I could reach that place I had to negotiate the changes that my pyramidal ascent had, on me, on my friends, on my family, and on my wife.

Changes

Because of the fears I had already overcome, en route to the top step, *who I was* fundamentally changed. Of course. I was a man on a mission, chasing down and claiming shadows. This kind of quest would change anyone, it certainly did me. Only a little at first, but, later, as I undertook more radical change, and placed my heel on the neck of societal dogmas, small change became the catalyst for metamorphosis.

Inevitably, the change was enough to inadvertently distance me from some of my old friends and family members, especially those closest to me - specifically my lovely wife.

It must have been frightening for her to see her docile, waddling, half-asleep husband flex his wings and take to the air. When you move, everything moves with you. As Leonardo da Vinci said, 'when a bird lands in a tree, the whole world changes'.

My wife did not like the new me.

The old me talked a good game, but never really left the safety of the bleachers. The new me was venturing out on to the field of play. The old Geoff always talked about becoming a writer, but never wrote as much as a note for the milkman. This new, invigorated self not only wanted to write, but had actually started filling pages with words. The cowering personality of old was no more, and the new man in the house would not acquiesce to marital dominance. When my wife threatened to kick me out and change the locks on the door (this was the standard threat), if I didn't jump when she commanded it, instead of folding, instead or bowing down to fear, instead of becoming sycophantic when she withdrew her love as punishment, I took a chance and said 'change the locks. See if I care.'

Like all fears that are dragged into the open by the rope of courage, this fear disappeared when challenged. All the things I'd wanted to do, all the things I'd wanted to explore or experience suddenly became possible, because I had discovered the courage to do them.

Admittedly, this led to a few wild and (later some dangerous) personal expressions. I got myself an earring (the shame), and some tattoos, lots of tattoos, arms and legs full of tattoos. Sadly, my exuberance also led to some clumsy and ignorant personal oversights. Once I started to realise my massive potential, recognising that it lay on the other side of fear, I did not hesitate, to my shame and regret, to trample over the sensibilities of others in order to get there.

One of these people was my wife.

A word about my first wife...

I loved her very much.

I should start with this because it is true.

I have never met a more selfless mum. I have yet to meet a more protective parent. For a time we were both asleep, spiritually speaking, and when I woke up and she stayed in her fearful slumber, it created an inevitable dichotomy in our relationship. When she told me that I could leave anytime I wanted to - something she said often, when we rowed - when she said that she didn't need me, and that she'd do just fine without me, I believed it. I really did believe it. Looking back, I can see that she really believed it too. When the inevitable happened and I finally left the marriage, in the most disgraceful way, after the most awful betrayal, she realised and I realised that she did not really believe it at all. She couldn't do without me; in fact she fell apart without me and it remains to this day the most painful episode of my life. She was damaged by my leaving, beyond repair, and, if I'd known back then that she was posturing when she told me to go, that she was afraid of and felt threatened by my growing ambition, the blossoming me, if I had known then that her every moment was filled with anxiety because she was terrified that I might abandon her, I would have been kinder, I would have taken care of that delicate and beautiful soul. As it happened, my self-esteem was non-existent so when she said *don't think I can't manage without you, I don't need you*, I believed her, I believed everything she said.

She said all this to me because she was afraid.

If I'd have known *how* afraid she was - attack is always a sign of fear - I would have rallied to her pain, I would have made fewer announcements, I would have slowed my ascent, in order to keep her in sight.

It's easy for me to read this and judge my ex-wife, but I can't. I will not. She was ten times the parent to my children than I ever was. The idea of me writing this book is so that I can process the raw data and sift out the essence.

I left, she stayed.

If I am going to measure a character, this is the only detail I need to consider.

She stayed.

When you go beyond the paper-thin familial posturing you will not find unkind malevolence, but you will find naked fear. Although she was physically beautiful, her self-image was not; it had been damaged by a number of negative experiences when she was growing up.

Today, in the last year of my sixth decade on spaceship earth, I would have seen beyond her spontaneous expression. I would have climbed into the wound of that beautiful, beautiful woman and I would have loved her completely and her fear would have dissipated like a shadow under the glare of the midday sun.

But I was not fifty-nine years old. I did not have the self-knowing then that I enjoy today. I believed her blind rhetoric, *every word of it*, and it inspired me to invest extra effort into climbing my *hierarchy of needs*, looking for, *if not complete self-realisation*, certainly a release from fear, anxiety and crippling self-doubt.

Unfortunately, somewhere on my ascent I completely lost sight of her. As a consequence our marriage hobbled through the world and our relationship drew its last laboured breaths. It was not specifically articulated at the time, but I had definitely and unequivocally withdrawn emotionally from the marriage. I started to do all the things I really wanted to do; writing, training more and changing jobs.

I changed jobs.

Before the pyramid, I complained a lot about the kind of work I could procure, with my particular skillset, and I dreamed of better employ. But I never did much more than dream, and gripe about my dreams not being realised. Although I would not have thanked you for noticing it, I was with the masses, I was I one of those job-for-life guys. I'd been working the soul-destroying continental shift system at Courtaulds, in a stinking (literally) chemical factory. I stayed there for seven years because for seven years I was afraid to leave. Now that my courage had expanded, and my perspective changed, I was no longer imprisoned by this angst, so I left the factory.

I took a job as a hod carrier on a building site.

Later I trained as a bricklayer for the same company. And, later still, I taught martial arts classes, to supplement my income.

I was starting to see that anything was possible. If I could pluck up the courage to stand up to my wife, then I could muster the nerve to leave my steady employ. I could abandon the menial work, a job I took 'just to see me through', the temporary stopgap that, for most people, quickly becomes a permanent abode, even a prison sentence.

Most people I knew went into these dreary jobs, never imagining that in thirty of forty years' time, they would still be there. Few, if any ever left. Most became institutionalised, fearful of the great unknown beyond the factory gates. Every time one of the lads got fed up and threatened to leave for pastures new, the others would congregate and whisper like co-conspirators: 'you don't want to leave here': 'it's tough out there': 'this job is safe': 'you've got to be grateful for any work you can get these days': 'jobs like this do not grow on trees you know'.

I allowed the factory fear-mongers to keep me in small places for a very long time with their hysterical rhetoric. Looking back now, I can't even remember their faces. I can't even remember their names. And yet I allowed the nameless, faceless amalgam to completely determine my life. Most people live and die in the towns where they are born, because they fear the great beyond.

When you change frequency, you are both missed and noticed. Missed by those in your vacated frequency, noticed by those in the density you matriculate into.

You are engaged by the higher frequency.

Unfortunately, those who shared your old life often fall out of step. You are no longer congruent with them and you both sense it. It's not that you leave people behind as you grow, that's not what happens, it's just that some people do not come with you. This is their choice and not yours.

This can cause pain and upset and often conflict.

The people in the old frequencies feel abandoned. They feel slighted (often jealous or envious), or patronised. They think it's your fault that they are stuck, so you get the blame, they make a monster out of a windmill, and the lance is tilted firmly in your direction.

I have to admit that this fear of judgement, my own fear that I was (as some people suggested) getting above my station, or that I was *up myself*, or pretentious, held me back for a long time. It was only when I realised that this too was a fear, that I placed *judgment* on my pyramid and advanced on it in the same way that I did with all my fears.

I learned too that I didn't need anyone else's permission to live my own life in my own way. You will never grow if you are waiting for permission.

You will never excel if you need the approval of others.

You will not move even one iota while you fear other people's judgement of you.

Each victory over a fear that had once immobilised me, added new urgency to my mission. I wanted to test every boundary. I aimed higher. I went wider and broader and deeper. I realised excitedly, and I realise again now as I write, with greater excitement still, that this expansion can go on and on ad infinitum.

The pyramid of fears taught me that our capacity to grow is boundless.

But growth comes at a price.

That price is everything, everything, everything.

We cannot create the new reality without first destroying the old. We have to be prepared to empty out the old house, if we are ever to kit-out the new.

The Torah warns us that we can't be taken through the doorway by anyone else, we have to lead our self in. If someone else leads us in, then someone else can lead us out again.

The entranceway is a gate-less gate, a narrow door. When we enter, we enter alone.

Others may follow in their own good time, but we can't make them, no matter how much we would like to, no matter how much we care for them. All we can do is go through the gate ourselves and leave them with the proof that it is possible.

I recognised later that this was part of the journey. People will not always understand. They do not always understand. I can't make them understand but ultimately, I don't need them to. I just need to pioneer new lands. I just need to colonise those new densities with my life. If others want to follow, at least they can see it is possible. I will be the first proof.

Waiting for permission, waiting for others to understand means you will do just that; wait.

I had reached the penultimate step of my fear pyramid: the fear of violent confrontation. You might say that the fear of violence is a healthy angst and that most reasonable people share the same fear, and you would be right. But my fear was beyond reasonable, it was massively disproportionate, I would say that it was debilitating.

To reach the summit of my pyramid, I knew I had to confront my ultimate fear of violent confrontation. I did this in the only reasonable, sensible way I could, I took a job as a night club bouncer.

5

The Door Years

When I tell people that working the doors was a metaphysical pursuit, they think I'm jesting. I am not. Hopefully, you will have already ascertained from the tone of the book thus far that we are not in the world of fisticuffs and fights outside chip shops on a Friday night anymore. This chapter (this book) will be no fight-fest; there will be no bloodletting on these pages, and there will be no body count at the end of the telling. There is too much of that already in *Watch My Back*, so I will not be repeating it again here. In this outing - my odyssey from the exoteric doors of Coventry clubs to the esoteric halls of academia and beyond - I'd like to explore not just why I suddenly found myself in a very violent employ, but how it came about and more specifically what I learned as a bouncer that was worth a decade of personal investment, and the risk of life and limb. Looking back on it now, thirty years after the fact, what were my essential lessons, the reduced concentrate of my sojourn into the seedy world of Coventry night clubs?

The most revelatory aspect of my ten year secondment was pivotal and informing, it was life-altering and inspirational.

I will come to this essential imminently.

You could say I was lucky when I decided to take a job as a bouncer. The planets were aligned in my favour. A room of requirement opened up for me and quickened my learning in a heightened field of play. I was lucky because, at that particular time (the early 1980s) there was a growing necessity for bouncers in the local pubs and clubs of our fair city. Coventry was experiencing an unusual and unprecedented spike in unprovoked, unsolicited, drink-related violence. Men got pissed, specifically at the weekends, and when they did the hard drink turned into hard violence - lots of it. Certainly, the spill was too much for the local constabulary to mop up, so, like the Wild West, men good in a fight were in high demand. That was the only stipulation on the job sheet. No specific schooling was necessary, no O or A levels required, there was no call for a college diploma or a university degree; the only question on the job sheet was *can you fight*? If you can, apply within.

I'm exaggerating but not much.

Initially, my black belt and my growing note as a martial artist vouchsafed me a little work. I picked up a shift here and there; pubs on match day, when the City was playing at home, a bit of door security for a kids' pop concert at a posh hotel, and the odd shift at a friend's pub. This eventually led to a regular night at the tombstone of Coventry night clubs, the infamous Busters, which hosted the toughest door staff in a very tough city. Initially I was offered the chance to cover one night for a friend. The head doorman at Busters was a legendary character called John 'Awesome' Anderson or, as he was known thereabouts, 'One Man Gang'. He was a beautiful, quiet, monosyllabic, absolute powerhouse of a human being. I loved him the moment I met him. I loved him through six tough years of schooling in the art of door management and self-management and the effective subjugation of violent threat. Forty years on, writing about John now, I still love him and I recognise today more than ever before how pivotal this angel was.

I won't go into detail about the thousands of encounters I had in those heady, unsteady, unready bloody days of violence because it is a subject beyond the remit of this book. I have already written 552 Sunday Times Best Selling pages about it, published back in 1992 when the sweat was still damp on my palms and the pavement sticky-red with the fresh bodily fluids of the low brow, low blow Coventry underclass.

This book starts properly where *Watch My Back* left off, so what follows is an overview of the door years, and a prelude to what came after. Enough to say that the black belt I held in Shotokan Karate got me the gig at Busters, but the martial arts skills I'd honed in the previous fifteen years on the dojo floor did not survive even the first night under scrutiny of nightclub neon. My whole method of training and my way of living in the world changed after the first shift.

I can still remember it now, going back to my karate class the next day, after that first shift. I had by now attracted a small gathering of dedicated students who were already drawn to my 'mask-less' philosophy, but now I was about to crank the truth barometer up by several degrees. I stood in front of my students, like a pilgrim who had just seen the light, and said, 'we are doing this all wrong! Everything has to change.' That first night at Busters, a carnival of lashed, pissed, drunk, drugged, semi-drunk, and downright fucking crazy human beings passed before me as I stood and guarded the entrance to the club, searching people for weapons (if they didn't have any, we gave them some; it was that kind of club). The common joke was, 'Busters night club? I worked there for five years, one night!' I experienced several long lifetimes in one five hour shift. They were the most intoxicating, exhilarating, frightening and ultimately revealing nights of my life. I'd only ever intended to work the door for a few months. It was a means to an end, it was not some crazy, suicidal, kamikaze career choice. I did the doors, just so I could face down my fear of confrontation. It was the pinnacle of my ascent. I wanted to peel away the fear-carapace and look below the scab so to speak. It would enable me to get a better understanding of the wound below, maybe gain a little psychological desensitisation to the fear of a real fight en route. Then I could tick it off my list and move on having successfully climbed a pyramid of fears without being terrorised by a spider, tortured by my dentist, abandoned by my mum or battered by my wife.

That first night was purgatorial. Dali's metaphorical clock melted the seconds, minutes and hours so slowly I thought it must have stopped. I feared the tick might never tock, and the night might never end. The fear, the anxiety, the constant constant threat of imminent violence made the eternal night pass in torturous slow motion. My arsehole was like a manhole. My adrenals were doing double and triple shifts and my inner dialogue (the chattering voice in my head) was telling me every five minutes that 'this is not for us, this is not for us, this is definitely, definitely not for us'. But I was sitting cheek-by-jowl with the power, ah man, the power of standing on a nightclub door, surrounded by five hundred potential threats to life and limb; standing there, taking abuse from living, breathing, angry, posturing, threatening monsters (some of them were bonafide monsters), and not running away, not freezing and not burning up in the fire of my own fever. I can't tell you how powerful that felt.

As I mentioned in the last chapter, at the time violent confrontation was my ultimate fear and I was not only standing in front of it, I was standing up to it, actually I was up to my squeezy-bottle neck in it.

There is a huge difference between intellectually understanding fear and actually embracing it, deliberately and willingly suffering it as a choice.

The doors in Coventry in the 80s were disproportionately violent. On paper, standing on a nightclub door, taking on all-comers, might not seem like the feat of titans, but people were being battered in these clubs, stabbed, glassed, even shot, and no small number had been murdered there. Customers, staff and door security, especially door security, were the red rag to every bull in the city who fancied themselves as a *de toros* of repute. During my decade's stint in the club arena four of my friends were murdered in and around the click of our employ.

To stand there all night, was the greatest feat of courage I had ever displayed. The dynamic changes completely the moment you take the leap from *saying to doing*. They are two entirely different landscapes. I'll admit, it was also an experience standing next to Awesome Anderson (Clint Eastwood in black), Ricky 'Jabber' James, a professional heavyweight boxer and No-Neck Maynard who could bench press 400lbs and was as wide as he was tall. It was such a privilege. And to be in charge of the entrance of a club with the power to say yay or nay, to deny or to allow access, and be prepared to battle for that authority was a completely new and revealing experience.

In order to take charge of a nightclub door you have to take charge of yourself. That's the first thing I learned.

The Chinese philosophers tell us 'better and more powerful to control the self than to lead ten thousand armies'. This is because the self is vaster by comparison; this human tabernacle is literally made up of trillions upon trillions of conscious, individual cells all of which are controlled and compelled by human perception.

When you control the self, you control perception.

When you control perception, you are not merely in charge of ten thousand armies, you command a legion beyond reckoning. You captain the microcosmic human-universe, a seemingly small and insignificant bundle of nerves, muscles, organs and sinew that connect through a web of consciousness to every other particle in the macrocosm.

At the time I believed I was merely standing on a nightclub door to confront my fear of violent confrontation; later, much later the absolute and utter significance of what I was being taught truly set in. In learning to protect the doorway of a nightclub, I was learning to protect the mind-door which was the literal entrance to my very being, my centre.

Despite the clear understanding that by standing on Busters' door and confronting my fear I had done something good, something worthy and brave, despite the obvious glamour of the work - there was a seductive mix of curvy girls, heady music, dance and party - I decided there and then that it was not for me. A black guy confronted me halfway through my first night on the door and threatened to tear me a new arsehole because I'd refused him entry to the club. He looked capable of doing it. He was wearing trainers, our dress code was 'no trainers', so he couldn't come in. We had standards: this was a nightclub not an all-weather football pitch. When he postured and made large, baring his keyboard-teeth and bunching his fists into ugly clubs, he looked the collective-manifestation of every demon of scripture. But before he could make good on his promise to maim on a whole new level of agony, John, perhaps reading my sensory overload, told the demon-amalgam that if he didn't step away from the door, he would personally play a tune on those teeth of his. John had the kind of tone that convinced even the dimmest of intellects that he was serious. Later that evening another drunken customer tried to attack me and more out of luck than skill, I managed - in a messy kind of kick-bollock-scramble - to drag him through the club and evict him from the premises.

I experienced more adrenalin in that one single night than I had felt in the previous three decades.

This job definitely was not for me.

The violence, certainly the very real, constant and visceral threat of the red stuff being spilled on the beer-sticky carpet at any moment, *my* red stuff, was enough to convince this comprehensive school reject, this young husband and father, this soft doting son that the quiet life and the factory and the nine-to-five, beer on a Friday night, takeaway once a month, sex now and then (if I begged) was good enough.

I decided that my first shift would be my last shift. I just wasn't cut out for this. It was overwhelming; it was too much for me. I planned to hand in my notice at the end of the evening. I could tick the box I wanted to tick, assured that the depression had taken the last train for the coast and most of my obvious fears had been laid to rest. This work, this *world* was not for me and the moment my eternal dark night ended, I promised myself that I was going to tell John and the other boys 'thank you for the experience, but it's a no from me'.

When the night finally did end I felt one hundred years old.

As the last punter staggered out and the iron doors closed (yes, really, they were iron) and the staff sat down together for an after work drink, the club became a new world, a different world, a quiet and reflective island of whispers and quiet chatter and relieved laughter, as though the night of revelry and threat (an oxymoron, but accurate) had been an incarnation we'd all shared and this was our after-room, some kind of waiting area, the resting bardo between the world of club and the world of home that we would all return to as soon as drinks had been swallowed and the night had been laid out on the table and discussed and processed.

I was to find out that every night on the door really was like a single lifetime.

Some nights unfolded uneventfully and nothing much happened, other nights had the odd drama here and there, a fight, a flirt, a vomit-fest in the toilet (the customers, not me), an emotional domestic on the dance floor after a pretty teenage girl held the gaze of a pretty teenage boy for too long and a jealous scuffle ensued. Other nights were like the war of the roses, with Sodom burning and the orgies of Pompei all in one five hour shift.

Every night, eventful or otherwise, was processed over staff drinks at the end of the shift.

I was still working out how to tell John 'this is not for me' when he unexpectedly threw me the bone of a compliment. He said that, although I was an absolute fucking greenhorn (John's compliments were often heavily cloaked with insult) I'd stayed on my feet, I'd stood my ground, I had not run away or shamed myself or embarrassed the rest of the team. 'You did well', he added, and in that brief assessment of my very tame and under-average performance on a very average and under-tame night, he was telling me that I could stay. If I wanted to. I could be part of the team. But man, this was not just a team, this was *the* team and the implicit invite to join them was like Ferguson throwing me the red shirt (number 11) in an Old Trafford locker room and signing me for United. I was so thrilled and so surprised by the compliment that my fear just went, it evaporated into thin air and I thought to myself in a moment of sheer folly, 'I'll stay, yes, I will, I'll just stay for a week'.

Nearly a decade later I was still working the doors, still learning, still finding out who the fuck I was.

Well, there's a question: *Who the fuck was I?*

A nightclub bouncer, that's who, or certainly that's who I was for a moment.

Nietzsche said that we should be careful when hunting the dragon that we do not become the dragon. I'm ashamed to say that somewhere in pursuit of my ideal, I lost not only my way, I also lost any identity that I might have caught sight of on those early adventures climbing my pyramid.

I had taken the job to overcome my fear of violence and in doing so I became violent myself.

I thought I'd found a calling, my real self. In truth, I had found both on my pyramid of fears, but lost them again on the violent doors of Coventry. I had been tricked out of both by a carnal tempter, a parasite that fed off violence and the suffering of other beings.

As is always the way I could only see this in hindsight. I could not have seen it at the time, and I wouldn't have thanked you for it if you'd pulled me to one side and told me what a despot I had become.

If you were going to stand on the doors in a tough working-class city like Coventry, you had to be tough yourself, no doubt; certainly you had to be at least equal to the hardest men the city had to offer. You wouldn't survive otherwise. If you were going to accept a wage four times above the hourly rate of the factory worker to protect a club, to protect the staff, to guard the building, shield the customers and safeguard the drinking licence, against hard men, against hard drinkers, against hardy fighters of repute, this was an entry level expectation. If you wanted to keep your job and your life for more than a few days, you had to reach this standard and maintain it for the duration of your tender. In fact, you needed to maintain it for the rest of your life, if you were to stay in the same city after you hung up your dickie bow and retired your knuckle-duster. When you made enemies in this game, you made enemies, and you kept them for life.

I, of course, was not tough in any sense of the word, not at the time. I was not at the standard required for this bastard trade, and if my mustard had been tested at that very early stage it would not have cut it. I would have been found wanting. I'd have been kicked and punched and pilloried and rolled down every step of my erstwhile pyramid with neither pomp nor ceremony. As it was, the testing in those early, initial weeks did not crush me. It was testing enough to file off any nicks or burs in my character, and remove any stains, any weakness in my metal. But the tempering was steady and proportionate to my ability to handle it. And, of course, I had John by my side, and unless he was registered blind, he would have seen that I was not the finished article. I guess he must have been encouraged by the fact that I was there in the first place, that I'd had the courage to fill in the forms, as they say, and apply for the job. John took a shine to me and I (unofficially) became his young apprentice. He helped develop and prove the few raw skills I already possessed, and he added many more to my growing arsenal. Not so much physical skills. Men like John were not collectors of exotic techniques, they relied on basic, boring but effective skills, and usually survived thousands of violent affrays on one perfected technique, with a few rainy-day tricks tucked up their sleeve as back up. Anything more than that and the work became complicated and untenable. For John this single technique was a cannon of a left hook, and I never met a man who could throw a left better.

I adapted the skills I'd learned in the martial arts so that they would find efficacy in this unforgiving environment. Working the doors also gave me my first introduction to a process called apophatic theology, about which I learned later. It is the theology of negation, a method of locating God by means of reduction. We recognise what God is by first identifying what God is not. I accidentally discovered this method and employed it to locate true self-defence through negation. The door teaches you this process without announcement or protocol or even the need to label itself as a method. Nightclub security is a highly pressured environment where only the truth will prevail. The muttering untruth is chewed up and spat out unceremoniously. Pressured arenas demand truth, they leave room for nothing else - anything less might cost you your life. The moment you enter the cauldron of microcosmic war you know it; man you know it so quickly and so keenly it is shocking. Immediately, you automatically and intuitively reduce everything in your arsenal until all you're left with is raw practicality. It is like an acid bath, burning away the extraneous and leaving only the essential. It was so exhilarating to be so close to such raw truth. No, actually, let me rewind: at first it was not exhilarating, exhilaration came later. For now, faced by men steeped in violent intent, prepared to use any means, method and tool - sharp or blunt, contrived or incidental - to achieve their end, was frightening. Frightening because the metaphoric bag I was carrying was full of crap, it was brimming over with pseudo tools - techniques that worked in a controlled environment, but fell apart the moment they sniffed pressure: frightening because I was instinctively and immediately aware that this was the case: frightening because although I knew it, I didn't want to know it, I did not want to admit it to myself. If what I was seeing was true. What about all these years I'd spent training, what about all the time I'd wasted developing useless, plastic skills that melted in the blaze of a real fight? And if what I knew to be true was true, what about all the teachers and the masters and the systems that had schooled me, were they lying, were they ignorant or were they just simply blind?

To be completely frank, I was so hungry for truth that I immediately embraced it. I didn't care how many of my teachers I offended, how many protocols I smashed, etiquettes I disrespected or dogmas I exposed; I wanted the truth so I took the apophatic as my new method of practice and reduced my fighting art to the level of rude practicality. For me this meant pretty much one technique: a heavy right cross, and a method of delivering it to its optimum effect.

The effects were devastating.

The reduction of technique to its pure essence was so potent that it damaged everyone I landed it on.

It is uncomfortable to write about it here on this page, but I must. I am embarrassed and ashamed to express it again after all these years but still I must, and I will qualify my reasons for this shortly.

Everyone I hit I knocked unconscious. Sometimes they regained consciousness within a few seconds, sometimes it was taken from them for long, long moments, and other times they were taken to hospital on a stretcher and I had no idea how long they were out for, only that they were out when I hit them and they were still out when the ambulance carted them away. Believe me, that they did not die, that I did not kill someone in these vicious affrays, was a matter of divine providence and not a stroke of good luck.

I was protected from homicide by some unseen force that must have known my dharma lay elsewhere, somewhere other than a prison cell.

I located the best technique, the most vulnerable target area, and I developed the optimum method of delivery and intent. Once this violent alignment was in place, I made it my job to perfect the process so that eventually I could knock an attacker out at will. The technique became so consistent in its efficacy that eventually I was scared to use it for fear of killing someone, for fear of ending up in prison.

I learned to place my whole consciousness into my fist and close down worlds with it. I also learned to do the same with the use of sound (my voice), placing so much negative intention into the projected voice that I could place people into a state of freeze or flight without having to lay a glove on them. With the use of specifically directed word-intent I could deliver a violent rhetoric that would make people time travel. I call this *shaped sound*. I could force a person's imagination to leap forwards in time, literally lift him out of his body and jolt him into the near future, make him witness the dire prognosis of entering an affray with me, then allow him to come back to his body again, with the future consequence of his current actions clear and present in his mind. This would usually be enough to convince him to step away - often it would compel him to run away. The use of directed and specific sound allowed him to see exactly where his intercourse with me would end. I had to engage full intent for this to work. You couldn't fake it. The opponent had to believe, you had to believe what you were threatening otherwise the sound-attack would not have the desired result.

I would tell a potential attacker that if he didn't walk away. I would find out where he lived, I would find out where he worked, and I would come to his house and his work and I would enact unspeakable violence on him. I would also use violent yoga mudras. I'd twist my body into a hideous shape to back the words and create either dissonance in them or forced withdrawal. I did all of this innately. I could tell you that a mysterious eastern master taught me it, or that I read it in a secret doctrine, I could say I learned it in a private club, from an elite, invitation only clique but none of this would be true. This kind of learning came from a teacher-less realm. The environment taught me, the natural pressures shaped me, the demands of my situation delivered its own solutions.

Later, when my hands became too dangerous to use in a fight, sound became my weapon of choice and I could defeat most people with nothing more than my voice.

Later still, when violence became sickening to me and fighting my anathema, I would use sound as a negotiation tool and employ intelligence and guile to talk people out of a physical confrontation. And, much later still, when violence was no longer in my vernacular at all, and the sage in me was born, I used the same principles - sound, mudras, physical touch - to inspire people, to instruct people and often to heal people.

Everything I was learning now on the doors, to debase and destroy, I would later use to create and heal.

For now, I was using sound as a weapon of war and whilst it is reprehensible, it was where I was. And, as I said, later, knowing its potency for destruction, I was able to see its potential as an anabolic instead of a catabolic tool.

If this all sounds a little crude, a tad carnal it's because it is. You may also be thinking it is peripheral to the arc of this story; this book after all is not about the efficacy of fighting techniques in a hostile environment. But for this book to work, for me to reach the pinnacle of my endeavour, I do have to first travel briefly through the basecamp, the hell regions of my origins.

All the adepts I met on the door were of the same ilk. All of them were the very same; they all relied on a single, perfected, pre-emptive strike to take their opponents off the planet before they even knew they were in a fight. This was a secret hidden in plain sight. Whilst martial arts teachers everywhere were teaching their students the art of defence - block and counter, trap and counter - I was implicitly being schooled in the art of the pre-emptive strike, attack as the best means of defence. Pre-emption was the only consistently effective strategy in this savage environment, and this was common knowledge amongst the door fraternity. But it was unknown, even frowned upon in the sanitised systems of martial art being taught in church halls and sports centres all around the world. It was so obvious, and it was so immediate and so effective I was shocked that I had never been shown it before: I had been taught by some of the best martial arts teachers in the world, why hadn't they told me this?

Because they didn't know.

This was what excited me. They did not know the truth, even though it was there, on display, every night in clubs and pubs and bars up and down the country. So (I asked myself) what else was I not being taught? What else was hiding in plain sight, what other truths had I not been taught, had I not been shown?

What I learned very quickly about the efficacy of martial arts in the field of combat, I started to teach in my class in Coventry. I eventually wrote about it in magazine articles, and books. I produced videos, extolling the virtues of reality martial arts and the superiority of the pre-emptive strike.

Pre-emption was not all I learned from the doors, but it was pivotal, even seminal, because it unlocked a wealth of untapped potential, the likes of which I had never even dreamed of uncovering. With the discovery of pre-emption, I had split the atom of my training and discovered massive and hidden energy potential.

But pre-emption was just the start of it.

In hostile environments like this, you learn more about yourself in one single night, than most people discover in an entire lifetime. You had to learn about yourself. The environment demanded it. You would not survive for an hour if you were not acutely aware of your weaknesses and strengths, and if you did not quickly discern the rules of this neon jungle.

Knowledge of yourself gives you knowledge of the other. It is an automatic extension. We are all pretty much the same physiologically, biologically and neurologically, so what you learn about one, you simultaneously learn about all. This knowledge comes with benefits, but it also contains inherent dangers. The boon of elevated knowing, earned certainty, can be used or abused; certainly it can be transferred across into every other area of your life. Command over yourself allows you command over your environment, and to a large degree over the people who occupy that space. People everywhere largely lack any kind of centre, or self-command. To recognise this lack of internal leadership in others, enables you to lead them, to control them, and, if it is your intent, manipulate them, and herd them with their own fear. You can literally climb inside people and hijack their inner voice, and control their thinking and with the use of mudras - body movement, facial expressions, intention implied by an expression of movement - you can destroy them. You can take control of their adrenals to such an extent (switching them on and off at will) that they completely burn out. Depending upon how long this control is applied, this can either result in the simple withdrawal from a confrontation -you manipulate their adrenals to trigger the powerful 'flight response' so that they bottle it - or complete mental breakdown: imposed control over another person often leads to psychosis.

I have seen many people lose their minds when placed under this kind of external control. It is violent and it is base, of course, that goes without saying, but on the doors the skilled use of this kind of information kept me alive. Later, after my door years, when the folly of violence became apparent, I employed the same commands and intentions to heal myself and to guide and heal others.

The same self-control and the skilled management of my adrenal response later took me out of Coventry and all over the world. It was all a matter of perspective. If I was able to stand in front of a violent aggressor and control my nerve and make my techniques work under such extreme pressure, how much easier would it be to stand in front of an audience and teach, or lecture or deliver a keynote speech, whilst at the same time mix with amazing new people and earn thousands of pounds for my efforts?

All of these extensions of personal control were completely transferrable. If challenging my old and redundant beliefs could transport me from the magnolia walls of everyday existence, to the no-man's land of Coventry nightclubs - something I would have believed impossible only a year before - what other beliefs might I challenge, what other life shrinking, gaol imposing perceptions might I expose and shatter? Perhaps I could write the book I'd always dreamt of writing when I was a kid, maybe I could become a playwright or a screenwriter of acclaim. Was it possible that I might realise my lifelong dream of giving up the day job, eschewing conventional work and writing for my bread? Suddenly anything seemed possible, everything was up for grabs because in challenging my fears and perceptions and beliefs, some of them millennia old, I was challenging reality itself.

Facing my fears taught me to perfect intention and command. I had exercised, to a large degree, both intent and command by climbing my pyramid. On the doors it was asking me to extend and perfect these skills to deal with people who would take a hammer to a brittle intention and defy any command that did not transmit at least one level above their own. The dogs of society - the fighting men I faced on these doors - were sodden with drugs, drink, adrenalin, with displaced rage, twisted entitlement and an unhealthy disregard for authority; usually a cocktail of all the above. They would not tolerate weakness, they despised fear and anyone who displayed it, and would attack it on sight. Fear was an abomination to them. They innately taught you to control your fear, to disguise your fear, to develop an eye wall, so that the storm of fear could be contained from your centre. These mutts always acquiesced to the most stable energy in the pack. The dog with the calm, assertive energy always became top dog.

Working the doors taught me this.

But it showed me too that this calm assertive energy could not be faked, certainly not for long, it had to be won, it had to be located as a frequency, it had to be claimed as a station and it had to be maintained. A top dog will soon become a dead dog if his frequency is not held in the most conscientious manner. By extension, it was clearly implicit that before you can become the top dog in the pack, you had to first become top dog in yourself. If you could not command yourself, how could you command others?

Intention in this game meant the difference between winning and losing, living and dying, being first to the punch and being first to the mortuary.

Working in violent environments taught me that we are our own atmosphere; we take our microclimate with us wherever we go. If the atmosphere we exude is weak, we will be dominated by the strongest atmosphere in the room, in the house, in the workplace, in the world.

For the majority, their atmosphere is neither stable nor constant, so wherever they go they are vulnerable because dominant energies – what Saint Francis called *the roaming lion* and Sri Aurobindo called *the adverse forces* - are always sniffing the air and scanning the plains on the lookout for weaker energies to dominate and exploit.

If this sounds mercenary, it's because it is. If it sounds personal, it really is not. Nature abhors a vacuum. Gaps will always be filled by prevailing energies, just as water will run towards the lowest point.

Ultimately working the doors exposed my blemishes, fractures that needed to be redressed, sealed, improved, removed or upgraded. Pressure is the ultimate test of character, our most diligent teacher, and there really is no pressure like that of a maniac with a knife threatening to kill you.

In short, the pressured environment separates the wheat from the chaff, in you.

It is not personal, even when it appears to be very personal.

This was significant information. It was arcana, and it was won only by those who entered the room.

But this was not the most important thing I learned, not by a long shot. What I learned and what I know is this: the doors, the clubs, the pubs, the customers, the friends, the enemies, even the infrastructure that supported all of these disparate elements, all came from me, all of them. I created them, I maintained them, and I dissolved them again.

I created the reality I found myself in. All of it.

I didn't know this at the time, of course. I was still too invested in four-dimensional reality to even contemplate the densities beyond. I had no way of understanding this magical phenomenon. It is only now, in retrospect, that I see it as clearly as the page beneath my pen. We sketch our world, we fill in the colours and, like the myth of Wu Tao-Tzu, we climb into the world of our own design and disappear.

It is all very miraculous. It might sound ridiculous, you might think this the stuff of fiction, the result of a delusional mind, a trip of authorial fancy.

It is real.

The only problem is, people don't know it is real, they don't believe it is real, so they are in no position to manipulate their world and make it the world of their ideal. Instead they create randomly, accidentally, sporadically. Sometimes they create a horror show with their unchallenged beliefs, occasionally and for brief moments they craft a nirvana, other times they manifest the inferno; and in the case of some of the people I know, all nine circles and the Iblis himself.

What I realised from facing thousands of violent aggressors was that I was not creating the world of my ideal; I was creating the world of my projected damage.

Because of strong and abusive influences in my youth - class discrimination, limiting education, and sexual abuse - I was implicitly taught that the world was hierarchical, that I was in the lower echelons of it, it was dangerous, and that no-one could be trusted. This impression was grafted onto me as a belief that I did not question. What was there to question? As far as I could see, it was just the way it was; nothing personal. Consequently, I went out into the world, directed unconsciously by false perceptions, and built myself into a one-man armoury of muscle and sinew, a warrior with a raft of exotic martial abilities that I would use on anyone that challenged my space. I also covered myself in war paint - my body is a billboard of garish and violent tattoos. My nose was broken in three places (I won't go to those places again!), I won two cauliflower ears and I made myself into a frightening gargoyle. In short, my very powerful belief, powered by a strong imagination and a will to volition, built a world around me that was in the very image of my perceptual blueprint. I was unknowingly creating monsters with my mind-projections that were so visceral and so real that they manifested as actual characters in my life. Then I set out to defeat the very monsters I had created, and said to everyone that would listen, 'isn't the world violent, it is so full of monsters.'

I created them. I forgot I'd created them. I went out into the world to combat the *wonderful creations* that I had birthed and forsaken. I stood on a nightclub door for all those years devising techniques, strategies and philosophies to deal with monsters of my own making, projected trolls that only existed in the mines of my own Moria-mind.

I was involved in thousands of violent affrays and bloody encounters and life-and-death struggles before I was able to recognise this.

If discovering the potency of the pre-emptive strike was splitting the atom, discovering that I was the one creating the violence in the first place, took me into the quantum realm.

It was revelation beyond revelation.

As I sit here now, writing these words, I am inspired all over again by my understanding of human potential, for both good and bad. I am astounded by the creative power of belief, especially when it is united with imagination and faith and powered by human volition.

I am certain of this potential. I have proof. For many years I placed my entire consciousness in the belief in monsters, and I subsequently manifested a daisy-chain of trolls in all their guises, who literally made queues and took turns to assail me.

I created all of this with my unchallenged belief. When I finally understood this, when I eventually came face to face with the fact that the world was violent and sick and it was all my fault, I killed the belief dead. I stopped feeding the erroneous perception that I had enemies in the world and that my enemies were sitting in rooms somewhere trying to make life difficult for me.

When the belief was no longer fed the belief no longer lived.

I withdrew my faith in the lie, and it was emaciated by my refusal to engage it. As it became skinny and frail so too did the violent world these beliefs had created.

I created them, I maintained them, which meant that I could kill them dead, simply by turning my focused attention, my consciousness, in another direction. It was like denying weeds soil and light. They do not last long if they are not fed. Consciousness creates reality. What we tightly focus our energy on we create. When we hold that focus, we maintain what we have created. When we withdraw attention, we deny and decrease the reality we have created.

This, by far, was the most important thing I learned from working the door.

Another important lesson, leagues above and beyond the lessons of martial efficacy, was this: when I took my bones onto the doors of Coventry, **I was noticed**.

Not just by the enemies of my employ, and not just by the new teachers that appear to any student who does the work, but also by people, nice people, especially female people. I didn't have very healthy self-esteem. I mentioned this earlier. I also mentioned that this made me into a conjugal punch bag. Actually it had made me into a societal punch bag; even my own inner voice kicked sand in my face. My esteem was kept low by myself, and by the people in my world who felt duty bound to place their heel on my neck every time I tried to raise my confidence from horizontal to vertical: the woman I woke up with in the morning, the foremen and the bosses in the factory, the middle classes I'd been taught to fear, and the lofty upper classes who seemed to regard me and my ilk as dangerous animals in a cage. Then, suddenly, esteem lifted by the new platform at the top of my fear pyramid, I was noticed. I was being fed a little bit of attention. I liked it. In fact, I gobbled it up like a hungry ghost. People were suddenly paying attention to the guy on the door, the man who says yay or nay. The soft-spoken skinny bloke sweeping around the lathe in the engineering factory was no longer 'that skinny twat with a stoop and a broom'; rather he was 'a bouncer from the town'.

To be a bouncer in this neck of the woods was to be someone. If you could *have a fight* you were respected. The greater majority of men couldn't fight the tide in the bath, so anyone good with their fists, was admired, looked up to, feared even.

Attention grows something new in you, especially when you have been starved of it. A new element awakens. Something deep and vital is nourished, something hidden and it challenges the parasite of self-loathing, that man of misery who squats inside you, the one that insists you are a piece of shit and then feeds off your squirm.

The girls notice you too.

Ah the girls, yes, the girls, they like an assured man, a man of position. They certainly took a shine to me. I may have had a hairline that went back as far as the first world war, but they liked me, they flirted with me, some of them gave me drunken flashes of frilly knickers (it was that kind of club) just to delight me, a few fell in love with me, and more than one beauty formed an obsession with the cute bouncer, the soft-spoken one *who stands on that club door.*

This sort of attention, as flattering as it was, would later seduce me, and get me into all sorts of trouble when a healthy esteem bloated into a gluttonous and shameless adulterer.

But more on this a little later.

Initially, the attention did me the world of good. It took a bat to the part of me that insisted I was as ugly as a bridge troll and beat it into submission.

My self-esteem grew on a (not always healthy) diet of admiration and attention. It also grew as my ability to manage violent situations burgeoned. When you can control yourself and that control extends itself to others, your confidence becomes naturally muscular and alert. It walks proud in the street, it turns heads when you enter a bar, and it finds favour with people of influence.

I realised that my world had expanded. I was now entering new rooms, many new rooms, but not all of them were good.

I didn't realise until much later that new rooms in the world appeared because I had created new rooms in me. When you make space in you, you create space in the world. When you make a lot of space in you, the new space in the world is proportionately expanded.

This is no metaphor, this is metaphysical.

When I say that by removing old fears I created room, I am not being entirely accurate. Their removal did not create room, as much as they revealed the room that was always there. It was blocked by the invisible fatbergs of fear and false belief, by perception and cognition, unresolved hurt, simmering grudges, familial inheritance, and ancestral bias - the congealed mass of human detritus that blocks the narrow gate we must all enter through in order to reveal the esoteric, the fabled clear view.

When you challenge and dismiss fear and false belief new doors open up to you. Through these new doors you meet new teachers who guide you and direct you to other rooms and other realities in the many mansions promised to us in mystical eschatology.

Space is made for new birth when we remove outdated and redundant perceptions. All the old beliefs have to go, the lies we have been told, and the lies we tell ourselves over and again in our minds. The moment we expose a non-truth and disprove it, the fatberg is penetrated and conscious awareness automatically rushes in. The lie we all nurture about limitation, is a house-ghost that stands sentry at every esoteric doorway. When we have the courage to face him down, he has no choice but to allow us entry.

This access is automatic when we kiss the leper. Recognition and liberation are simultaneous.

I had inadvertently stumbled upon this truth the moment I wrote my fears, my non-truths, on a pad, at a time when the only world I could see was one of scarcity. When I removed even a single fear, consciousness rushed in, filled the vacated space and everything previously hidden became immediately accessible.

I would have to repeat this exercise many times before I became properly aware of the process and my own potential within it. Once I understood that arcanum was hidden inside fear, like Rumi's *Night Hunter* I went in search of my own fears in order to liberate the effulgence they held.

The doors being opened by my freshly awakening consciousness were often very literal. The door of the night club. That was first. Next was the door to a new job. I mentioned this earlier. Instead of working shifts in a factory - a job I'd been miserable in for seven years - I started working days on a building site, learning new skills and constructing grand buildings that strangely mirrored the infrastructure being newly erected in me.

I was working the doors at night and on the building site in the day.

I would maintain this two-job reality for many years.

It sounds gruelling I know, but I loved every minute of my new freedom. I was like an excited puppy taken to the beach for the first time: I didn't know whether to run or piss or paddle in the sea. I was living two lives at the same time, both of them in extremis. The building sites were as unrelenting in their own way as the doors, but this meant I was getting twice the learning, twice the pay and two times the life experience.

My learning growth was off the charts.

This young factory worker, frightened of change, working in menial jobs for a miser's wage, was suddenly the change-meister, commanding great money as a bouncer, and learning a highly skilled trade as a bricklayer. Before I finished my stint on the sites, I would be able to build a house from scratch. I could construct a full house from a detailed blueprint. Not bad for a floor sweeper, who left school with no qualifications. By the time I left the doors, I would be able to control my central nervous system, in situations where my life was threatened. Pretty good for a quivering wreck, a man that was once afraid of a spider in the bath.

I made friends on the building sites, real friends. These were hardy working men, each of them living in a separate reality to mine, each of them looking out into a different world to the one I inhabited. Each of these people opened the door to their own very private reality for me and I entered yet another world and I found yet more teachers who knew of other teachers who taught of other doors that I could explore and enter, ad infinitum.

The building sites, like the doors, were demanding, the labour was back-breaking and relentless and the work highly skilful. A man had to have tremendous control of his faculties if he was going to stay in this employ for any length of time. Again, it demanded real self-control to exist in this room. The men were extremely physical. Often they were challenging. Many of them came from violent backgrounds and they brought their ferocity with them to the workplace with their sandwiches and flask. It was in their manner, in their gait, in their highly colourful vernacular, and in their fists when hard language spilled into hard violence. In these mucky brick-and-mortar domains, the brutal workload often attracted large egos with small intellects, so offence was often and easily taken; physical conflict was the usual result.

Every night after work on the site, lying in the bath like a beaten thing, fingertips torn and bloody from the labour, body crying out its alarm, you had to develop a hardy centre to stop your inner dialogue from throwing you into outright chaos. I have lost count of the amount of times I soaked in that bath, close to tears, and told myself *I just can't do this*. But you learned quickly about the inner voice of doom, the man of misery, always running from fear, always searching for comfort. You learned by necessity to control those rogue elements, the fears that keep extraordinary men locked in the ordinary. In short, you learned command.

The new doors I was opening, the new teachers that were finding me, the worlds that I was entering were always potentially there. More specifically, these infinite rooms of reality had always existed - they were in me, they are in me. The sage teachers that sit in their lofty rooms, waiting to hand over the cloak of learning, they were always in me too, willing to guide, eager to instruct, but also ready to cut me down if I strayed too far outside of my due.

I realised that there was not a single door I could not access by removing the obstacles that stood in my way.

Later, using this new-found knowledge I would open many exciting doors. Some led me into the halls of academia, others revealed the secret places, private clubs hidden in plain sight, and more still led me into the homes of mysterious gurus who appeared in my life at pivotal moments to guide me towards a particular truth, or to nudge me away from a specific danger.

Some of the rooms I entered were dangerous, none less so than the nightclubs I worked which had proved to be an invaluable human Petri dish. Initially, I only intended to keep myself under the microscope for a very short time, but I became so immersed in my personal testing that I lost all track of time. Weeks became months and months became years. Suddenly, the neophyte became the adept, uncertainty was replaced by confidence, sometimes arrogance, and the kid working the door in search of salvation soon became a monster running the door in need of redemption.

I went on the door looking for myself and somewhere along the way I lost complete touch with any sense of self.

Over time, subtly, by piece- by-piece, I became darker and darker. The humble became hubris, the confidence bloated into arrogance, and the 'care' became 'don't fucking care at all'. I had learned how to have a fight. I had unearthed secrets but was unconsciously seduced into exploiting these secrets for my own ends. The physical confidence I used to guard club doors became a violent and ignorant method of problem solving. If there was a situation that could not be fixed with badinage or a little over-the-table negotiation, I used violence or the threat of violence as a means of redress.

I was obsessed perhaps possessed with my new-found power. I became known in the city of my birth, a fighter with a reputation. I was a nice man but if people got in my way, if they opposed me, I knocked them back or I knocked them out.

I was known for it. It was what people respected me for.

I thought it was what people respected me for.

It was not respect. They feared me.

I didn't realise this until much later; they feared me because I was violent.

I was no longer the admired bouncer from the town that people loved. I was the violent maniac that people recoiled from.

And rightly so: I was insecure, selfish and with a violent hair-trigger. I would think nothing of laying you out if you pressed me too hard in the places where I was still sensitive.

I was an infamous bouncer with a degree of local celebrity and I was about to spread the infamy by sharing my stories in ink.

I wrote my first book.

6

Watch My Back

While I was still working the doors, I started to teach my *certainties* in local martial arts classes. These quickly expanded into regional, national, international and eventually global training courses. People queued to learn these new arcana. And, when the classes got sufficiently big and more and more people wanted to hear my stories of derring-do and learn the lessons from my sojourn into the seedy underbelly of nightclub security, I wrote a book. I placed my learning onto the pages of three notepads and recorded it in ink.

When I was first depressed as a sad and lonely young man, looking for answers, searching for balm and finding neither, some people told me that I should acquiesce and accept my condition, that I should give in to the inevitable; I had got this depression (or it had got me) for life.

Forgive me, I lost the line of honesty for the briefest moment there and tried to generalise a particular.

'People' did not tell me that my life would be determined by the disease of my ancestry, my lovely mum told me.

I was trying to protect her and in doing so I fell. Forgive me.

My mum was my human source. She is where I came from. Her truth, her word, her sound is my sound and it is undeniable, therefore it should never be challenged. She is the oracle, she is the font of all knowledge, and she is always right. Except… except she is not always right. Perhaps she will never be right. I don't know. I don't really care. All I know is she was not right in this case. She was wrong when she insisted that a family condition must by decree become an unavoidable ancestral inheritance. She was trying to protect me I suspect, trying to prepare me for the unfathomable lottery of life. I love my mum's bones. My love for her is unconditional. But that doesn't mean I should lay the burden of omniscience on her. She can't be right about everything. She is not the alpha and omega of truth. I can't trust my mum, I cannot trust my dad, or my friends, my peers should not be trusted, nor my priest, nor my guru or their bibles and philosophies or lore. I definitely can't trust myself, that is one thing I do know, I cannot trust the being known as Geoff Thompson. This leaves only one place to go if I want to find trust proper; God. And as He exists, He speaks to me, He speaks in me and through me. His means of communication is revelation, vision, epiphany, clarity and intuition. My mum told me that depression was my inheritance and that I should just accept this as nature's curse, as there was nothing I could do about it. She didn't lie to me, my mum, but she did not tell the truth. She told me what a doctor had told her when she too was fighting a debilitating depression and the unquestionable impression of a middle-class authority figure never left her. He told her that depression was a chemical imbalance and that only by replacing that chemical with a prescribed anti-depressant would her neurology be redressed.

The doctor was wrong.

My mum was wrong.

When we enter the battleground against perception, no one can be spared; man, woman, mother, father, clinical doctor, church priest or even the pontiff of Rome. All perceptions have to be challenged. All existing cognitions must qualify themselves or fall to the arrow of truth.

So, some people told me to swallow it, others said suck it up, many patronised me with their pity, and thought me a weak mind. More than one persona said *pull yourself together*. Others offered me their answer in a little brown bottle of pills. And the books that I devoured didn't tell me anything at all because they didn't know either. Or, if they did know, they were not saying. This made me so angry that I made a promise, a holy vow: when I find the truth, I'm going to write it down and

I am going to tell everyone.

Watch My Back was my way of honouring that vow. I wrote my first book in the middle cubicle of a factory toilet block where I was employed to sweep floors.

By now I had left the wild but unreliable freedom of the building site, and taken temporary work in a factory again. I went from laying bricks, to sweeping floors, and I will explain why. On the sites, I spent probably two years doing the most gruelling physical and mental work of my entire life. It was hugely challenging and extremely exhilarating but ultimately it became untenable as a reliable method of earning a wage. I was still married at the time. My children were very young. I had a mortgage to pay, so for now I needed a steady wage. Building work was largely weather reliant, which meant unless the job was inside and under cover (very rare) your weekly wage was entirely determined by the temperature. You couldn't lay bricks below a certain degree because the mortar would not set. You couldn't lay bricks in the rain either because the water would run into the mortar joints, ruining the facia. So, if it was too cold, you didn't work. Ours was self-employed piece work (we were paid by the amount of bricks we laid), so no bricks laid meant no wage collected. Even worse, the moment a drop of rain fell from the sky one of the keener drinkers in the gang would announce joyfully 'lager clouds!' and everyone would down tools and seek refuge in the nearest pub. An afternoon session ensued, subbing money from the foreman that we hadn't even earned yet. By the end of the week, whatever money we'd borrowed to fund the session was subtracted from whatever money we had managed to earn on the dry days. The balance was rarely enough to meet our weekly bills.

The men I worked with were the hardest working, most charismatic, funny, dark, colourful characters I had ever met (outside of working the doors) so I was sad to leave - but needs must.

I took a job as a factory labourer. I never intended to stay there for long, but I needed a steady income, and this job was the right fit. The work was tedious, it was unchallenging but regular and that made it, temporarily, very appealing. At that time, it was the means I was looking for to meet my financial ends. It was here, at The Apex on Red Lane in Coventry, that I first started sharing the nightclub stories with my friends and colleagues over a tea, leaning on the broom around the lathe and across the table at breakfast and dinner breaks. My stories were fresh from the oven. I was often sharing experiences that had occurred only the night before. I told of friends and fiends, I re-enacted the bloody fights fought at the club door, the debacles that spilled out onto the street pavement and ended up at the city hospital or the local police station. I painted visceral pictures of frenzied maniacs, seductive sirens, beautiful prostitutes, menacing pimps, men turning up at our door with guns, knife battles on the beer sticky club carpet, showdowns with notorious gangsters and all of the other nasty and nice occurrences in that world of disco lights and loud music. They took to my stories like voyeurs, my friends, and I revelled in the telling. One particular day, one of my new friends, a lathe turner called Steve, said, 'Geoff, you should write these stories down, they're really good'.

And that's how it started.

That is all it took.

A casual suggestion from a friend. His words blew fresh oxygen onto the sleeping embers of my dream of becoming a writer and suddenly I was all aflame.

It did not have to be suggested twice, I know that much.

Hours later, I found myself excitedly sitting on the factory toilet writing my first book. The stories were there to be told. They were rude, they were loud and challenging, some of them were very funny, some sad, many read scary even in the pages of a book, but above and beyond everything else, the stories were all true.

It was not a difficult book to write because the stories were box fresh. As they happened, I wrote them down. I didn't know anything about writing protocol. I had no schooling in the rights and wrongs of layout or form. But at the time I'd just finished reading a series of autobiographical books by a retired policeman called Harry Cole - *A Policeman's Lot* – and a series of books written in a similar vein by an author called Helen Forrester - *Twopence to Cross the Mersey*. The former were the anecdotal tales of a London bobby in the 50s and 60s and the latter a series of autobiographical books about a young middle-class girl whose family fall into poverty in the depressed north of England in the 1930s. I loved both authors. I was inspired by the humour of Harry Cole and the pathos of Helen Forrester, drawn to their collective style. I was inspired by their un-upholstered honesty and I loved how accessible each read was, so I followed their format, I modelled the layout and I wrote my book, in my own voice.

I loved every minute of writing that first book. Ever since school my dream was to be a writer, and now, here I was, sat on the loo writing. It came very naturally to me. There was no effort, other than making the time, and sitting down with a pen and pad. The stories told themselves, in exactly the way they wanted to be heard; I was just there to facilitate them, a vessel through which they could find expression.

I have to admit that, not even in my wildest romantic reverie did I ever imagine that my working office would be a stinky factory toilet, and neither did I envisage that I'd be writing a bouncer's story on cheap notepads (seconded from the factory stores) using a biro with a chewed lid. But the writer writes. That is first and foremost. And he writes about what he knows, he uses whatever material he can find, and if he really wants to write, he will find somewhere to sit and make his book; anywhere and everywhere is his office.

That's how you know he or she is a writer.

In a couple of months, *Watch My Back* was finished. I was very proud of the fact that against all the odds I had written a book. Well I say a book, it was the beginnings of a book. And it was a book of truth. It was not a work of fancy or fiction. I'd remembered my vow, during the depression years, the promise I'd made to tell the truth when I found the truth and share it with others as it was revealed to me.

I injected the sharp nib of my cheap biro into the rich inkwell of truth and refused to stop until everything was on the page. I told of my depressions, my fears, my anxieties and my doubts. I did not present myself as a brave or fearless warrior with Teflon skin and concrete will. Quite the opposite. I wrote about how nervous and timid I had been and how afraid I still felt. I also spoke of my curiosity. I was hungry to understand and keen to learn. I presented myself as I was: naked. So much so, that my brother Ray, after reading an early draft asked me, 'Are you sure you want to publish this Geoff?'

'Yes' I answered, 'why?'

He looked at me with the genuine concern of an older sibling: 'Because it makes you look very vulnerable'.

Those were his words.

Vulnerable.

That was his assessment. What an unintended but beautiful compliment.

'Ray' I said, 'what is the point of writing a book if I can't be vulnerable?'

He nodded. He understood, and in that moment I too understood why most people do not write books or even attempt to write books. Or they start but fail to finish their work. The whole process from beginning to end is one of gaping vulnerability.

'Who is it going to help Ray, if I am not honest?'

I realised too why all the books I'd previously read had not been truthful: the authors were afraid to be vulnerable.

If you can't show vulnerability in the life of art and in the art of life, what is the point and how will we grow?

Every crustacean worth its pincers knows that it has to shed an old shell in order to form a new one. Every crab in the sea understands that when it sheds its shell-world in order to expand into a new world, it is vulnerable to risk and open to attack, not just from natural predators but also from its own kind, other crabs.

And so it was. This was my first real look at why people fail to grow, because they fail to risk.

It was interesting too how wildly variable my own opinion of the book was, as I read and re-read it on different days and in changing moods. It was as though the quality of my writing changed according to which personality was reading the text.

I can remember sitting in my car one day reading a particular section of the book and smiling. 'This is good', I congratulated myself, 'this is very good'. The very next day, in my car, sat in the very same place, reading the exact same page of words, I remember thinking, 'This is shit!'

It wasn't until the book was eventually in print, in the shops, and before the eyes of discerning readers that I was able to read it with any kind of objectivity. And it wasn't until many years later that I was able to fully comprehend what a box of delights this small book contained.

Watch My Back was complete, but once you have a book written down, what next? How do you get a book from ink on a notepad to print on a clean sheet of copy paper? My world was still very small at the time. I was a working-class kid, working in a factory sweeping floors. I didn't know anyone with a typewriter. This was the 1980s, no computers yet. Only posh people owned a typewriter and I was certainly not one of them. In the world of 'us' and 'them', I was definitely in the former category. Without a means of taking my notepads to print I didn't know what to do next – I was at an impasse. Where should I go from here?

Obviously, where my head is now, where my consciousness is right now, I would have done the rigour. I would have found a professional typist and paid them to transcribe my words, or I'd have earned the money to buy a typewriter and developed the skillset to type them out myself.

I didn't know that the book was calling me to educate myself in the world of publishing. I didn't understand yet that it was encouraging me to expand my conscious net and find the contacts I needed (they were out there), and learn the skills necessary to get my book transcribed.

A few months later, book written, safely ensconced in my three notepads, Steve - the friend who had initially encouraged me to write - asked me how I was getting on with it. I told him the book was finished but it needed typing. Typing was a posh job, I told him, and I didn't know anyone posh. Out of the blue he said, 'my sister's got a typewriter. Give me the pads and I'll get her to type it out for you'.

I now knew a typist.

Before long, I had my book in black type on white paper. '**WATCH MY BACK**' in capitals, in bold, on the front page. 'Watch My Back - by Geoff Thompson'. I looked at it and I looked at it until it felt real in my head.

Where I came from people did not write books. They did not have books published and in the shops. And those that thought they could write a book and become a published author were either deluded fools or pretentious twats. Deluded I could deal with, but the charge of pretension was a growling beast in my mind, the fanged mutt-of-fear that was as frightening as a loose tiger in a small room. The thought that anyone might think me pretentious was a very real terror. The idea that anyone might accuse me of getting above my station had always stopped me from contemplating what a station was, let alone perusing the potentials of personal development. My conditioning had groomed me as a people-pleaser, a timid follower who would rather fail abysmally than be seen to be trying too hard.

The moment you put your tall poppy-head above the social crowd, there was always someone in the field - often the whole field combined - who would want to cut you down to size.

I kept looking at the printed manuscript until it became real in my head that this was my book and no matter what happened next, I had written it. It was very real. It was a manifest certainty. And just because I didn't know of anyone of my ilk who had published a book, that didn't mean it wasn't possible. Hadn't I climbed a fear pyramid, against all expectations? Hadn't I picked up a spider and sat in a dentist's chair and stood up to my wife and mother and changed jobs, and experienced all kinds of unlikely miracles en route? Hadn't I risked my life by standing on a nightclub door?

I had stood up to my wife! Anything was possible.

I reminded myself of the successes. I recounted the things I'd learned thus far and reached back to those reference points for guidance and inspiration. My fear of being considered pretentious was just that, a fear. And, if I'd learned one thing already, it was this: when you intercourse with your fear, when you embrace your fear, it becomes your footstool; the whole world at large becomes your footstool.

So, the nebulous fear of seeming pretentious went on my mental pyramid and I set out to dissolve it by finding a publisher for my book.

There was a new part of me, a growing self that, frankly, didn't give too much of a fuck what other people thought about me, pretentious or otherwise. And when that personality rose, the throbbing fear of being seen as a bighead withdrew. But it did not disappear completely, it just hid, and lay dormant and waited for an appropriate time to rise again, and feed on my insecurities like a winter lion. Actually, this fear was less of a roaming lion, and more of a stealthy scavenger, waiting for convenient prey to pass its way. It was to feed on me many more times and for many more years before I was finally able to recognise this parasite as 'not self' and send it on its way.

Like all shadows, they rise to claim or be claimed.

This one was so subtle, so quiet, and so clandestine that I hardly noticed it. It was a humming constant in the background of my life. Looking back, I can see it was always, always there, perhaps that's why I hadn't noticed it. Something that is so present it becomes invisible.

It might seem innocuous, even ridiculous, this fear of getting above my station; it might seem benign. But sitting here now, at the age of fifty-nine and looking back, I can see that this fear was like a cancer in me, a growth on my psyche that just kept on expanding and taking up room. It left me with a cold, hard belief that I was not good enough, that asking for more was greedy, that aspiration was selfish, that the desire to explore was irresponsible (you've got a job, you've got kids to feed), that belief in possibility was juvenile and naive and that only a village fool would believe in impossible things. I can still feel the sting now, rising up in me as I write these words. I can see the look on the faces of certain individuals, friends and family, when I shared my aspirations - dissonant, disappointed, pitying, exasperated, judgmental, fearful, angry, incredulous, despising, reprimanding, and enraged. Yes, some people, key folk in my life, were enraged by my aspiration. Not necessarily an aspiration to be socially mobile, I think even then I knew that class was little more than a gossamer-thin idea, a perception that anyone but the blind would see through if they really opened their eyes. No, not social mobility, that was too small, it was situated on a lower rung of the ladder that I was eager to climb. Evolution was what fascinated me. The potential of me, a human being, to be fully realised, even though, at the time, I didn't have the understanding or the language to articulate this. I knew there was a place beyond grasping and I wanted to experience it.

This was all good for me of course. Even if I couldn't see it at the time, it was cleansing because, metaphysically, the light I was receiving by removing the shadow of my fears was not only exposing the vices in my friends, it was highlighting the same vices that still existed in me.

Their dissonance and rage etc. were my dissonance and rage.

I later learned that one of the Siddhas, the miracles of expansion, was the ability to recognise people as mirrors, reflections of oneself.

Of course, their dissonance triggered my own dissonance.

'Why are they behaving like this, I don't understand?'

Their disappointment in me triggered my disappointment in them.

'Why can't they just be happy for me?'

Their fear brought out my fear.

'What if they are right? Am I being unrealistic, am I being a pretentious twat?'

I quickly learned to despise the despisers and criticise the critics and attack the attackers. Their vice became my vice. Their poultice my poultice. Once I saw this, once I recognised the world as a reflection, and its people the mirrors, I used them to locate areas in my own game that I could improve. They became the whetstone on which I sharpened my consciousness. They became a vital tool in my apophatic theology, my religion of negation, the perfection of the self via reduction.

The core problem here was that I didn't believe I was worthy. The reaction of my friends and family, and my reaction to their reaction, told me as much. It was an ancient belief passed down as the baton of the ages, confirmed by the very scarcity it produced, and aged in the barrel of my ancestry. I did not feel worthy of anything better than my designated lot. Belief is reality and if reality is to be changed, then belief has to be changed first. If belief is to be changed, it has to be located, it has to be drawn out of the swamps of our minds and exposed to the light of scrutiny.

They lay hidden, these monsters. They feed on obscurity. They live in the dark and the only way to bring the vampires into the light is to head towards the things you dream of doing. If the blocks that stand between here and there are hidden, if the shadow-hurdles between man and his ambitions are not visible or if they are present but vague, or vague but lack clarity, head towards the dream and watch as the blocks appear before you. Observe as the invisible hurdles become visible impediments. Witness the devils of scripture appear in their full regalia.

They are there these blocks. They are present but we can't see them. They are dominant but disguised. Approach the object of your desire, the dream job, the book you want to write, the love you'd like to win, the life you dream of living, approach them, move forwards and the blocks - the wrong beliefs, the fears, the doubts, the denials, the distractions - they will appear before you ready to claim you or be claimed.

The defilements that stood between me and a better job, between me and good mental health, between me and being brave had already risen on my fear pyramid, and I had overcome them.

I saw them because my approach drew them out. I claimed them by confronting them and denying their validity. Now I was approaching something that I'd always dreamed of doing and the fear of elevation, my belief in my unworthiness, the curse of my class, rose and I trampled over them in the stampede towards my goal.

I was worthy of anything, that was the truth.

I was worthy of everything, that was a fact.

At my very core, in the depths of my soul, my ground of being, below the perceptual waves of vicissitude, not only was the vast ocean of everything available to me, I was that vast ocean, I was everything.

Back then, trying to publish a book, crippled by doubt, I did not know any of this.

Beyond the impediments that stood in my way, there was a certainty that was my ground of being. I knew it was there. I could smell it. I could feel it. On a good day with a clear view I could see it and touch it. Occasionally I held it in my hand, but it was ephemeral, and it dissipated before I could ever get a full grasp on it.

The certainty I needed to publish my book was already mine: I just needed to remove the society imposed, self-maintained roadblocks, those pesky fears, and reclaim it.

I needed to get myself closer to having my book in print.

The jump from writing words on notepads in a factory toilet to seeing a finished book in a Waterstones shop window was too much of an ask. I just couldn't get my mind there. Every time I stretched my imagination to the idyll it flipped back like snapped elastic. If I could get some actual manifest proof of my potential, real proof, an external validation from an authoritative source, something bigger than an unpublished manuscript, but smaller than a published book, it would surely bridge the gap, and take my self-belief a little closer to the next station. I needed to expand my current belief so that the gaping chasm between here and there could be lessened, but how? My good friend, a brilliant martial artist called Ian McCranor, massively helped me at this point. He read the book. He loved every page and he unreservedly championed me. He was an international karataka, a member of the British squad. He was very erudite, he had much more experience than me and I trusted his word. He encouraged me to persevere, he felt certain that if I did, my book would find a home. His words greatly helped me to expand my imagination, so that I could visualise myself in print.

But even with all of Ian's infectious enthusiasm, the gap still seemed too big to jump. I had a moment of inspiration.

The construction of my pyramid triggered an idea.

I wrote an article about my quest to overcome fears and sent it one of the martial arts magazines I'd been following. The article I wrote was called *Confrontation Desensitisation*, and the magazine was Terry O'Neill's *Fighting Arts International*.

Terry's magazine was glossy. It was full colour with hard-core editorial, written by and featuring some of the best martial artists in the world. I ordered the magazine every month. I bought extra copies and sold them to my own martial arts students. I wanted them to be inspired and the magazine was brimming over with inspirational manna.

Magazine writing was new to me. I had never attempted it before, but it felt a lot easier to write an 800 word article than a 45,000 word book.

Terry, the editor, was a walking phenomenon. He was a senior grade, world class Karate teacher. He was also my hero. I sent him the article. I was chancing my arm really. I had no idea how to write an article, I understood neither formatting nor magazine etiquette. I just wrote the words, I got them typed out (I knew people who could do that now) and I sent it off, with fingers firmly crossed. It was a risk. I was very nervous about sending my short piece off to a prestigious publication. If a man as influential as Terry had written back and told me that I didn't have it (whatever it is) and that I should leave my number in the bin, it could have been enough to abort my confidence at this embryonic stage. I may have sacked the book as a bad job, and shrunk back to the weak specimen I used to be. It can happen. At this stage in your development a strong word from a respected influence can make or break you. In this case it proved to be the latter, and my risk paid off. A very short time later I had a phone call. It was from Terry.

Yes, Terry rang me!

It probably won't mean a lot to you if you don't know martial arts and you've never heard of Terry O'Neill (what is wrong with you?!). If you were an aspiring amateur footballer, it would be like Gareth Southgate calling you to comment on your amazing football skills and inviting you onto the England squad. Or if you were a budding thespian, steeped in am-dram, it would be the equivalent of Scorsese ringing to offer you a part in his next movie, and saying *you can really act kid...* it was that kind of thing.

Terry rang. He loved my article. He was going to publish it in his next edition, and he wanted to let me know personally that he thought I had something.

Terry O'Neill.

He thought I had *something!*

He told me that his editor at the magazine, a non-martial artist, had marked the article out as one to look at, he said it was a piece of writing with note. I was thrilled. Not only was my work being published but the man I'd idolised my entire martial arts career had called me personally to pass on the good news. Someone else could have made the same comments and it might not have got past the walls of self-doubt. But a man like Terry must have known that his platform and my respect for him would have magnified his words enough to penetrate the bubble of insecurity and impress themselves on my hard drive as a proof of potential.

In other words, if Terry said something was true, there could be no doubting that it was true.

Within a couple of months Terry O'Neill published my first article. It was in print. I was a real writer. This personal proof weakened my doubt and took me one step closer to the dream of publishing a book.

If you can publish one article and get paid, you are a professional writer. You are professional because you have been published and you have been paid. If you can publish one article, you can publish two articles, why not? You can publish three. I eventually went on to publish hundreds of articles for martial arts magazines, men's magazines, right up to a two thousand word feature for the Sunday Times Newspaper. If you can publish an article, you can publish a book, a book after all is only an extended version of an article. If you can publish a book, why not ten books and if you can publish a book, surely you can write a stage play and a film - what about a musical for stage?

One article in a small reputable martial arts magazine might not seem like any big shakes, but for me it opened the vault doors, and everything inside was now mine for the taking.

This was a massive, massive moment for me.

I didn't know why it felt so important to me at the time, and I didn't know exactly where it would lead. I only knew that something had happened, and it was going to be the catalyst for wonders to come. Ezekiel said, 'Look to the nations and be amazed, for I am going to bring you things in your days that you would not believe even if you were told'.

This is how I felt when Terry O'Neill published my very first piece of work.

My wife didn't react very well to my published article.

Actually, to say she didn't react well is an overstatement. She didn't react at all. She was quiet and subdued.

If I'd known then what I know now, if I'd known she was afraid, I would have still followed the new path, I have no doubt about that; but I would have been more delicate and understanding, I'd have been careful with those close to me, the loved ones who would not join me on the coming adventure. There was a very sad part of me that quietly knew my wife would be one of them. She would not travel with me.

I would have to go on alone or not go on at all.

My dharma compelled me to drive hard and drive forwards, even if I didn't know how particularly, or where to or why. I intuited that the optimum route would reveal itself to me, street by street, road by road, and city by city: it would all make sense eventually.

The article was published and, once again, I was noticed.

I was no longer the wilting flower hidden in the shade, I was a blooming mass of colourful petals, bathing in the full glow of the midday sun.

When you take yourself out of the shade, of course, you are automatically noticed.

People read the article, people of influence, folk that understood the nature and the calling of public platform, and the courage demanded of those who accept the invitation. More new doors opened. New teachers noticed me, and they made their approach. I had entered a new density. Over the next few years, I would leave my small patch of Coventry soil, and explore ever-broader pastures.

The article also got me noticed by people who wanted to stand in front of me and pay money for my instruction. If writing the article had forced me to condense and quantify and qualify what I'd been learning on my fear pyramid and on the doors, then teaching forced me to deliver this learning in a way that could be understood and practiced by large groups of people.

My classes swelled. Students came. Students told other students and they came too. My confidence, in myself, in what I was teaching, also grew and I fell into the role of guru very comfortably.

At the time I was still working in the factory by day, the clubs by night, teaching classes, and bringing up my beautiful children.

Perhaps this is where I should talk about Sharon.

I will come back to *Watch My Back* imminently.

It is important that I pause for a moment because Sharon was not only the catalyst to me eventually finding a publisher for my book, she was also the reason why I was eventually able to eschew bouncing and end my covenant with the violent way.

About Sharon

What can I say about Sharon that is not immediately evident in every beat, pause and hesitation I feel in approaching this aspect of the book?

What can I tell you about Sharon?

I can tell you that in this world she is my alpha and that she is my omega.

On the mountain of purgation, she is Beatrice in the empyrean, and I am the poet who climbed out of the fire to claim her.

She is my religion; she is the bringer of joy.

This all sounds very nice.

I like it, and it is true of course, it has been true and no matter what the future might bring, it will always be true.

I was the maverick combative teacher, breaking all the rules, making-over a martial arts milieu that was archaic and untested.

I was the teacher. Sharon was my star student. She was brilliant and sharp and funny and beautiful, with her short, spikey hair and the most beautiful, enigmatic face.

She was everything I'd ever wanted in a partner, a lover and a friend.

But I was married.

I was twenty-seven years old at the time, and married. I had three children. I had responsibilities; I had made the holy vow of matrimony before a priest.

Sharon still lived at home with her parents.

The spark between us was instant. We both felt it, even though our relationship was not physically consummated until sometime later.

I was the one that initiated the affair not her.

I was a hypocrite. Of course. Teaching budo, teaching self-knowing, and self-control, ethics and morals and virtue, and I swept all of that good talk aside and fell violently in love with Sharon.

And her with me.

If there was a moment, one single instant where the relationship tipped from attraction and admiration into full-fat, in-your-face love, it was when I gave Sharon the typed manuscript of *Watch My Back* to read. She read the book and loved it, and I loved her for loving it. I told her I wanted to be a writer; she said 'Geoff, you already are a writer.'

Sharon had taken my fledgling words and proclaimed me a bonafide scribe, and I was so moved by her simple and fearless affirmation that I fell in love with her instantly. If there was a consummating moment in this marriage of souls, it was outside Buster's Nightclub, on a quiet Wednesday night, when this astonishing vision turned up, on her own, just to hand back my manuscript, just to tell me that I need search no longer for the grail, I was it.

I can still see her now, walking towards me. I can still feel the tingle of love rising in me. I can see her face and hear her voice and the absolute certainty in her words when she delivered her assessment. It was the innocent and unconditional nature of her delivery that moved me, as though she was speaking the most obvious and undeniable truth in the world. I was the laughing Alice in a strange looking-glass-world proclaiming that 'there is no use trying, one can't believe impossible things.' And Sharon was the white queen of certainty, telling me that, regarding impossible things, 'I daresay you haven't had much practice.'

Sharon believed in me.

In that moment, at the front door of a city club, before the peak-hour rush of customers, just me and her sharing an eternal moment on a Coventry pavement, she believed in me, way, way before I was ever able to believe in myself.

I was so fucked up from my past, the sexual predator of my youth who invaded my thoughts and taught me that no one could be trusted, and the fists of my class pummelling the belief into me that I was not worth protecting anyway.

I was so emotionally damaged that even on this violent platform, I still did not believe in myself.

It took a young angel to fill me with her belief until I could grow my own. I loved her so much in that moment that I lack the literary dexterity to bring it to the page.

I loved her. And today I love her absolutely, my sage, my Alma.

I have to tell you that I was so in love that I forgot myself. But I also forgot my marriage, and I forgot my children. I am ashamed to recall this now, to place my sin onto the parchment of this page. It would be easy for me to project at this point, and rationalise my behaviour and criticise the behaviour of others to forgive my own. But that would be disingenuous, that would be an unforgivable lie; and I have already told enough of those over the years, more than I can ever hope I be forgiven for.

I was selfish. I was deceptive. I lied. I hurt my family. I wounded my wife. I traumatised my children when the marriage eventually fell apart. I hurt my mum and dad. I offended Sharon's parents. I dishonoured my students and I defiled and defamed myself by physically consummating a relationship whilst I was still vowed to another person - and all this whilst preaching the virtues of Budo to students who trusted me.

If you look the word hypocrite up in the Oxford Dictionary, you may very well find a photograph of me in place of a definition.

This is clear to me now.

It was not clear to me then.

I rationalised my behaviour. I blamed other people for not caring about me. They didn't care about me, so it was their fault that they lost me - **this was a lie.**

At that particular time, I had woken up to many things in my life; my potential, my ambition, my ability to create. But emotionally I was still a boy. I naively believed that I could hide my relationship with Sharon, leave my wife - I told myself that she didn't want me anyway, she'd told me as much, so it wouldn't matter - and then pretend that Sharon and I had fallen in love, post-divorce and everything would work out perfectly.

This is not how it works.

That is not how karma, the self-levelling, reciprocal universe operates.

This was certainly not how it worked for me.

I had already left my wife on other occasions, long before I ever met Sharon. Our relationship was volatile, and we were prone to rows, arguments and fallouts. When I left the first time I didn't know where to go. All I knew was that I was not happy, and hoped that, beyond my marriage, I might find contentment. I'd get a flat where I could have my kids at weekends. I could start again and eventually, officially, bring Sharon into the picture, job done.

This was not my experience.

I told a friend at work that I was leaving my wife, and he said matter-of-factly, 'You will be in for a very difficult time.'

I can still remember smugly thinking, 'Difficult how? She doesn't even love me.'

That's how naive I was.

Eleven years married, four children, I thought I'd be able to leave the marriage-pool without creating any ripples on the surface.

Ripples!?

Man, there was wave upon giant wave, and after the waves, large ripples that carried themselves across time and space, that would have an effect on me, my wife and my kids (and Sharon) for years and years to come.

Divorce always incurs damage. Of course. But if I'd been brave enough, If I'd been wise enough and decent enough to control myself, and end my marriage with honesty and integrity before consummating my love with Sharon, I know that karma would have been kinder to me, and kinder still to all those around me that got caught up in my whirlwind of indefensible deception.

At the time I didn't have that kind of courage in reserve. I had neither the integrity nor the emotional intelligence to understand what the fuck I was doing, and the hell I was about to bring down on myself.

This is not written in the tone of regret.

I was where I was.

Spiritually, I was asleep. I can no sooner change who I was back then or what I did than I can change the weather. To regret even a moment of my past, would be to regret who I am today, thirty years along on my journey - wiser and kinder for it, sitting in a Coventry café, trying to make an honest fist of my notes.

I am blissfully happy.

I wake up every morning talking to God. I talk to God all day (I am talking to God now: *hello there!*) and at night I go to bed talking to God. Had I not defiled the virtues, had I not gone toe-to-toe with karma, believing that I could win, had I not made every single solitary one of those mistakes, in my marriage, on the doors, in my life, there is no way I would have (eventually) turned so acutely towards the divine and embraced a holy life, and made my Hippocratic oath to 'do no harm'. None of this could have come to light, had I not first gone through those painful dark nights of the soul.

I am the sum total of all my parts. I regret none of my past, though I vow never, never, never to hurt someone like that again. Never.

When I eventually left, my lovely wife took it very badly and I took her taking it badly very hard too. I wanted the transition to be smooth and without incident. It was neither. It wasn't until I actually announced that I was leaving, that I'd be staying at a friend's flat, and packed my clothes into two black bin-liners, that my wife realised she didn't want me to go after all, that she did love me, and she wouldn't cope 'just fine without me'.

She broke down, and her breaking down wounded me.

Even though I didn't *love* her, I still loved her; I love her to this day. I have four beautiful children with her, these kids are my blood, they are my life, how could I not love her? But I didn't *love her* love her. The romantic love we'd once shared had perished a long time ago, and it was not going to return any time soon.

I left. I set myself up in the bedroom of a friend's flat. Much later I found a shitty paradise in an itchy bedsit.

I left, and I was gone. I was gone like a soul set free from its coil.

For twenty years after I left, I was still having nightmares about being back in the marital home, in some purgatorial Groundhog Day, having to leave her again and again. It was painful. It was heart-breaking for all concerned, especially my wife who had to live with my mass-deceptions and betrayals and - when she found out about the affair - the fact that I was seeing Sharon.

The deceit was made worse by the fact that I was still sleeping with my wife sporadically, right up until the time she found out about Sharon and the marriage was finally over.

I have no defence for this behaviour, no clear explanation, because I didn't love my wife. Only that in the interim, between leaving her and uniting officially with Sharon, I was the archetypal, selfish, estranged bastard-husband, who did not want his ex-wife, but did not want anyone else to have her either. I can still remember how unkind I was, and how horrible I felt and how cruel it was to keep her holding on. I sat in my car one day, knowing that I had to make a decision: go back to my wife for the sake of the children, (family and friends were trying to *guilt* me into this decision) or officially divorce, and end this dance of misery and deception. I thought about both my wife and Sharon. I tried to imagine life without one and then life without the other. When I imagined how it would feel if I never saw Sharon again, just the thought killed me dead. I could not bear it, not even for a day.

I rang Sharon from a phone box outside the shitty bedsit that had become my new home, the token of my freedom. It was a shithole of a room, in a shithole house with a shared shithole bathroom - and it was the most amazing, beautiful, exhilarating space I have ever lived in. It was my space, and it was a free space. I was free. This shithole was my shithole. And it was to become the foundation stone on which I built the rest of my life. I told Sharon that I had left my wife, and that I was getting a divorce. The phone went quiet. Sharon said nervously, 'I didn't ask you to do that.' I said, 'I know you didn't. But I did it anyway.'

I asked her if she could come around and see me. I heard hesitation in her voice. 'I'm at home,' she said, 'I don't think my mum and dad would be happy.'

I was twenty-nine by that time, Sharon was nineteen. She still lived with her parents, who thought I was just her karate instructor. They had no idea about our relationship, and had they known (they would soon enough) they would not have been happy. Sharon realised in that very moment, as I had realised myself, that in order for us to be together, she would have to give everything up.

Being with me would cost her everything.

When she put the phone down I presumed that this was too much to ask, it was more than she was capable of bearing. Whatever Sharon decided to do, my decision about leaving my wife would not change. Now that I was away from her, I knew I would never be going back.

An hour later Sharon tuned up at my door.

She had made her decision.

If it seemed as though the whole world was against us after this, it's because it was.

Certainly, it was that way, at least for a while.

Friends took sides. Judgments were made. The world changed.

It happens.

At the time it seemed as though the world was needlessly torturing me and Sharon; there was a lot of hate in the air, a lot of finger-pointing, especially from the people who should have known better, those who were least qualified to judge. Friends, good friends, old friends, acquaintances, enemies, peripheral characters in our lives and complete fucking strangers in the street put the boot in. Many of our harshest critics were people who'd had affairs themselves and confided in me about their lovers. One or two had even used me as an alibi in their illicit liaisons; they were now married to the very people they'd left their previous partners for and yet still they pilloried us.

Our old friends became keen enemies.

We took it all on the chin.

No complaints.

You can't complain about judgment when you've committed sin, even if the people judging were breaking bread with you the week before. The cavalcade of abuse we received, the social rebuttal, the abandonment of all established friendships, powerfully bound me and Sharon together in a way that no other confluence of circumstances could. We were tongue-and-grooved and glued together so tightly that you couldn't fit a breeze between us. She became everything to me, and I became everything to her. We were all we had in the world (it seemed) and so our world together became all.

I will spare you the details of the subsequent fallout, and the ugly encounters that occurred in the next year when I went to the family home to fetch my kids, and the embers of our marital bonfire were re-ignited in sparks and flames and sometimes wild-fire arguments. Enough to say that, over time, my ex-wife proved to be the better person, and allowed me to have my kids three nights a week, even though every bone in her body ached at the thought of her children sleeping under my roof. And over the years, her grace extended to accepting Sharon, being kind to her and even though we were disparate - I married Sharon, my former wife married a new beau - between the four of us we did the best job we could to raise our children.

I can see in retrospect that my meeting Sharon was a spiritual intervention, a divine intercession. It is unlikely that any other circumstance or any other soul would have been equipped to lead me along the road I was now walking. More specifically, Sharon led me away from the destructive path of violence I'd been on for so long. She was the first person to recognise something more in me. She was the first to encourage and nurture my creative spirit.

When I was violent on the door, when the violence spilled out in anger and she was a peripheral witness to it, she would tell me directly and in no uncertain terms, that she loved me very much, but she did not love my behaviour.

'When you get like that,' she said to me one day, 'it makes you look ugly.'

Ugly!

Ugly you say?!

I can't tell you how disconcertingly affecting it is to hear those words coming from the lips of the girl you love. All I got before this, from other people, in response to my violent outbursts was admiration, back-pats and free beers on the bar like winners' cups.

Ugly!

I didn't want to be ugly, especially not in front of Sharon.

This one line of brutal truth went a long way to freeing me from the addiction of violence. Or more precisely, vacating the element in me that was insecure and scared and elevating it, transfiguring it into something beatific, something splendid.

If I was Saul of Tarsus on the road to Damascus, then Sharon was my redeemer, the living bridge, my means of conversion on the path.

She also encouraged me to untangle myself thread-by-thread from the base elements I was so enmeshed in - heavy training, heavy eating, and violent living - and immerse myself instead in culture, which was my true nature. She encouraged this, even though at times my new path would confuse and frighten her, even though the way ahead often forced her to face many of her own shadows. She led me towards places that I knew she was scared to go. And much later, with my radical ideas about love and forgiveness, when I was attracting criticism, anger and hate from a new enemy and even family members and senior students were assailing me, she still stood with me, and once again chose me over everything else.

The latter was a very interesting period of our lives, but it is a separate story which I will return to later in the book, in the appropriate space.

I don't think the split from my wife could have happened in any other way. The subsequent fallout deemed us veritable outsiders, which was uncomfortable in the extreme. Later I realised what a gift this was. If you are to do anything vital in this world, at some point you will, by choice or by default, have to become an outcast, you have to eschew the mores, you must break worldly covenants and ignore rules…and this by definition is what an outsider is.

It was a good training ground for the future.

I would not be who I am today or where I am or what I am, without every previous encounter. The intercession was brutal and beautiful, and I would not like to repeat it, but I am grateful for it.

It was painfully kind, a divine shock that much later led me to God, and I was privileged to have gone through it.

At the time it all seemed unnecessary, random and needless. Looking back, I can see that it was designed, bespoke and perfect; it was a rescue mission, I would not have escaped the darkened rooms of mendacity without it.

But enough of that for now, back to the book.

Watch My Back still needed to be addressed.

I had a printed manuscript, all I needed now was to find a publisher crazy enough to convert it into a real book.

8

Getting Published

Confrontation Desensitisation had been published In Terry's magazine and my third level of Yaqeen (experiential proof of certainty) proven, but I still didn't know how to get a book in print, published, and into shops. I was getting closer though. *Fighting Arts International* (the magazine) was sold in newsagents all over the country, so technically speaking I was already in the shops. I could go into WHSmith, take the magazine off the shelf, and see and touch and smell (it was a glossy magazine with the waft of quality) real manifest proof that I was a published author in a respected journal being sold in the shops.

An idea alighted.

As your awareness expands, I have noticed, ideas just pop into your head like divine post.

Who would know about writing?

Who could I speak to about publishing a book?

Who would have that kind of information?

This was the dying years of the 80s, 1989 to be precise; no World Wide Web, no internet, no search engines, no pocket computers. If you wanted information, you had to work really hard for it.

Where I lived, we had a local daily newspaper, *The Coventry Evening Telegraph*. If anyone knew anything about writing and the process of publishing a book, surely they would. I was nervous about going to the Telegraph. It felt to me like a middle-class world full of snooty people who might just scoff at a council kid like me who thinks he can write a book.

Another lie. Another fear. Another unofficial addition to the eternal pyramid.

It's very easy, I have found, to allow shitty perceptions to crop-spray the manure of unqualified beliefs over everything that frightens you, just to prove to yourself that the world stinks. In thinking negatively of a place or a class or a person, you make it so, just by proxy of your pre-existent belief. How many doors to how many wonderful rooms do people fail to open because they either believe the room does not exist or that it does exist but not for the likes of them? The rooms are there. They are open for anyone who cares to find them, they are there for anyone who dares to enter.

I flicked the working-class chip off my shoulder and pushed my hysterical and unlettered prejudice to one side. I transferred the confidence I'd found on the door to the courage I needed to enter this foreign space, and I went to the Telegraph offices in Corporation Street, Coventry hoping for advice. Some of that chip I'd flicked away earlier jumped back on again as I entered the reception area and sat like a throbbing wound on my shoulder. A frown, an unwelcome look or any sense of judgment from the Telegraph would have been enough to throw me into a self-pitying tizzy of paranoia, and my new door would have slammed closed-shut before I even got a chance to say *hello! I think I might have written a book*. It is hard to describe how painful it feels, when you have been groomed on social hierarchy, and told that you are merely a foot stool in its lower echelons, when you have been taught implicitly and explicitly that there is an underclass and that you are it, and everyone is looking down on you. The force of class certainly had its heel pressed firmly on my neck. All the people who held the power when I was growing up were from the educated classes, the social elite; these were the foremen and the factory bosses who determined whether or not you worked and earned a wage and got to eat and make the rent for another week, they were the doctors who held the power of health and illness in their prescription pads, they were the teachers who guarded the gates of academia like the three headed Cerberus (and us not knowing the right music to make him sleep), they were the policemen who could steal your liberty in the beat of a bent-cop heart, the politicians who literally governed over us, and of course the reporters, the newspapers. We had all witnessed enough death by tabloid to fear the poison pen of an unscrupulous journalist.

It felt perilous walking into a room stocked with posh people, when your whole life had been spent in fear of middle-class professionals. It was akin to an intellectual no man's land where you ran in fear of the next bullet, bayonet or bomb. You might accuse me of exaggeration or embellishment, but any such charge would betray an astonishing lack of understanding: conditioning is an electrified fence that borders every individual reality. I have lost many friends to negative conditioning, people that tried to leave their designated class, cast or culture, and fell into the deathly terror-bardo between here and there. Some lost their lives to sudden-suicide, violence at their own hands; others like my brother Ray, died of slow-suicide, violence at the hands of an unknowing accomplice, who passed chunky jars of lager-hemlock across a club bar. The feeling of worthlessness, of insignificance, the thought that I was shit under the shoe of a higher cast, made me squirm in discomfort as I walked into the Telegraph and asked to speak to a reporter. Any reporter would do.

Minutes later my fears were bug-quashed, they were found without substance when a lovely young woman reporter stood before me. Her name was Sue Lary, and she had a welcoming smile.

Good start.

I told her the story so far: I'd written a book. I wanted to get it published. I had hit an informational roadblock. Did she have time to read it? Would she tell me if she thought it was any good and if so, could she offer any advice on the path to publishing?

I realise now, looking back, that this was a brave thing for a burgeoning artist to do. As I may have mentioned somewhere else, aspirants risk much when they lay their head on the chopping block of public opinion. The search for validation not found has proved the undoing of many a prospector. I was already balancing precariously on a dodgy rung on an unsteady ladder, so if Sue had told me my book was no good, and *don't give up the day job*, if these words or sentiment were even implied, I think it may have toppled me over, and ended my aspirations before they had even really begun.

One of the reasons that writers often fail to finish a book is because they know that, once complete, they will have to send it out into the world, and this is to risk much, not least rejection. The very idea of *another* rejection is enough to keep people locked forever in the gaol of an unfinished manuscript.

Another fear for the pyramid pyre.

I'd developed enough courage by now from facing down and fighting the mad men, the harridans and the maniacs in Coventry bars to lend a bit of it over to the task at hand. I think that Sue, as a professional writer for a newspaper, must have understood the dilemma of an aspirant, and I think I may have prefaced my request for guidance with an unconscious call for sensitivity, by saying something like, 'I don't know if it is any good' before I handed the manuscript over. I don't know, but her kindness and her words certainly put me directly at ease.

'Up there' she said, pointing to the floor above, 'in the Telegraph offices, we've got fifteen reporters, and all of them want to write a book. None of them have managed it yet. So, no matter how this book reads, remember, you have written it. That puts you one step ahead of every one of the professional writers in this building'.

It was such a caring and knowing thing to say.

I left the book with Sue and waited nervously for her call. A couple of weeks later I was standing before her again. She was *a real writer* so her words meant something to me. Yes, I knew a real writer now. And I was a handshake away from fifteen more real writers in the Telegraph offices above; my world was expanding once again.

Just the courage to find Sue, to stand before her, to risk rejection and the heartache of a crushed dream and another binned manuscript, dissolved walls of fear. My own volition unlocked doors and a new reality had opened up to me. It was a room that was always there, I just couldn't see it before. It was a world that had always existed; it was my requirement that made it appear.

The room was always there.

Fear had been the terror barrier that had road-blocked me.

Sue loved my book.

'There's a real voice here' she said, 'an original turn of phrase.' She thought it was funny too. It made her laugh. I was delighted. It was an exhilarating moment. I felt the inspiration enter me and unlock myriad other possible rooms that I would soon enter. Sue felt that the book could be longer and whilst my description was good, there was not enough of it, she suggested that I go back into it and add more, in the same vernacular.

I thanked Sue. I went on my way and I started writing again. The hopes of being published were getting ever stronger.

Taking into consideration Sue's notes I near doubled my book, it went from 25,000 words to a respectable 45,000 and new stories were added, some that I'd forgotten first time around and some new ones that had occurred in the interim. I also went posh, and invested in a fancy Starwriter, an automatic typewriter with a thin band screen that displayed about a paragraph of writing at a time. It was basic. It was a decade before computers were properly introduced, but it was a beautiful machine that allowed me to put my work immediately into type, ready to send to a publisher.

But what of a publisher?

Where do they live, these living bridges between a scribble on the page and a book on the shelf at Waterstones?

No one seemed to know.

They lived in the *Writers' and Artists' Yearbook*, that's where they lived. And they lived there all together in an alphabetically-ordered family. I don't even remember how I found out about the writers' yearbook, perhaps Sue had directed me to it, I don't know. All I know is that I bought a copy from the bookshop and it transformed my life.

Suddenly I had access to every publisher operating in the country. The yearbook explained how publishing worked, what publishers expected, what they were specifically looking for and perhaps more importantly, what they were not looking for. It told me how to present my work, when to present it and to whom it should be specifically addressed. It informed me about small publishers, major publishers, international publishers, agents (a strange and rare species of humans who act as an intermediary between writers and publishers). It also spoke about self-publishing and the dreaded scourge of all literary output, *vanity publishing*.

Each publisher had a small section that informed the aspirant about the type of books they were looking for; no point sending a book about cats if they only publish books about dogs. No small folly in submitting your opus on motor cars if your publisher of choice is only interested in books on exotic plants.

It supplied me with addresses and phone numbers. I could actually speak to someone who published books.

If you've ever wondered if there really are different, co-existent frequencies on this spinning planet, other densities or dimensions, wonder no more my friends. They are there, and in their multitudes, perhaps just not in the way you might have expected.

In the year of our Lord, 1990, I held in my hand a magical book that gave me access to a Milky Way of potential, a new galaxy littered with glittering stars, black holes and worm holes and many other strange literary anomalies (that no one quite understands yet). More importantly it contained portals that delivered me front of house to thousands of publishing houses. It was exhilarating to say the very least, it was exciting.

I was asking for guidance. I was knocking at the door. I was seeking.

Do the work, do the work and the doors will open.

I must admit, in the beginning, I did send my book to all the wrong places. I did the equivalent of sending a book about meat to a publisher on radical veganism. I did not read the detail. I did not follow the protocol. I sent my book to companies who stipulated that they would not receive unsolicited manuscripts. I either never heard back from them, or I received a snooty reply and my manuscript - unopened, unread (you can tell) - plopped onto my doormat with an impersonal letter of refusal enclosed. Sometimes publishers even sent a bill charging me post and packing for the return post. Other times they simply sent back a standard, 'I'm sorry but on this occasion...' type rebuttal, the body-blow to many a scribe. More often than not, I never heard back from publishers at all.

The rejection tempers you. It hardens your resolve. When you are going through the birth canal into the world of publishing, every preparatory nutrient is supplied en route; information (read the publishers requirement, you fool) direction (each rejection is one path less to try) baptism (by fire often, but necessary for this tough domain) endurance (you can only learn to endure by enduring) faith (rejection often leaves you with nothing but faith as your force) and a very powerful mental hardiness - struggle in the birthing gives you the lungs for the higher altitude that you seek to attain.

You also learn savvy and wisdom.

In the beginning, you imbue every publisher and every agent with the reverence of the one-eyed Odin, and you heed their word like it is wisdom drawn directly from the well of wyrd. They guard the majestic, enormous halls of publishing, they hold the keys to the kingdom, so if you want to get in, you do not question their council.

They hold all the power.

That's what you believe, and the belief can turn you into a subservient fool.

Later you realise that they are not the almanac to all things literary, they do not hold the keys to the throne room (only one doorway to their own particular room) and their word is not law. If their word was law, some of the best books in the world would never have been published. Harry Potter was rejected by many publishing houses in London before eventually finding a home with Bloomsbury, and even they warned its author that they would probably only be able to sell a few thousand copies.

The people behind these doors, at the end of that London telephone line, those receiving your email proposal or letter by post, are people. People like you and me. Some of them are kind, others curmudgeonly and decidedly unkind. Some of them know what they are talking about, others haven't got a Scooby. More than a few of them are elitist snobs. Some will be grand teachers for you, great guides on your journey. Others, the clumsy ones, the jealous and the blind types, might take a bat to your sensibilities and beat them to death like a beached seal, so beware of investing too much faith in the opinions of publishers and agents. Ultimately, they are people like you and me, who go home to their families every night and dream the same dreams and nurse the same complaints.

Eventually - to save myself unnecessary discomfort - I read the small print, the addendums, the publishers' requirements and I started again.

In the year book, unsurprisingly, not all of the publishers listed were looking for a book like mine. In fact, most of them were actively not looking for a book like mine. This was good news; it would save me a lot of time, and no small amount of postage stamps. The revelation reduced the list of possibilities vastly and made the task of choosing a print that would fit my book's genre, much easier.

Actually, at that time, there was not a specific publishing genre for a book about the tales of a nightclub bouncer, and that was part of the challenge. A decade later, the category that my book would precipitate would be called 'the hard men genre' and it would attract a large market of voyeurs who wanted to hear the stories of derring do, of fighters and villains, from the safety of a page.

There was no genre. So, I had to inadvertently create a new one; or certainly I had to find a publisher that might create it for me.

In the yearbook I noticed that there was a section towards the back pages called *small publishers*. I deduced that, if anyone was going to take a chance on a virgin author and a book without genre, it was more likely to be a new, maverick, guerrilla print, someone unfettered by the small thinking of the old way.

I saw the name Summersdale Press. I felt something, an intuition, an inner light and I thought 'maybe....' I rang them up and I spoke to one of the young directors, a guy called Stewart (his publishing partner was Alistair) and I told him about my book. He sounded intrigued. Even though they were largely interested in travel books, my manuscript about the colourful adventures of an unlikely Midlands bouncer sounded, well...*different*.

Stewart asked me to send some sample chapters.

They were in the post the same day.

I waited.

I waited, but it was not long before Stewart and Alistair contacted me again and asked if I could send the rest of the book. They didn't say much more than that, but you didn't have to be Holmes & Watson to deduce that they must have liked what they'd read so far, otherwise, why ask to read more?

The rest of the book was sent in very excited anticipation and a short time later I received a page long letter on Summersdale Press headed paper officially offering me a publishing contract.

There were a couple of small caveats; the book needed a conclusion, could I add one? They felt the story ended too abruptly and they wanted me to round it off. They also felt that the book needed a sub-title. They suggested I call it *Watch My Back - A Bouncer's Story*.

I don't know if I can even begin to describe the level of excitement this created in me and in my world. It led onto so many amazing, immediate and distant experiences and opportunities and changes, not least giving up my job (after the book was released) to write and to teach full-time.

I'm not sure anyone fully believed my news at first. I'm not sure I did. I pored over the letter from Summersdale again and again, looking for tricks, looking for traps, checking that the offer was legitimate, making sure there was no hidden clause, or covert requests asking me to pay for the print or cover the publisher's costs. Even Sue Lary at the Telegraph seemed initially suspicious about my offer of a publishing contract and warned me to make sure that Summersdale was not a vanity company who would print any old book for a fee.

It was none of the above. It was a genuine and sincere and legitimate offer and I was in a state of exhilaration for weeks afterwards. A new energy entered me. I was deeply, profoundly inspired. I started to write more and more and as the release date for the book approached I began making phone calls to newspapers, and magazines, TV shows and radio. I had an unquestionable belief that if you gave me a telephone for a morning I could get myself into any newspaper and onto any talk show.

I now had incontrovertible proof that it was possible for a man like me to publish a book. Before, when I only had intellectual proof (other people's successes), those proofs could be quashed easily enough by external criticism and internal doubt; but now I had proof of experience, I had certainty proper. It didn't matter a fig what anyone else said to me, it didn't matter if the Queen of England or the Pope in Rome or the Redeemer himself tried to cast doubt in my mind, it would not have worked. I had proof. I was certain. My belief in possibility was fire-resistant.

The samurai Mushashi said that to master one thing was to master all things. He knew then what I knew now, that certainty in any area opened up the potential of certainty in every area.

I could and I did (and I still do) use this one experiential proof as a template for all proof. I use it as a reference point, something to draw on when I struggle to penetrate boundaries.

No-one can convince me of the limitation of possibility. Publishing one book showed me that limitations are merely interims, and with the appropriate proofs, certainty in any area was mine to claim. But I still had to do the work. And the work is not just in obtaining certainty; the work was also in coping with the consequence of revealing a certainty before the world.

Certainty is a divine revelation, no doubt, and revelation gets you seen; you are noticed.

The book was published.

I held it in my hand.

The year was 1992.

I was thirty-two years old.

The new me held it; not the old me, he was already long gone. The factory worker, the snotty comprehensive kid, died with the birth of my new certainty. I held the book and looked at the cover: a black and white photo-juxtaposition of *Geoff the bouncer* - tuxedo, dickie bow, the hard eyes - standing back-to-back with *Geoff the scholar* - soft face, neutral clothing, and kind eyes peering through rounded spectacles.

The cover image - self designed - should have told me something even back then. I should have heeded what my unconscious was glaringly pointing out to me.

In my naivety I thought I was displaying the yin/yang of my persona, the warrior-scholar, the man who could rip your head off and shit down your neck whilst reciting ancient Hindu scripture. I can see now that this was not what my growing consciousness was alerting me to. It was letting me know that I had done well, I'd birthed a new angel identity, but I still had a devil in me the size of a dog. I was still divided against myself and if I was ever going to become a fully realised human being, this darker self would have to be confronted, controlled, and ultimately subjugated. The higher part of me would have to go to war with these unconscious elements.

In his Red Book Jung said that until we make the unconscious conscious, it will always direct our life and we will call it fate.

The cover showed me this, although I'm not sure I was ready to hear it yet, let alone understand it. But this was a grand beginning. The book was in my hand. I had given up my day job in the factory. I was still working on the door and my karate classes were swelling proportionately with my new-found certainties. I was certain about what worked in a real fight, I was certain that fear could be managed and driven as a living creative force and now I was certain that it was possible to write and publish a book.

Do you know what happens when you start talking with certainty?

It attracts people.

Genuine certainty is rare.

Folk are drawn to the rare like iron filings are attracted to a magnet. In a world full of incongruence, dishonesty and greedy opportunism, certainty shines like a beacon.

But you can't fake it. You must *be* it.

I was still divided in so many ways, of course. I was definitely an unfinished David, my best features still hidden beneath the raw marble, ready to be revealed. I was being moulded by the Michelangelo of my growing circumstance. But there were things of which I was certain. I was teaching them, and my truth attracted a crowd.

When the book was finally released, about a year after the initial offer of a contract, the attraction increased and intensified. Suddenly I was on the television talking about my book, and about my experiences. I was on the radio. The newspapers took pictures of me and wrote words about *Watch My Back*. Radio One sent a reporter (Mark Whittaker) to the Siberian outskirts of Coventry and they ran a feature on the bouncer who had published a book. It was an anomaly I know, an oxymoron; a knuckle-dragger who could walk and talk at the same time, a pleb who could turn a phrase. I didn't mind. I enjoyed appearing on screen and on the radio. And those expecting monosyllables from me, the hosts who anticipated their lumpy guest to be an inarticulate thug were in for a shock: I could talk, I liked to talk, and I talked most of them under the table. Not all of my hosts liked the fact that I could hold a conversation, and those that tried to humiliate me with *intelligent* questions they thought would highlight my ignorance, were quickly chagrined when I countered their subtle assault with direct counters that exposed not only their own ignorance, but their dire lack of preparation. One woman wanted to take me to task about a particularly offensive comment I'd made in *Watch My Back*. I asked her if she had read the whole book. She said she hadn't had the time to read it all. I said, 'Then you are in no position to take me to task, because the offending line qualifies itself in the overall arc of the book.' She had no more questions about the contents of *Watch My Back*. On a national radio show, I was being interviewed via telephone by another *astute* host who accused all bouncers en masse (and by implication me) of being little more than paid thugs. He wondered if I could refute his claim. I answered his question with an enquiry of my own: 'Are you playing devil's advocate, or are you just plain ignorant?' My unexpected riposte sent him into a stammering tongue-tied tizzy, and he cut me off air, leaving his embarrassed producer to apologise for his rudeness. Another famous radio presenter delivered an on-air diatribe about the gangster Dave Courtney, and when he asked me to join in the verbal assail and validate his views that Dave was indeed a monster, I said, 'haven't you read the violence in my book? I am in no position to judge Dave Courtney or anyone else.' There was a tumbleweed moment, before the host found his footing and rapidly changed the subject. One rather snooty interviewer with a large following, said he hated the fact that *certain people* (read that how you will) - because of position, money or power - were able to enact the most heinous crimes on society and still escape the law: *they get away with everything* he bleated. I said I felt his statement was untrue, it was very naive, it was certainly not what I had experienced. Reciprocity has a faultless memory, it may delay, but it never forgets. 'No one escapes the human condition,' I assured him. My honest philosophy vexed him. He didn't know what to say by way of response, so instead he blurted out angrily, 'My listeners wouldn't understand what you are talking about. They wouldn't know anything about the human condition.' In one blundering sentence he managed to insult his whole demographic. On yet another occasion, a local host who'd invited me on to talk about my book, made a peripheral, introductory comment about the local football team. They were arguing over whether or not they should sack their manager, who hadn't won a game in the last six. 'Do you think we should change manager Geoff?' he asked. The team in question (like most football teams) had a very fickle fan base. They wanted to change manager more often than the team changed their strip. 'I don't think they should change manager,' I said, 'I think they should change fans.' The phone lines lit up like a Christmas tree, every fan in the city ringing at the same time to voice their dissent. Yet another unprepared interviewer, an older gentleman, suggested that there was no room in civilised society for bouncers, they were a violent aberration. I asked the host if he had children. He said he did. I asked how old they were. They were all adults, he told me, in their twenties. 'And do any of your children visit pubs and clubs?' He nodded mutely that they did indeed frequent drinking establishments. I think he was getting a hint of where this was going. I asked him the killer question: 'Who do you think protects your children from the darker elements of society when they drink in these pubs and clubs?' He took a deep breath. He looked away from me for a moment of thoughtful ponder, and then looked back, sheepishly. He nodded. 'I apologise,' he said with redeeming grace, 'I'd never quite thought about it like that.'

During a battery of back-to-back interviews I held with a rag-tag of intrigued journalists, one took a particular dislike to me. It wasn't so much what he said, rather it was his disparaging looks, the demeaning tone, and his accusatory questions. He wanted to know if I had killed anyone. I parried his question with joviality: 'I haven't killed anyone, but I have hurt a few peoples' feelings.' Did I feel any sense of shame about making money from a book that extolled violence? I wondered if he felt any shame himself making money from writing in his newspaper about a book that extolled violence. It went back and forth like this for a while, until I realised that this lovely man was quietly disgusted by me, he was fat with judgment; but he was not a bad man, he was not an unkind man, just conflicted. Despite his low opinion of me, I liked him, I felt sorry for him. He was probably close to seventy years old, about the same age as my dad, and he looked genuinely perplexed about having to interview a man like me. After the interviews and questions had finished, as we all made our way across to a buffet that had been laid out for the press, I put my arm gently on his shoulder and said, 'I made a lot of mistakes when I worked the doors. But I did save a lot of people too. I saved people.' I saw the scales of judgment fall from his eyes. For the first time he looked at me like I was a human being, someone's husband, a father, an uncle, a brother; I was someone's son. I was no longer the beast from the black lagoon to him.

Another esteemed gentleman, a highbrow lawyer, an expert on criminal law and a fellow guest on a show about crime and its punishment, commented that, 'Of course, people are convicted for the crimes they commit, they are convicted for what they do, and that is only right and proper.' I told him that I'd had many first-hand dealings with the judiciary, on the wrong side of it, and I didn't think his statement was entirely accurate. 'People are not convicted for what they do,' I explained, 'people are convicted for what they say.' He squinted his eyes, opened his mouth to reply, but he remained mute. He contemplated for what seemed like an eternity, and then said, 'Yes. You are quite right. That is very true.' When you are working on the frayed edges of the law, and when the people you are trying to contain in violent situations actually choose to step outside of the law, you often have to go to that place with them. And in order to exit the encounter with your liberty still intact you need to understand that it is not what you do that gets you sent to prison, or released without charge, it is what you say on your statement sheet. I have known people ignorant of the law receive long prison sentences because they did the right thing but said the wrong thing on their police statement. I have also seen criminals steeped in the exegesis of written law, do the wrong thing, but say the right thing on their arrest sheet, and evade even a single night in a police cell.

It is not what you do that gets you convicted it is what you say. *

If I was making waves on telly and radio, I was definitely ruffling chicken-feathers like a fox in a hen house on my old stomping ground in Coventry, the setting for *Watch My Back*.

You don't really think about this when you sit on a factory toilet and pen a book in your spare time. You write your stories with a certain naive impunity, because, well, realistically you don't ever think it's going to get published, so no-one is going to read them anyway. Then when it does get published, and it's being talked about on the telly, and on the radio, and written about in the newspapers, when the book is actually in the front window of Waterstones on the high street, you suddenly think...'Oh fuck, yeah, I'm not the only character in this book.' There were lots of other personalities peopling the pages of my autobiography, people that I'd had a fight with, that I'd knocked out, humiliated and embarrassed, people that hated me and would no doubt hate me even more when they saw what I'd written about them. Some of them were gangsters that had tried to kill me and would probably try and kill me again when they read my *honest* depiction of them.

---

* The law of self-defence is covered comprehensively in my book *Dead or Alive*.

More than a few of the people I wrote about in *Watch My Back* were incensed and insulted by my description of them, of their city and of the situations I resurrected in the pages of my book.

When you publish stories that involve other people, particularly if those other people are real, and they are violent, you really should (but I did not) think about how they might react to your assessment of them. Most of them have their own grand ideas of who they are. They see themselves as fighters. In their thwarted mind's eye they imagine themselves as brave, Robin Hood type characters. Most of them are just plastic gangsters, violent chancers, weekend bullies and failed criminals. When they read how someone else sees them, and that seeing is not favourable, it is jarring. I suppose it's a sign of my sheer naivety that right up until publication I was oblivious to the fact that some of the people I'd locked horns with during my time as a bouncer, some of those I'd upset (or battered) would not be happy. It was just before the book came out that the realisation hit me. I can still remember now that feeling of 'Fuck! People are going to read this'. They were hardly going to not read it were they? I was the first night club bouncer in the country to write about the doors, so there was a great deal of publicity and anticipation around it. In fairness, most people got it, they understood the book, they thought it was honest, funny or visceral. Some just loved reading about the violence, it was what they knew, it was what they witnessed in the pubs and clubs of their city every weekend. Some that starred in the book were happy to see their name in print even in a negative context. Others read about themselves in the pages and immediately went into denial. Even though I described them so closely that everyone knew it was them, denial was still the defence mechanism of choice. To be honest some of them were dumb-and-dumber, and unless I printed a current photograph of them with an arrow pointing to the photo saying *this is you*, they wouldn't have recognised themselves, not in a million reads.

I used initials and pseudonyms in the book to protect the guilty and to shield friends who deserved anonymity. Mr S or Mr K or Mr T. One killer I'd rolled with, someone I expected to be violently unhappy, simply shrugged off my heinous characterisation by saying, 'That's not me. My name begins with K not C.' Another fella I'd fought at midnight in a factory car park had apparently told people - prior to the book's release - that his bloody encounter with me had been epic and heroic. When I wrote about how it really went down, that he was a coward and (to quote a witness) 'squealed like a pig being slaughtered in the factory car park', he was embarrassed and full of angry revenge. The cachet he'd received from his own version of our encounter was relegated to the bargain basement when my book did the rounds in his local bar. Another fighter, a man I'd knocked out in the roughest pub in the world, sent a similar message of revenge. This was a dangerous man who really could have a fight. I only beat him the first time around because I was quick to the punch and did not stop punching until he stopped moving.

I sent a message back saying that we could 'do it again' if he was unhappy, anytime, anyplace. His last message, and the last time I ever heard from him was, 'I am unhappy, but not that unhappy'.

Other fighters and criminals who did enjoy me recording their legend for posterity bought ten copies and gave them out to friends and family as gifts and told everyone what a splendid and truthful fellow I was.

Those most affronted were less offended by the fact that their defeat was listed in my book like a local almanac and more angry at the fact that I'd described their aesthetics ('face like a Toby jug', 'bully of the first order') in an unflattering light. They were throbbing at the neck with rage, and some of them never, ever let it go.

When you write the truth, the enemies you make remain enemies for life. Even now, three decades later, there are people who would attack me on sight given the right circumstance, and there are certain bars I would not visit day or night unless I wanted to see claret on the carpet.

Almost immediately after publication and more so over time, the stories and the characters in *Watch My Back* fell into myth and legend. People somehow got it into their heads that I didn't write the book (how could I, I was a bouncer), someone else must have written it for me. They also convinced themselves that the stories were either untrue or greatly exaggerated. It was common to hear people say, 'yea, but he didn't write it did he', or 'the stories are not true, nowhere is that violent'; or my absolute favourite and said to me on more occasions than I care to remember, 'the book will die in a couple of months, who wants to read about a Coventry bouncer?'

As it turned out, a lot of people wanted to read about a Coventry bouncer.

The book gets you noticed of course, but the subsequent articles and interviews - the effects of your cause - also place you before a widening audience.

People buy the book. They see the interviews. They read the articles. They are intrigued. They want to know more, to put a face to this *new sound*. In my interviews I was talking about the one thing that, at the time, no-one really talked about… fear. It struck a chord. They were expecting me to talk laconically about the underbelly of nightclub life, but I was talking about conflicted and frightened men. Most of the hosts on these shows were quietly afraid themselves, but they didn't always know why or specifically what they were scared of, but they were living with fear, so what I was saying piqued their interest. And here was I, the bouncer, a man paid to contain violence in busy clubs, saying that I was afraid too, but that I'd learned how to recognise fear, I'd learned to control fear and direct its energy.

Folk completely underestimate fear in the world as a controlling force. The masses are unconsciously cattle-prodded and herded into social-pens by the farmers of fear. Fear is the controlling element in society, and yet no one wants to talk about or even consciously recognise it, they are more likely to show their pus-oozing knob on a reality TV show about embarrassing bodies than talk about the things they fear and fear itself.

People wanted to know what I thought about fear.

They wanted to learn about fear from someone who was certain that fear could be managed. Most folk didn't know quite what to think of this Coventry kid writing a book. Some thought I was a local novelty, they said my story would remain local, and I'd disappear again as soon as interest waned.

But Radio One was not local. Sky News Live was not local. Daytime TV talk shows and cool BBC documentaries were not local either, and I featured on them all. Some people were thrilled, as though my attention was their attention by proxy. Others decided that I was up my own arse.

As well as constructing a platform for the subject of fear, it also gave a voice to bouncers all over the country who had previously been relegated to the lower echelons of society. It created the beginning of a reality movement in the world of martial arts too, which had until now been a bunch of disparate arts, all certain about the potency of their system and the sovereignty of their art, too many chiefs, as the common idiom goes, but not many Indians.

Watch My Back was selling in the shops. I was on radio and TV. I was appearing in newspapers and magazines, all whilst still bouncing in the pubs and clubs of my city. It was a strange experience. I was swimming around a small fishbowl with the big eyes of baffled voyeurs staring in. People I'd known for years were looking at me like I'd grown a second head, as though they didn't know who I was suddenly. Others, who didn't know me before the book, wanted to know me now. One pretty girl asked me, with a nudge and a wink, 'Geoff, how do I get into your next book?'

'You either have to fight with me or sleep with me', I quipped. Sharon was with me, she was listening in: 'Well,' she said dryly, 'I've done both and I'm not in it.'

Men and women were actually starting to travel from distant cities, just to observe me. Others who'd read the book and liked the violence wanted to meet me in person, if not see me in action. One night, a stranger hovered around the door I was working on, ogling me.

'Are you waiting for something?' I asked him. It was 11pm, the pub was closing soon, perhaps (I thought) he was waiting for a friend or a taxi.

'I'm waiting to see you *go*,' he said, with a heavy emphasis on the word 'go'.

In our world *go* was an acronym for 'have a fight'.

'Well,' I said, playing on the colloquialism, 'if you wait for another fifteen minutes you'll be able to see me *go*; I'll be going home'.

With more and more people turning up at the pubs and clubs I was working, to look at me, meet me, shake my hand or simply stare at me and whisper conspiratorially, I realised that working the door was no longer tenable. Even my very small amount of local celebrity was making the door an impossible employ.

So, with some relief and with much sadness, I left the doors for good and took with me all my experiential certainties, of which there were many. These I put to good use as a teacher, as a writer of stories, and as a conflicted human living on a strange and mysterious planet.

Before the publication of *Watch My Back*, the idea of becoming an author was a distant dream, like winning the lottery. It felt exciting but unlikely. It seemed vaguely possible, but frustratingly random. Now I was published and everything changed. Everything. If you've been brought up with a specific truth and that truth is suddenly, rudely, demonstrably and publicly disproved, you experience a complete paradigm shift. If even one incontrovertible truth is proved to be blatantly and consummately wrong, you find yourself asking, *'so...what is true then?'* What other lies have I been told, what other life-limiting beliefs have been holding me captive?

A piece of information taught to me, passed down as a belief, enforced on me as a truth, had kept me in a place of human scarcity for the first thirty years of my life. It had kept my brothers there too and my sister and my friends, my peers. Even my teachers were imprisoned by the steel bars of unquestioned perception, and they unknowingly used their beliefs to teach us how to build our own prisons - the factory job, the drinking culture, the dog-eat-dog ideology - lock the doors, hide the key from ourselves, then wander around in an existential dissonance saying, 'why do I feel so trapped?'

I'd challenged a powerful and cultural belief in class and in possibility. I had proven this belief to be wrong and in doing so started an avalanche of further and deeper and broader enquiry. I questioned every belief. The ones I had inherited. The ones fed me on the school-curriculum. The fibs I'd been bottle-fed by my parents. The bullshit impressed upon me by my peers. The half-truths, the mistruths and the full fat, blood red lies that society had programmed me with every day of my life. I didn't just open the door to the publishing world, I kicked down the doors to personal emancipation. This was not simply a change of job, it was a change of reality, an individual new world order.

Removing old truths left me with a clearer view, and I could see potentials that I'd never seen before.

I felt compelled to pursue them all concurrently.

In the Buddhist canon, we are advised that there are no problems in the world. The only problem is that people believe there is a problem, and this of itself becomes problematic.

There are no problems, but there is a clear view.

When we clean the ignorance, and remove the lies, the limitations on our perspective vanish and the clear view appears.

By challenging old beliefs, and removing my own personal defilements, I was seeing clearer and clearer every day. As a consequence of my broadening vision, several distinct paths opened up for me at this point: teaching reality martial arts and writing books about combatives were just the first of many, and I pursued them all with vigour.

Much of the martial arts I'd been taught for the last twenty years were at best naive and at worst dishonest. Not a blatant lie. That would be a harsh and disingenuous statement. The greater majority of my peers really believed in the honesty and the potency of their teaching. What they were flogging from their school halls and sports centres was neither honest nor potent, but at the time they couldn't see this, so they taught what they knew. They passed on what had been passed on to them. I had no argument with the old guard or the new wave or even the *flavour of the month type* martial art. I was not the martial arts police. I had no desire to be the judiciary, ruling over martial efficacy. I just wanted to tell the truth. I felt it was my duty to pass on what I'd learned so that people might be better prepared if they should ever bump into Mr Mugger down a dark alley on the way home, or Mr Pisshead outside the chippy on a Friday night.

The most exciting path that appeared on the new landscape was the *way* I'd longed for all my life: writing. The written word, it held an allure for me all of its own. I'd felt its calling since I was a boy at school, and in the not too distant future, like the jealous mistress of fable, she would demand all of my hours.

But before that I still had unfinished business. Whilst the rise and fall of my relationship with martial arts ran in direct parallel with my ascent in the world of published writing, I need to separate them at this point, if only to make clear what could easily become clumsy and busy if I try to explore them both concurrently. So, if you will oblige me, let me start with the martial arts and the Budo metaphysics.

I will return to the year 1992 imminently.

I will come back to the books, the articles, the films, the stage plays, my path to the BAFTAs and all that followed the publication of *Watch My Back*.

I will make my way back to the literature as soon as I have made my way through the martial arts.

9

Martial Arts, Metaphysics and Chuck Norris

My message in *Watch My Back* was as simple as it was clear. It was brutal regarding martial arts and it was without apology. The art you play in the dojo and the dojangs, will not work on the pavement arena, it will fail you. At the time of my book's release, everyone in the MA universe believed that their arts were deadly. The rationalisation for not qualifying or testing this theory was the belief that the arts were as dangerous as a wild bull. They daren't let it loose in the china-shop of a controlled environment in case something got smashed, for fear that someone might be killed. They were sold this lie by their teachers, by their gurus and in the books left as lore by the masters of antiquity, all of whom should never be questioned.

Let me be direct: the majority of the arts were not deadly.

Most of the artists themselves were not physically or psychologically conditioned to be deadly either, they were suitably equipped to stand in front of partisan students, training recreationally, in a warm sports hall on a Sunday morning training session, but they did not have the boots for the muddy battlefields of war, neither in the microcosm nor the macrocosm. And the arts they practiced and passed down were not the arts originally developed for the theatre of war either, even though the core of those disciplines were still evident below the flaccid ostentation of what was left.

It was a case of the emperor's new clothes.

At the time, Martial Art was a naked potentate, but nobody wanted to be the first to point it out. They lacked the child-like innocence to say *the emperor is wearing no clothes*. Even though it was patent and obvious, no one wanted to speak the truth, for fear of looking ignorant or seeming unsophisticated. Teachers could roll out ridiculous theories and proffer obscure moves and unworkable techniques - *a laughable syllabus* - and the most astute and otherwise intellectual professionals would buy it. They would not question a word, a comma or an ampersand, if it came from the pen of their master. It was delivered with such certainty by the convinced or the already converted that there was little room left for question. By and large, the martial arts world was insecure and sensitive, so a challenging question from a student could lead to a bloody nose or worse from the offended teacher, or from his senior students who were dissed by proxy. I could see this very clearly. I could see, but for a time, like everyone else involved in any dogma, I did not want to see. I certainly did not want to be the first to voice it.

With my new-found certainty and a platform to speak from, I started telling the truth. I told it as it was. I told it in martial arts magazines. I told it in martial arts classes. I told it on television interviews and in public classes and on organised courses. I spoke openly about martial efficacy, and the urgent need for honest rigour.

I also talked a lot about fear.

If the martial arts had a bastard child hidden away in shame, its name was definitely *fear*. As a martial artist, especially if you wore a black belt around your waist, you were not supposed to be fearful anymore and if you felt fear, you denied it, you hid it away, and you attacked others if they tried to infect you with theirs.

People learned never to talk about fear. It was a declaration of weakness, of failure, and you were quickly regarded as a coward if you broke the silence and admitted that you were shitting your shorts.

I spoke about pre-emption too. The pre-emptive strike. Hit first. As an empiricist, I knew that this was the only reliable constant in a real fight. My message flew in the face of traditional MA, which considered attacking first both immoral and unethical. It was frowned upon. If you hit first, you were a thug, no questions asked, no qualification provided.

To get my reality message across I started to teach (what became known as) Animal

Day classes. They became popular all around the country and beyond.

Animal Day was basically a no holds barred, no rules fighting class where people were able to practice their technique in a pressured and testing environment.

My critics claimed that my classes were a 'playground for bouncers and bullies' (to quote one newspaper). We had a rare mixture of folk in these sessions, all wanting to test and prove themselves. We had professional people, doctors, policemen and women, we even had priests and pastors.

The training was hard. It was extremely challenging. It was honest. It was direct but in no way was it thuggish. It was new, and most people at the time didn't understand what we were doing, so they cherry-picked elements of my method, and drew hysterical and provocative conclusions. What we were doing back then was a form of apophatic theology. A method of finding pure technique via negation. The pressured Animal Day fights that we organised allowed us to locate what was real, by first identifying and eliminating what was not. The pressure of full contact, rule-free scrimmage acted as an acid bath, it was a controlled caustic that stripped the rust from the metal, in the fighters and in the system.

My Animal Day classes preceded the UFC and MMA fighting which, a decade later, would become respected, mainstream viewing. But at the time they were deemed controversial, and I upset lots of prominent people, both in and beyond martial arts. What we taught was pioneering. We were first through the door and of course first through always gets a bloody nose.

The local press heard about my 'infamous' classes and made certain unkind and unqualified judgments about me and about my method of teaching. They never once sought clarification or explanation nor did they visit a class or talk to me or the students. They simply ran garish newspaper headlines that incited public fury. One newspaper demanded that the local MP bring me up in parliament and get me banned. This was the first time that I was witness to the blatant dishonesty of the popular press. Everything they wrote about me in that article (and many more to come later) was either hearsay, highly subjective or a blood-red lie. It just shows you my naivety at the time. I genuinely thought that people in positions of authority always told the truth. I genuinely thought that. The idea that a reporter might lie never even entered my mind. To me these people, along with the politicians, the police and the judiciary, were above question.

I was wrong. They lied.

The news of my training sessions became notorious and I also (inadvertently) offended some of the old guard of the martial arts elite. They too considered me a thug of the worst order. One stalwart described me in an MA magazine as *a slug that you might find crawling around in your salad*. Nice! This was upsetting, of course, not least because the man in question was someone I greatly admired and when I spoke to the editor of the magazine about the slight, he defended my defiler, saying he was a man of great intelligence, and had a right to his opinion. If someone is reduced to using a base insult to describe a fellow artist, who also has a right to his opinion, I think we have already lost the line of intellectual debate.

First to employ an insult loses.

His comment could be deemed many things, but intelligent is not one of them.

It was never my intention to upset him or anyone else. I was very direct, that's true, and my message was as blunt as a weighty bailiff, that is also true; but what I said was honest and it was qualified. If I have learned one thing it is this: there is no better way of raising people's hackles, than with an uncomfortable truth.

My intention was always to tell the truth, but whilst the truth can set you free, it can also highlight to those who thought they were already free, that they have mistaken complacency for emancipation.

So, the papers told lies about me to make a headline and sell a paper.

A Member of Parliament tried to get me banned on the strength of a rumour.

And a small seaside resort on the south coast barred me from teaching there, before I'd even set foot on their shores. They'd heard rumours that I'd been invited to coach in their town and forbade my entry before I was even officially hired. How this would have been enforced, I have no idea: a bobby on the town border? Photocopied wanted posters on every lamp post? A small reward for anyone who spotted me near their sands? A WHSmith book token perhaps, or a one-day pass to the local Pleasure Beach, for anyone who dobbed me in. I don't know. But I do know I was being noticed again and that not all the notice was good.

The articles I wrote about my learning, the book and the talks led to instructional DVDs and martial arts courses. The courses led to more articles and more books, that would see me teaching all around the country, in schools, in military bases, on bodyguard courses (I worked for a wonderful company called Excel for six years delivering self-defence to their trainee bodyguards) and in universities.

I was in high demand.

Sharon came with me.

She was my personal uke.

She called herself my bag carrier, because she always carried the equipment (bags and gloves) into every seminar. She was the perfect uke, because she looked like Tinkerbell, but she punched like Mike Tyson. She looked like a cartoon elf, but when she hit a pad, man, the room would stop. She threw a right cross like a seasoned pro. Sharon was my way of demonstrating that limitation was an illusion and that power came from intent and was not determined by weight or gender. She acted as a first proof of Yaqeen (intellectual proof of certainty) for those in the room who believed otherwise. She was light in weight, slim, feminine and pretty, but her punch defied all the old archetypes, her power was immense. It did not conform to stereotypes. It was not bound by weight or gender. When she punched, it was just bodyweight and intention, a perfect exchange of energy between fist and pad. She inspired people. Not just because she punched hard, but because when she punched, she lost herself in the movement, she was no longer there, just a perfect explosion of energy, the ideal transmission of force. The rhythm and the focus of consciousness in her technique took her out of the room and into the abstract. It did the same for people who saw her in action.

It was around this time that I met Peter Consterdine. Actually thinking back, it was just before this. I met Peter when *Watch My Back* was still in manuscript form, waiting to be published, but I reconnected with him again around this time. I'd contacted all the martial arts magazines, told them about my book and asked them if they would interview me, and perhaps commit to a review of my work. The editor at Martial Arts Illustrated - Bob Sykes, a savvy, rugged, knot of a man - was a great martial arts exponent but knew little about the doors or reality combat, so he passed my request on to his in-house self-protection expert. The next thing I knew, I was in a café somewhere up north talking to Peter Consterdine, a block of granite with a posh accent that I'd only ever heard legend of. If there was a James Bond in the world of MA, he was it.

What can I tell you about Peter Consterdine?

It's hard to even write his name on the page without smiling. I only have to hear his voice on the phone and I'm laughing. He has a squaddie-type humour that is based mostly around *taking the piss*. I knew it well. I appreciated and welcomed it, because I knew where it came from. Black humour is the natural by-product of working in dangerous environments. On the doors and on the building sites of my youth, the humour was savage, unrelenting, and it was a very necessary adjunct to surviving in harsh and violent environs. In these hardy worlds humour offered necessary relief, when the black of a situation got too much and emotional overwhelm rushed the door of the heart, it could be chased away by a joke, a pun or a savage piss-take. Peter was ten years older than me when we met (I think he is still ten years older than me now!) and one of the most senior, revered and outspoken martial arts practitioners of his generation. He was a professional bodyguard, a very successful businessman, erudite and articulate. He was everything a rough diamond like me needed. He helped me to bur away some of my rough edges.

He read my book. He liked it very much, especially the uncompromising honesty. He felt that martial arts had lost its integrity somewhere along the line and *Watch My Back* might go part way in helping to regain it. He even agreed to write an intro to the book.

We spoke for a few hours in that northern café, and there was an instant connection; we were each speaking the other's language. He did a profile for me in the magazine and we parted company, me promising to send him a copy of the book as soon as it was in print, and he promising to stay in touch.

I think he might have been surprised when the finished book finally landed on his doormat. The unpublished manuscript was a little rough around the edges when he first read it, certainly it was not the polished and edited version we ended up with, once the editors and designers at Summersdale brought their magic to the project. When I had first sent the manuscript to Peter there were enough typos to give a pedantic palpitations. I'd typed it out in at least three different fonts and printed it on two different shades and grade of white copy paper. In fact, his first words to me when we met in that Manchester café were, 'who's going to clean this up for you?'

The printed and bound book however shone like a new penny. It was professionally produced. I think he must have been impressed because almost as soon as he received the brand new copy, he called me and said, 'I'm thinking of starting a self-defence association. Would you like to come in as a joint chief instructor?'

Joint chief instructor!

With Peter Consterdine?

Would I like to join him?

Does a one-legged duck swim in circles?

Of course I would like to join him. It was the greatest honour, just to be asked.

For me this was no mere business proposal, this was not a jolly frolic that I might embark on, just to see where it might lead, it was an invitation to the top table, it was affiliation, a tip of the hat from an immortal, the martial arts royalty, the Budo elite. It was an invite onto the British stage, proffered by a stalwart, a veteran who had occupied a spot on the world stage for the last two decades.

As a martial artist, I still felt like *that club player* whose big dream was to wear the silk black belt around his waist and hold a certificate to teach at the local YMCA. Now, somehow, because of the fear pyramid, because of the doors, and the book and the subsequent profile, now I was being invited to take a seat alongside the martial arts gods. At first I panicked. I didn't feel good enough. I didn't feel worthy enough. I wouldn't be able to handle it. I knew that Peter was a revered and respected former British Karate squad member and a pioneer of full contact karate, he pretty much wrote the book (one type face, one grade of paper, no typos - Peter is very particular) and I knew that the moment people heard I was working with him as a joint chief instructor, heads would turn and I would get noticed all over again. I would be in a whole new Petri dish, being scrupulously examined, poked and prodded by a different level of being.

I would be noticed.

I'm aware that I've said this a lot throughout this book, and the repetition has been deliberate.

The false ego wants to be noticed. Of course it does. It feeds it, it gets it fat and sated, but, at the very same time, the false ego is terrified of being noticed too. Not enough attention and it feels ignored; too much attention and it feels pressured. The false ego is never satisfied. It is always afraid. It is always divided against itself. So, the fact that being noticed at this new level of play created resistance in me, was a good sign: we do not grow without resistance, and big resistance is always a powerful sign that you are on the right track.

One of the reasons people do not deviate from the status quo is because to move is to be noticed. To be noticed is to be scrutinised. To be noticed it to be tested, and criticised. When you are noticed there is also an inherent expectation in the noticing entities; they will want to exchange energy with you - business, personal, private - even if you don't necessarily want to exchange energy with them. When you are noticed at higher levels, you also have to field a massive new influx of energy.

In Catholic mythology this is often referred to as being Christed.

To be Christed means to be magnified by 1000.

But, if we are not prepared, if the infrastructure is not stable, this surge of current could pop your bulb; 1000 watts of electricity going through a 100-watt bulb will explode the element.

The offer to join Peter was an invite onto the big field with the big boys, where the game was tougher, the players were better, and the expectations were proportionally greater.

As a business advisor warned me once, when I'd been invited to deliver a talk to his ultra-successful associates, 'Geoff, they will challenge you!'

If you are not congruent, if you are not living at the third level of Yaqeen, don't bother even turning up, because you will be found out and you'll be unceremoniously *turned on, and torn to pieces.*

Peter reminded me, many years later, that often we are invited into the higher echelons not just because of what we have done before, but more importantly, we are invited for what we will be expected to do next. You can't just reach a new level and then coast. What we attain we must maintain. As the Torah reminds us, 'that cannot continue which is not being renewed.' We are tested at every station. New demands are placed upon us, we are given new responsibilities and duties. Every reward brings with it the charge of more work. If I took the invite to be Peter's wingman, I'd have to at the very least maintain the standard that had attracted the offer, but more likely, I would have to up my game. I would have to place greater demands on myself.

I knew this innately, hence my nervousness.

If I enter a room and hold a course, and I am not the best in that room at what I aim to teach, I have no right to be there. Disparity of ability in a room full of excellence is very quickly noticed and you won't stay in the room for very long. Altitude will suffocate those who have not developed the lungs for thin air. Only the acclimatised will be able to breathe and even then it will demand great and sustained effort.

But (I figured) there were as a lot of things I didn't know, that I had not yet experienced, lessons I had yet to learn, but altitude was not one of them.

Working the doors had already demanded this of me: people had tried to kill me!

I presumed that working with Peter would be tough, but no tougher than that.

The doors had already forced me to step up or ship out, and I had stepped up. I was also training with pro-boxers at the time, and they taught me all about fighting at altitude -I was slurring my words for days after every session with these knock-out merchants. I was training with those savage Thai-boxers too, and these madmen would chop you down like an old oak if you entered their atmosphere with anything less than the highest standards. During this period of ascent, I also started training at a wrestling club in Birmingham where the maniacal and beautiful fighters there tested me to the point of exhaustion. I'd only enrolled to improve my close range fighting game; these superb athletes gave me flying lessons.

On the door the technique I'd perfected was the widow-making pre-emptive strike. With it I had hard men, big men and crazy men falling over like old ladies on ice so, despite my initial doubts, I took Peter up on his offer. I knew I had a lot to work to do, I was not the best I could be, but I knew how to have a fight, I knew about overcoming fear, I absolutely knew how to be uncomfortable, even frightened for my life, so I swallowed my doubt, accentuated the positives and between us we set up the British Combat Association.

It was an instant success.

We attracted lots of members and we ran courses together from one end of Britain to the other. But it was not the association of martial arts that acted as a catalyst to a much-accelerated personal growth. It was the association with Peter that transformed my life.

He was a cultured man, articulate. I was as rough as old arseholes, I was uncouth. At the time I was too embarrassed to be smart. Peter was erudite. I didn't even know what erudite meant, I'd hardly left my home city of Coventry. I was terrible with money. As a form of energy, it scared me, I didn't feel worthy of it. Peter had been a millionaire twice. He understood the fiscal way. He was not afraid of money. He knew how to make it, how to save it, invest it and when spending was appropriate he knew exactly how to spend it too.

I got my very first new car by modelling Peter. When I said to him, 'I can't afford a new car,' he said, 'What's that got to do with it?' He knew that by creating the demand for money, by living just beyond your fiscal reach, you created wealth, and the flow of money began. He taught me how to make money, and how to respect money as a living breathing energy. He taught me too, how to make money work for me by investing it wisely, in property, in equipment and most importantly in human capital. He encouraged me to purchase the very best gear available for teaching and training, and he showed me how I could use my own company to pay for it, where it was legal and appropriate. When we travelled together all around Britain, teaching the great and the good, Peter showed me how to labour just beyond my ability to labour, work harder than I'd ever worked before, certainly work harder than everyone else in the room, and then, at the end of the day, at the end of the weekend or the week's teaching, book myself into the most splendid hotels possible.

'If you are going to do the work' he told me, 'you need to enjoy the fruits.'

It was because of (and with) Peter that I made my first instructional DVD, which quickly became a very successful set of four. 'The Pavement Arena' series of instructional martial arts DVDs became cult viewing for anyone even remotely interested in learning to protect themselves. The films Peter and I made were raw, direct and startlingly honest. Those with delicate sensibilities were often offended by our message, but those who knew, they doffed their hats and welcomed in the new order.

I look back now, at the articles I wrote (hundreds of them), at the books and DVDs, and I can see why people were so offended: they were uncompromising.

But they were always honest.

The DVDs became their own revenue stream. I sold thousands, and copies were sent all over the world. The DVDs planted seeds. They attracted a large international (eventually global) following and they spoke remotely to those who could or would not make our classes and courses in person.

The revenue was ploughed into new DVDs and later more books.

I learned much just from standing with Peter, just by being in his company. He had so much experiential certainty of possibility that I didn't doubt that anything was possible when I was with him. Working with an elite player like Peter, elite in so many areas, encourages you to continually, continually improve.

The money I was earning (more than I had every earned in my life, more in a single afternoon than I used to earn for a full month's work in the factory) allowed me to invest heavily in my own development. I spent thousands on building a personal Budo library. Eventually I accrued thousands of books and would spend any amount of money if it was for the right publication.

I invested heavily in my own training too. Not just money, although I spent whatever needed spending to improve my skills, but I also invested time, in fact I invested all my time on human capital - the improvement of myself.

It was the most exciting time of my life. When other people were putting in their ten hour day at the factory, on the building sites or in the office, I was working every waking hour on the one thing I loved most, martial arts. All I was doing was reading, writing and training, and teaching combatives. And I was breaking bread with some of the best exponents in the world.

I was so hungry for new knowledge that nearly all my time was spent training in and studying different fighting arts, especially, at this period of my development, in the (so called) hard arts.

I was training in western boxing to improve my hands and my footwork. Boxing was *the* art for close quarter combat, largely ignored in the popular martial arts world because (they said) it concentrated on only one range. Secretly, people ignored western boxing because it scared the living shit out of them, it was very brutal.

You always know an art is effective when there is not a queue to train in it, even though the fees were so low that they were almost giving it away. Boxing was immediate and vital. You could expect to be sparring on your very first session and the people you were sparring with, you could also guarantee, would try to punch you in the face as hard as they could and knock you out if at all possible; ugly but effective. The art was stripped back to its rawest essentials. All that was left in the curriculum was what worked in a fight; nothing more, nothing less. For me, it was a great lesson in life: get rid of the superfluous and the unnecessary, leave only the essential, and keep testing that too. Like the apophatic I'd learned on the door, the theology of negation, the boxing taught me to get rid of what did not work and retain only what did. Because of its immediate nature - i.e. if your technique did not work, you got knocked out - the ostentation dissolved like a sugar pedestal in a rainstorm.

I was a good fighter at the time. My reputation from the doors preceded me everywhere I went, so when I first started at the boxing club (and then later at the wrestling, judo, Thai and Greco classes) I knew there would be some nervous tension caused by 'the bouncer in our midst'. I also understood that, because of collective fear and fat fighting egos, some of the more insecure players in the room might see my balding pate as a respectable (if sparse) scalp to take. I could see this and, in no doubt about my weak boxing abilities, I introduced myself to the other boxers and told them straight, 'I am a crap boxer. I am here to take your instruction. I would be very grateful if, when you see me doing something wrong, you could pull me to one side and guide me.'

Because of my honest approach everyone was put at ease and I found myself in a room full of very hard, very lovely teachers. My hands improved to the point where I was able to enrol in the four day ABA Assistant Coaching Course. I ranked joint first in the final exam. My only fault, they said in their assessment of my skills, was that every punch I threw was a knockout punch. They would prefer that I concentrate on point scoring, which is more in keeping with the amateur ethos.

I could live with that kind of criticism.

The ABA coaching certificate was very rare in martial arts circles so I carried my qualification with a satisfaction that can only come from complete exertion. I prided myself at the time on placing my ego at the bottom of as many hard classes as I could, training with the very best and devoting my whole life to whatever art I was currently learning.

The ABA qualification remains to this day the best combat course I have ever taken. It was relaxed. It was packed with the most amazing, pragmatic information. And the teachers were all dedicated veterans of the art. Some of them had been in over two hundred amateur bouts, and it showed. And, two or three times a day in the middle of these hugely challenging sessions, one of the trainers would come around with a tea urn and an assortment of biscuits.

Tea, biscuits and boxing!

I felt like I'd died and gone to heaven.

The sessions were on Saturday and Sunday for two weekends in a row. It was held at the Standard Triumph working men's club. The boxing club was in the back room. My dad had spent a large proportion of his working life at the Standard at a time when Coventry was the motor capital of Europe, so it felt fitting to be there training, walking the same floors in the same rooms as my dad. In the dinner break I drove two miles into the city centre to meet Sharon, eager to share the excitement of my new learning.

Later when I held mammoth courses of my own in very large sports centres, I would adopt the *tea and biscuits* ethos. I would lay on copious amounts of tea and more biscuits than you could shake a stick at.

I only stopped the boxing when I started to slur my words and the risks started to outweigh the rewards.

Judo was another art I had always wanted to study and wrestling too. These arts were real and exciting and full of hardy men, the kind of men you'd trust with your back in a bar fight.

The 'scruffy' training I was looking for in the boxing and the wrestling was the kind that would hold its integrity on slippery toilet tiles, or on a packed dance floor, or on uneven pavement slabs outside a kebab shop on a busy Saturday night. It needed to be potent in all environments, whether that was an acre of field where you had an arranged straighter or a spontaneous bust up in a public phone box. It was not just the physical fight itself I was concerned with, but also the nerve shredding pre-fight build up where control of the central nervous system was the only thing that would carry you through the affray. These were the arts that developed the wherewithal to handle the post-fight aftermath, where the consequence of a violent encounter could lead to the threat of imprisonment, violent reprisals, and even death threats. Again, you needed self-mastery to manage this kind of pressure, and the systems I trained in and taught needed to reflect this.

Because of the nature of the hard arts (knockout and submission) the exponents were much more prepared for the mental game than the general martial art practitioners. The latter was so constrained and protected by the caveats of their training etiquettes, that it left many of them out of their depth when faced with a street fighter who didn't care if you were a fifth Dan or a tenth Dan or even Desperate Dan.

The wrestling fascinated me.

I am talking here about real wrestling of course, not the show wrestling where men in tights jump from top ropes and land hard elbows on soft wriggling throats. As athletic and insanely skilful as show might be, it is not the kind of wrestling I am talking about. I was interested in the shoot, the hook-and-catch, the catch-as-catch-can, Olympic freestyle, Greco Roman, and American collegiate. These very honest arts are beautifully real and I wanted to learn them all. I scoured the bookshops looking for their work, and I searched country wide for teachers of these rare arts.

I later invested heavily in judo. As is always the way with certainty, when you possess it, everything you need literally manifests before your eyes.

I was lacking skill in jacketed wrestling. I knew that judo would give me the basic grounding I was looking for. Initially I only wanted to know my way around the art, that was all. A basic black belt standard would cover all bases. After a bit of enquiry, I discovered a judo club just two miles from my house. And not just any judo club either, but a judo club run by an old friend of mine, Neil Adams, probably the best occidental judoka of his generation.

To cut a long story short, Neil told me that he ran a full-time class in the day, mainly for international players, and I was welcome to join them if I wanted to train.

My powers of intention were so sharp at the time, my belief in potential so unswerving, that nothing felt impossible. It was as though I had fallen into the Matrix, and Morpheus ('the most dangerous man alive') was programming my mind with whatever arsenal I called for. If I wanted to learn boxing, I knew I could find a teacher; if it was wrestling, I could call the leviathans out of the pages of history to assist me; and if it was judo I needed, a class would appear within spitting distance of my home. I asked for a judo teacher and I was delivered one of the best teachers on the planet.

I joined Neil's class.

I was not brave.

I did not just fling myself courageously into his lessons.

I was nervous. I was worried about being out of my depth, of drowning in this Olympic pool of world class players. I was afraid of being dropped on my head from a great height. People often imagine when I tell them that I did full-time judo for eighteen months that I am a fearless action-man with Teflon skin, happy to throw myself into the forge of any new discipline at the drop of the proverbial hat. I was not. I am not. I took a long time to decide whether the risks of training at this level in an art I barely knew would be worth the rewards. I spent two years in preparation, taking private lessons from the British judo champion, an amazing athlete called Wayne Lakin, before I set foot in Neil's dojo. After only one lesson at Neil's I fell in love with full time judo. I bought five judo suits and I started training three times a day, some of this with Neil and his people, some on my own, and some with the students at my own martial arts class.

After my first session at the Coventry judo club, I said to all my students, 'get yourself a gi (judo suit), we're doing judo!' And, from that day on, for the next two years, that was my life.

I didn't have to go to work don't forget. I'd given up the day job to pursue my passion. While friends and family were up to their nuts in the oil and the porn of the factory floor, I was being schooled in the 'gentle art' by some of the most elite players in the world. They were all either Olympic squad members or players on the international stage. This was Neil's academy and he was revered the world over, so people travelled from all four corners to sojourn in Coventry just to be under the eye of this modern-day master. So, I was not only on the mat with Neil's immediate students, but I also rolled with international students from South Africa, Russia, Europe, America, they came from everywhere and I had the privilege of sharing the mat with them.

The gentle art!

Judo is known as the gentle art. How it ever got that name, I have no idea. Over the next two years I 'gently' got two cauliflower ears, gently wrecked my fingers, gently bent my elbow joints until they pointed in the wrong direction and squeaked when I moved my arms and collapsed when I tried to hold a cup of tea. It should be called the 'fucking hard art'... On my first session I was so bad that Neil actually stopped the class and said to everyone, 'please take it easy on Geoff'. Even Sharon was perturbed by my new choice of training and the level at which I was attempting to play.

'Are you sure you want to do this?' she asked.

Why was she worried?

Hadn't I worked the doors for a decade? Hadn't I trained with elite boxers, pulled with Olympic wrestlers, and gone toe-to-toe with every roaming maniac who turned up at my own classes and courses looking for a little contact?

Why was she worried?

'You might get your neck broken,' she said with genuine concern. 'Someone might drop you on your head'.

Well I could have saved her the worry on that count.

People were throwing me on my head every session. It was a very real concern.

These were elite athletes. I did not underestimate the danger I was putting myself in, but I wanted it. I wanted it enough to risk everything.

But, these lads (and women) were amazing with me. Every time I changed partner on the practice mat, I was facing a squad player or a British champion or a European champion. I even rolled with World champions. Every one of these splendid specimens took me to one side at one time or another and gave me private lessons outside of the usual class requirement. Within a year they took me to black belt level in judo. Within two years - and this is testament to their teaching and patience - I could stand my ground in this international class.

At the end of my time with Neil, I was so in love with judo that it was practically all I did. I was planning to go and live in Japan to further my training. Neil even offered to write me a letter of introduction so that I could train with Kashiwazaki, one of the best judoka alive. Although this was the most exhilarating two years of my martial arts training, I realised that judo and Japan was not my dharma. I loved it, I was even contemplating dedicating my entire life to it, but I knew with much heartache that it was not my path. I'd allowed myself to be distracted by the sultry allure of that mistress judo, but a marriage was not in the offing.

My bride, my dharma, lay on a different path and the judo was just another preparation for the demands that were to come.

This beautiful class and all these wonderful teachers appeared when I needed them. They disappeared after the need was met. Shortly after I stepped away from my full- time study of judo, Neil's class disbanded and has never come together since.

It was a moment, but ah, what a moment.

My circle was growing.

I was expanding at a fast rate. We spilled out of our small house. It was already too cramped for the growing industry of our work; we were sitting on boxes of books. We had stock spilling out of the attic. I'd started taking private students in my very small garage. If we'd owned a cat there would have be no room to swing it, so we needed to move somewhere bigger, a place that could not only accommodate our growth, but also our continuing spread.

We drove past a new housing estate one day on the very edge of the city, where every house was the size of three normal houses. *Posh houses*, my mum would have said. There was a brand new show home on the edge of the estate and it beckoned me. I noticed a sales office set up next to it. I said to Sharon, 'Let's go and have a look.' This was back in the days when Sharon was still thinking how she had been conditioned to think by her culture…small.

'There's no point looking,' she said, 'we could never get a house like that'.

A year later we were actually living in a house just like that on this posh new housing estate. The new place was beautiful, and it massively encouraged our further growth. We had space to fill and a large mortgage to find, our output increased by three hundred percent in the next two years.

Because I was teaching classes every night, and doing courses at the weekends, I was beginning to crystallise my martial art. I was formulating a detailed schematic of my own process. I was so clear on what I was teaching, and it was being so well received that I decided to write it all down in new books on the art of punching, the art of kicking, and the close range art of grappling. I wrote about judo and wrestling, in fact everything I'd learned since I left the day job found space in my growing canon of work.

I noticed too that people were really inspired by my concept of the fear pyramid, so I wrote a book called *Fear the Friend of Exceptional People*, and I detailed the exact process so that others could follow it.

I was so inspired after writing and publishing *Watch My Back* that I wrote five new books in quick succession. They were not big books, but they were good books, because I crammed them with technique, I furnished every line and every paragraph and filled every page with the essence of my learning. The MA books organically spilled out into books for the self-help genre, where I wrote about inspiration and aspiration, I wrote down my certainties about realising ambition.

I remember a time when I was still early in my development, my eyes full of stars, my heart longing to be 'in the room' with my martial art heroes. Sharon said to me one day, 'Geoff, don't keep trying to meet your heroes, *do the work* and your heroes will want to meet you'. Her words were sage; actually, it proved to be some of the best advice ever spoken to me.

Do the work.

I did the work. I was doing the work. And now my heroes were contacting me; I was working with Peter, and he was one of them.

Alongside my teaching with Peter, running concurrently with the books I was writing, was my twice weekly martial arts class in Coventry. It was bursting at the seams with local students, and visitors from afar, some people even travelled from abroad to take instruction.

My teaching in all its forms, the true truth about personal combat, travelled around the world and eventually alighted at the reading desk of Chuck Norris. Of course, like many martial arts fans, I'd been weaned on Bruce Lee and Chuck Norris. The infamous Colosseum fight in the film *Way of the Dragon* acted as both line and verse to my early combative vernacular. Chuck, apparently, had looked at my work, had seen the truth in it and he invited me to come and teach for him in Las Vegas, Nevada, at his association's national convention.

When Peter first took me under his wing, I knew I was being invited onto the national stage and I was appropriately nervous. When the invite landed in my message box from Mr Norris, I knew just as surely I was being invited onto the world stage. It unnerved me. You might wonder what there was to be afraid of. I had a lot of experience now, I'd worked nearly a decade on the doors, and I'd trained in multiple arts, hard arts where no quarter was available so the *asking and the giving* of it did not even arise. I was an experienced teacher. I knew where my certainties lay and yet still... when the invite arrived I did not want to go. I was afraid of the uncertainty. I was scared of what might be waiting for me there, across the vast pond that separated me from my next station. Sharon didn't want to go either and she went everywhere with me. I needed her. If not as my uke, as my wife, as my partner, as my council. Usually if she said she didn't want to join me in a venture, I saw it as a bad omen and I would sit down, take a moment, maybe I'd take a knee, and I'd assess the situation. She had a powerful discernment. I'd learned to trust her insight when mine was spiky and aroused by the dragon rattle of fear or dull and foggy with the clouds of unknowing. When I looked at the whole situation, the black and the white, and all those unknown grey areas, I realised that I didn't want to go to Las Vegas because I was scared, plain and simple.

I realised that Sharon was scared too, and that was no basis for turning an opportunity down, in fact, quite the opposite. In my new landscape, all red lights were green lights, all stop signs said 'go'. I told Sharon I was sorry she didn't want to go to Vegas, but I did want to, I had to. Destiny was calling me. I'd pretended not to listen for a while, but the divine acoustic eventually became a deafeningly loud call to prayer. I could no longer block it out. I told my girl that if she chose not to go, it was fine, I would understand. I'd have to go on my own. At the time, facing even temporary separation from Sharon felt harder to me than standing on a nightclub door, facing the wrath of drunks, druggies and homicidal maniacs. She had given everything up for me. I know how hard that was for her. I know the sacrifices she'd made. She was a shy girl, not one for grand gestures or overt displays of affection, but when I looked closely at her, when I studied her, I could see that she had quietly and determinedly dedicated her whole being to me. It was clear that there was nothing she did as a means that did not have me as its ends. They say that you know when you love truly someone, because you are no longer thinking about yourself, you only think of them. Sharon never thought about herself. She always thought about me.

I'd given everything up for her too. And I was equally dedicated to her. We were together twenty-four hours a day. This way of living doesn't work for everyone, but for us it was a tailored fit. When I studied my conscience, when I delved deeply into my fear of being separated from her, even for a short time, I caught a brief glimmer of my wound; I was not afraid of simply missing my girl, I was frightened of losing her all together. I quietly feared that if I went to Las Vegas alone, she might not be there when I came back. I harboured a debilitating fear that Sharon would leave me, that she'd wake up one day and think, *what am I doing with this crazy loser* and disappear. It was a fear that was not fully identified at this point, certainly it was not articulate enough to place on my pyramid as a future challenge. On my good days this pang was a dull background noise. On my bad days it was a crippling, life restricting angst that imprisoned me. It didn't stop my ambitions, but it definitely placed a caveat on them and made everything I did feel incredibly painful. At its height, when the parasite of insecurity flared, Sharon couldn't leave the room without me worrying that she would leave me or betray me. Part of this was probably the karmic legacy of how we met. I knew how deceptive I had been in my early liaisons with Sharon. I also knew how deceptive our relationship had forced her to be, so we both knew how duplicitous each of us could be before temptation. The residue of this distrust *for me* was jealousy.

I'd always had an unhealthy jealous streak.

I'd inherited it from my dad. He displayed his psychotic distrust with a violently curled lip, a maniacal glare and baseless, drunken accusations against my mum after the pub had closed, and there was no one there to curtail his posturing. It was an illness, and I was infected. Now that I was with Sharon, ten years younger than me and beautiful, the fear of being betrayed sat at the doorway of my heart like a squatting demon. Our circumstance did not help matters, and my green-eyed inheritance did exasperate things, but neither Sharon nor my dad were the true genesis of this terror. I was taught how to distrust the world by the teacher who sexually abused me at the age of eleven. He'd impressed this false belief on my psyche so hard that I did not know how to escape it.

Being invited to teach for Chuck Norris in the US might seem peripheral to my unnatural personal insecurity, but it is intrinsically linked. I didn't know it at the time, perhaps I sensed it, but something was waiting for me in Las Vegas that would hold the key to exorcising this defilement once and for all. Perhaps that's why I was so afraid to go. It was not teaching for Chuck Norris that frightened the bejesus out of me, it was what might be revealed when I peeled away this next layer of obscuration that sent my adrenals into chaos.

The fear was powerful. It must have been because even in accepting this generous offer, I still tried to unconsciously sabotage myself. I asked for more money than was reasonably acceptable. They said yes. I told them I needed to bring a uke and they would have to cover the airfare. They said yes. The Vegas convention was on for four days, Las Vegas was a long way to go for only four days, I asked them to extend my stay in a hotel. They agreed and put me up for ten days. Damn!

In the meantime, a 'friend' had hinted that the whole Vegas trip was some kind of conspiratorial ruse, an American ploy to get me over to the States where I would be confronted and challenged. More fear. Looking back I can see what a ridiculous notion this was, and how naive I was to even listen to it, let alone consider it as a real threat, but fear does funny things to a man, it magnifies everything, it will tell you that a spill is a flood, that a flame is an inferno, that here is better than there and there is better than here and that somewhere else, anywhere else is safer than where you are right now. It will convince you that what is far away is threateningly close, and that what is close, is very far away. *It lies.* Fear lies, and when it lies as big as this you know it is hiding gold.

If your life is a map, fear is the cross that marks treasure.

When I found out who was teaching with me on the same convention, my fear expanded again… the Machado brothers (of the Gracie family), the infamous Brazilian Jiu-Jitsu fighters who had taken the MA world by storm, and Benny Urquidez, a legendary full-contact fighter with an unblemished record. He was on the front of all the big martial arts magazines when I was still growing pubes.

Pressure!

Not just because I was teaching with the gods, but also because of the message I was teaching about reality martial arts.

Benny was a prolific kicker. I was teaching that kicking was a subsidiary art in the street, it was the poor cousin to close range punching, and it was a mere play-toy compared to the big-gun pre-emptive strike.

The Machados were grapplers, ground fighters. They were the best in the world, no doubt. I taught the truth: that grappling was a support system *at best*, and that going to ground in a real fight was not only dangerously naive, it was clinically insane. I felt sure that my 'honest' message would offend them, it would offend their art, it would be like digging their ancestors up from the grave and slapping them repeatedly across the mush with a comedy fish. I feared it would not go down well. As I said, martial arts practitioners are a sensitive bunch, even the threat of contrary opinion could throw them into an insecure frenzy of challenge.

When all these impossible requests were met by my hosts and the fears laid to rest (or certainly quietened), I jumped on a plane and I went to Las Vegas, Nevada. I had to go. I knew I had no choice even though I had every choice in the world. Strange isn't it, how your fears can magnify something small until it bloats completely out of all proportion. It will take a tiny mole hill and pump it into a Nanga Parbat. And strange too how this same fear, this gargoyle, the house ghost of progress, completely vanishes the instant you embrace it. And when I say embrace, I do mean a full on, hip-to-hip, lip-to-lip intercourse. You have to absorb ninety nine percent of the lie before it gives up its tenancy and proffers the truth. My fears have always been vanquished by the simple recognition that they are illusory. As real as they might appear, as manifest and three dimensional as they may present, they are still only projections of my own mind. The bigger and more frightening the house ghost, the greater the treasure it is hiding.

When Francis of Assisi was directed by God to kiss the leper of his nightmares, he was showing the saint-in-waiting this exact principle.

'I promise you Francis,' he told the frightened monk, 'I promise you that the things you hate and fear today, you will come to love'.

Francis was being shown the absolute unreality of fear. He was being shown that the mask of fear is not the face of fear and that the face of fear is not the core of fear. The real fear is always hidden behind those very elaborate projections.

This was where I was now. This is how I felt. But I was resolute that I must accept my date with destiny, so off to *the city of sin* I went.

Sharon did not want to come with me.

I told you this already.

And I was so certain that I must go that I was prepared to do so without her. To try and convince Sharon to join me, to make it a little easier for her, I invited our very close friends John and Ann to join us. Ann was about fifteen years older than Sharon and John was a decade older than me, so the company of seasoned friends who were experienced travellers was reassuring to Sharon. John was himself a veteran martial artist and a big fan of Chuck Norris, so he was keen to come. To make the trip even more special, John and Ann decided to buy a special licence and get married while we were in Vegas.

This tipped the scales and Sharon, whilst still reluctant, decided that she would come with me after all.

If you ever want to bond with people on a deep level, share a challenging experience with them and you will be joined for life.

I bumped into John and Ann just the other day, twenty-one years after Las Vegas, and the feelings of love were like electricity. Our friendship, our kinship and love, is so alive I doubt that even death could remove it.

They were the most splendid, supportive and steady influence for us. They got married in the White Chapel (Elvis was not there, he had left the building) and we celebrated with a meal in the revolving restaurant on the 106th floor of the Stratosphere Tower with panoramic views over the strip. It was so high that helicopters were flying below us. The only problem with a revolving restaurant is that when you go to the toilet, your table is gone by the time you return, it has moved. If you've had a beer or two you could easily find yourself sitting at a different table eating a dinner you didn't order and chatting to people you have never met before.

So, Sharon came with me to Vegas. John and Ann came too, and the whole experience was so much richer because our friends were by our side: they carried some of our stress for us, which made our load more manageable.

Las Vegas was a revelation.

It was an absolute eye-opening, jaw-dropping revelation, in more ways than one. There was never a moment where you didn't know that Vegas was not real, and I am sure that no one was trying to sell it to us as real; it was just a huge, colourful, fantastical playground that could only really be dangerous if you became intoxicated by its wares and believed its specious promises.

At the time, I absolutely loved the splendour, the opulence, the service and the big, big thinking. This place 'was' big thinking. Everything your material heart desired could be bought and found in this neon city with a simple phone call.

I could feel my mind expanding beyond comprehension. I was flooded with ideas and intercessions, with inspirations and aspirations. At times I felt as though I was physically watching the universe dilate before my very eyes. Everything was possible and standing in the dry heat of this lightbulb desert was living proof.

I was in Las Vegas. I was there to teach for Chuck Norris. I was walking around in my own living fantasy.

I would love to tell you that the teaching, and meeting Chuck Norris, and sitting at dinner with the Machados was solely responsible for the epiphany that I was having, and that would be partly true, but it was not the whole truth. Las Vegas, this wonderland of temporal delights, all played their part, no doubt. I could feel that the whole city was alive and sentient, even the buildings, even the bars and the constant song of slot machines churning out American coin were conscious and aware. Every molecule in that place was welcoming me, every single solitary one of those trillions of brightly coloured bulbs seemed to be lighting up and congratulating me. It was showing me the animated and golden representation of every treasure that was guarded by every fearful house ghost in me. Even the hotel we stayed in seemed to be dropping the metaphysical hint…Treasure Island. I was being given a five-star appetiser, a luxurious starter for the meal that was to come.

I filled pads and pads full of words while I was there. I was up every night writing urgently. Ideas were kerchinging out of me like those silver dollars in the slot machines in the casino below my room. I don't ever remember feeling so inspired. Every fear that had crouched at the doorway to my heart back in Britain, trying to stop me from coming, had gone. They had risen, they had shouted out like a ghostly town crier 'claim or be claimed!' And I claimed. I was here and the next day I was to teach the first of four sessions to five hundred of the top black belts in America.

The Chuck Norris people welcomed us like old friends. They were kind, courteous, and there was nothing they would not do for us. I met the Machado clan. The head brother Rigan immediately greeted me and gave me a private lesson in Brazilian Jiu-jitsu, then and there. He could not be more gracious. Later I spotted Benny Urquide. I approached him, introduced myself and told him how much I admired him. He was a gentle man. I could see the history of his brutal fight career etched into his very skin. His face was a scar of experience, a living record of every blow that had landed on him. Kindness was the perfume that permeated from this living samurai. I watched him as he walked across the room to the bathroom, it took him thirty minutes to move one hundred yards, because every few feet a fan stopped him, to shake his hand, to get an autograph, to pose for a photo or to ask advice. He stopped and took time with all of them.

Then a strange and wonderful thing happened.

Benny's beautiful wife Sara made a beeline for me. She didn't know me. Benny didn't really know who I was either to be honest, only that I was a guest instructor, but Sara took a shine to me. Over dinner that night, Benny to my right, Sara to my left, she sat for the whole meal with her hand gently resting on my neck, talking to me, advising me, offering me her wisdom. She was a Native American shaman. Her great, great grandfather was the warrior Geronimo. She told me of the spirits that she could see hovering around me, guiding me, prompting me and protecting me. When I asked Sara if my spirits thought I was on the right path, she looked behind me and then smiled, 'Your guides are laughing,' she said, 'they are saying, yes of course you are absolutely on the right path.' The laughter (I figured) was because I was perhaps missing the obvious: I was in Las Vegas teaching on one of the most highly regarded courses in the US. I was having dinner with Benny and Sara. The whole Machado family were sharing the same table. I was here at the invite of arguably the most famous martial artist in the world. 'Hello!' I could feel the Biff-knuckles of my ancestors wrapping on my empty skull, 'think, McFly, think!'

Of course I was in the right place. How many signs do you need you fool?

I thought I was going there for one specific thing - to teach - but once again, it was me that was being schooled, and in so many ways. Even now, two decades later, writing these notes, arcana that were seeded back in Vegas is just starting to flower.

I have collected thirty years of experience in a kick-bollock-scramble of beautiful living. This book, or the writing of this book, is helping me to process the essence of those moments and refine and bottle its perfume.

Eschatology opened up a room (that was always there, that will always be there) called Las Vegas, Nevada. It placed me before many new teachers, some animate, some inanimate, some walking, talking corporeal beings, some incorporeal, those energies and those guiding voices, who make up the invisible vanguard.

Fear will tell you that there is a monster lurking in the dark corner of your bedroom. Light, perspective, consciousness will show you that it is no monster, only a coat hanging from a hat stand dressed by the shadows.

I was being shown (once again) that light, perspective and consciousness are created by the dynamo of human volition. If I don't move, I will stay in the dark, and, my view will remain obscured. If I do not move, if I fail to create light, shadows will always shroud my imagination. If I do not consciously expand my awareness with courageous curiosity and deliberate movement, my earth is always going to be flat, limited by the folly of human conjecture.

And so it was in Las Vegas. No bogeymen, aggressively queuing at my hotel door to confront me, to challenge my ideas. No insecure stylists, wounded by an opposing opinion. I was not out of my depth. I did not and was not made to feel like an outsider. The very large classes I taught were not full of resistant traditionalists. I'd developed this strange fear that martial arts people in the States would be somehow different to the martial arts students in Britain. Different! The whisperer, the roaming lion of negativity did not even qualify what it meant by different, because (back then) I'd not yet learned to master sub-vocalisation (or recognise the voice of adverse forces) and I had yet to develop the kind of discernment that I enjoy today. I thought the whisperer was my own voice, a friendly chap who was trying to gently forewarn me of an oncoming threat, telling me that I should *watch my back* because the students in the US were not like the students in the UK, they were 'different'.

Standing in front of the Americans, I of course could immediately see that they were not different. They were just lovely people like the ones back home. They were people in a room, like other people in other rooms all over this planet and beyond. They welcomed me. They were gracious and open. Their chief instructor, Mr Chuck Norris, had invited me to the US to pass on my learning and that was credentials enough for them. One of my US students - Lito Angelis, a brilliant martial artist - even travelled over from LA to help me. Lito was the chief self-defence teacher for the LAPD, and he joined me as a very welcome uke.

There were nerves, yes, but the nerves were at bay. I had steadied them back in Britain when I found certainty about the purpose of both the invite and my acceptance of it.

As soon as I started to teach the flow came. I could have been in any room anywhere in the world, it would have made no difference. Sharon wowed the students the moment she dropped her first heavy right on the focus pad and they broke out into spontaneous applause. I spent the next four days teaching the essence of what I'd learned about martial efficacy, and the truth was welcomed and embraced like the prodigal son. What I realised then and what I realise now is that colour, creed and nationality mean very little; people are interested only in truth, certainty, and if you have the truth, you have the room. If you don't have it, better to pack your bags and head home, come back when you do.

Our days in Vegas sped by faster than a kid sliding down a snowy bank on a shiny tea tray. Between teaching sessions there were banquets and parties, and award ceremonies, and myriad other delights that impressed and entertained us in equal measure. I got the chance to sit with Chuck between sessions and chat with him one to one over tea. He was the gentlest man, very humble. It was a strange experience to sit with the man you'd watched over and over in the Colosseum fight with Bruce

Lee. It was life enhancing to sit with him face to face and confirm to my doubting self that we are all the same at the core, no-one higher, no-one lower, no inferiority and no elitism. This was not Chuck Norris, the superstar from the cinema screen, he was just a soul, passing on his story to another soul following a similar path. He said to me, regarding his success and his achievements, 'anyone could do this Geoff, this is here for anyone.' He meant it. Then he proceeded to tell me about his relationship with Bruce Lee, and how Bruce would call him randomly and out of the blue, 'hey Chuck, you wanna spar?'

Chuck told me that he'd only started martial arts because, as a kid, he suffered badly with a stutter and he thought that it might help grow his confidence. He went on to become a legitimate world karate champion, multiple times, and of course enjoyed a wonderful career as an action movie star.

People can tell you all day long that anything is possible, but when you sit with the frail, quiet, beings that have achieved seemingly impossible things, aware of the strides they have made and the boundaries they must have broken through to get there, you can't deny it.

What I learned, sitting with this legendary man over a cup of tea, was the power that third-certainty people hold. It is a divine force that radiates out and inspires all of those looking for certainty.

I taught for four days in Vegas.

I met and trained with many amazing people and I expanded exponentially. No doubt, the man that went out to Las Vegas was not the man that returned home to Britain again. I had shifted once more. My adventure showed me that there was another level of possibility, and I had just accessed it. I was living and teaching cheek-by-jowl with my heroes, men and women I'd seen on the movie screen and in magazines, and they were just like me: very ordinary. But that's what excited me. These were living, breathing, faulty and beautiful, frail and powerful human beings, who were living in the most extraordinary way. There were men and women teaching on this course who displayed near superhuman qualities, but they did so in such a way that you were made to see that the superhuman was actually super-normal: we all have these potentials, it is our ground of being.

As I already said, our friends John and Ann got married in the Little White Chapel (gaudy but strangely delightful). Me and Sharon acted as best man and witness. We went for a meal in the Stratosphere Tower to celebrate. We did the whole tourist thing. We stood like two awed ants staring into the Grand Canyon. We walked up and down the endless strip. We threw small change into the hungry slot machines. We ate too many slices of French toast, drank too many glasses of chilled American lemonade, and lay for too long by the hotel pool under a punishing desert sun.

Before we knew it, the adventure was over and we were heading back home to the UK.

When we got back to Britain, I was changed.

I didn't know why at the time, it was only later that I was able to see that Las Vegas, Chuck Norris, teaching at the highest, most demanding level had shifted something in me and the doubts and fears vanished. No-one was going to tell me what was and what was not possible. I knew now more than ever before that anything was possible, I had the proof. If I could publish a book, if I could give up my job to write professionally and teach globally, if I could travel to Las Vegas and teach for the man, what other possibilities were out there? What other possibilities were just waiting to be revealed. The belief in the possibility of all things was quite a siddha. I could see infinite potential, and even if I couldn't immediately reach it yet, at least I knew it was there.

I didn't know it yet, but this high was about to crank up another notch, when a mysterious midnight visit would send me into a whole other stratosphere.

Portrait of the writer

With Sharon

Running a combat course, my friend and student Wael Al-Sayegh watching on.

In training

Using the pads in training

'Notes From A Factory Floor' painted by the artist Ashleigh Farmer.

London premiere of Bouncer, left to right: Ray Winstone, Michael Baig-Clifford, Shaun Parkes, Ronnie Fox, Paul Green (producer).

Publicity poster for The Doorman

The BAFTA winning team, left to right: Mark Leveson (producer), Ronnie Fox, Natasha Carlish (producer), Michael Baig-Clifford (director) and Jo McInnes.

With the very cool LL Cool J

With the incredibly talented Renee Zellweger at the BAFTAs

Paris The Club premiere.

With Sharon on winning the BAFTA

Above: Craig Conway as Malky in Romans 12:20

Left: The original poster for short film Romans 12:20

Below: With Sharon, the Shammasian brothers and Craig Conway on the set of Romans 12:20

Right: With the incredibly talented Shammasian brothers

Left: James Cosmo on the set of The Pyramid Texts

Below: Poster for The Pyramid Texts

With actor James Cosmo at the premiere of The Pyramid Texts

Ethan Cosmo in The Pyramid Texts.

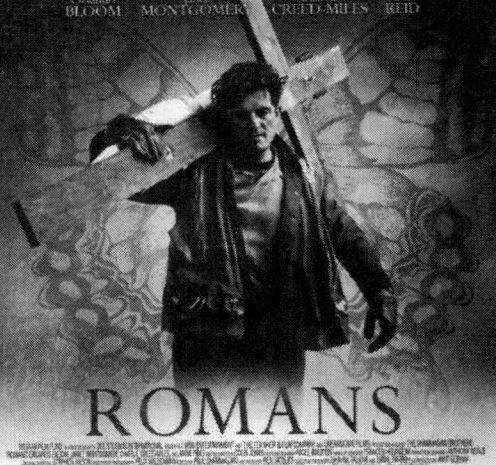

Left: With Orlando Bloom on the set of Romans
Below: The official poster for Romans

With Brian Rose

With Tom Clarke in the rehearsal room for We'll Live and Die in These Towns, at the Belgrade Theatre.

In the middle of my TED Talk debut
The TED Talk was thrilling but terrifying!

10

Post Vegas Epiphany

I was floating by the time our flight landed back in Heathrow. I was full of new stories to tell, hungry to teach and write and gobble up the future delights of this utopia I was now walking through. It was probably about a week or so after I returned home that it happened. A full blown, blow your socks off epiphany. I thought the feelings of happiness, excitement and inspiration were simply the effects of overcoming my fears and landing myself the prize of tea with Chuck in America. This, I can now see, was just the preparation for what was to come.

I woke in the middle of the night. That's how it started. I was wide awake and staring at the ceiling. Something was happening to my body, something was moving in me. There was an energy shifting through my being that was other. It was not mine, but it was in me. The energy was a pleasant wave that slowly spread from my lower torso up to my heart. It was like an orchestra had started to play, and I was its instrument. My back arched involuntarily, my chest expanded, as though an unseen aperture had opened perpendicular and along the full length of my breastbone, and when it stopped expanding I breathed in the whole universe. It was incredible and other-worldly and ecstatic. My chest opened into an invisible gape and I felt one with everything. Any residual angers and fears, any anxieties and pains, they just vanished. I felt peace, peace with everything, peace with everyone, peace with myself. I felt love too, but not in the romantic sense, this was not the sock-and-sandals of sickly-sweet evangelism, neither was it love as an emotion, this was love as a state, a frequency.

They say that the kingdom of God exists within us. That is what this felt like. I had opened up to the esoteric, and found my own personal throne room.

I am not sure how long it lasted for, two minutes, two hours, I don't know. I only know it eased in, made its full expression, and then eased back out again. I was changed by it, like a blind man waking up with 20:20 vision; I was very changed. I could see. The Siddhas (the holy miracles) flowed and I could see things - in myself, in the world, beyond the world - that were so evident to me that, at the time, I didn't even recognise them as Siddhas. I just knew I could see where others could not.

And I was given the secret to perpetual motion.

It was so simple it was almost offensive.

Selfless service.

That's it. That's the secret. What you do for others from a place of love creates a perpetual wave of volition that will go out into the world and work without any further effort. It was so easy. All I wanted to do now was serve people, all people, as many people as possible.

I said to Sharon the next morning, after the night-time excursion into the divine, after my interstellar sojourn, my trip between the stars of consciousness, 'have a guess who I was with last night?' 'Who'? She asked. 'God', I replied. 'That's nice' she said, as though my revelation was the normal badinage exchanged over every breakfast table. 'What do you want to eat?'

Her very-normal reaction to my super-normal experience helped me. It kept my feet firmly on terra firma. It was just what I needed at this time. Sharon's quiet and unannounced spirituality was never overt, but it did prove itself time and again when she proffered sage words in times of dire sensitivity.

Spiritual epiphanies can be very precarious if they are not handled carefully in the aftermath of their arrival. What starts as a beautiful and expanding clarity can quickly become a quagmire of dissonance, even psychosis if family or friends do not understand what has happened to you and overreact. One friend experienced a similar epiphany, and when, in his search for clarity, he shared it with his local priest, he was urged to join the priesthood immediately. It sent my friend into a confused tizzy: he was a bricklayer, he had a wife and a child, a mortgage, he didn't want to be a priest, he just wanted to understand what the F had happened to him. Another friend, a Christian, shared his *moment* with close family members, and they shunned him, they called him a liar and assured him that if God was going to visit anyone, it would not be someone normal like him, someone common.

Sharon just said, 'that's nice'.

She said it as though I'd found a pound coin down the back of the settee, or announced that I was going to Costa for a coffee. 'That's nice', as though meeting God on my *night journey* was the most ordinary and natural thing in the world. I am sure, looking back that if she'd flat-out dismissed my epiphany as a flight of fancy, or if she'd reacted with any kind of hysteria, I could have been wounded by her denial, or so affected by her delirium that I might have left planet earth there and then, floated above the firmament and lost contact with materiality altogether.

Epiphanies (moments of clarity, exposure to the Holy Dove, or Kundalini) can be disorientating. The world of wonder that you awaken to after a divine encounter, is not the world of limitation you went to sleep with the night before. This can lead very easily to confusion and dissonance which, if not checked, can very easily become a fearful disassociation, even an out-and-out psychosis.

Many people have fallen off the edge of sanity and landed in a psychiatric ward because their initial wonder lead to massive cognitive dissonance.

Sharon's balanced response stopped me from buying an orange robe and wandering the earth as a mendicant (nothing wrong with this, if it is your dharma) or rushing off to the East so that I could save a small village in India.

I was excitable after my experience, and frantic and in a hurry to act. I needed to tell everyone what I'd learned during my experience. I needed to serve everyone. I needed to do something big, something global.

Sharon reminded me of a simple truth. She held my arm across the breakfast table, and was deeply earnest, 'Geoff, when you spend 30 minutes on the phone, talking a stranger through depression, that is global'.

'But I need to serve people,' I said, as though she didn't understand the importance of the mission I felt.

'You've got a pile of letters on your desk Geoff. You've got a stack of emails in your inbox, they are all from people asking for your help. They are asking to be served, why not start with them?'

Wow, that was profound.

Only hours after my moment of clarity, and my ego was already trying to hijack this gift and claim it as its own.

My false ego wanted to steal the freshly delivered divine essence and do something visual with it, something grand and ostentatious, something that people would see and say, 'wow, did you hear? Geoff Thompson just saved a small village in India. What a guy, what a humanitarian, what a splendid fellow he is'.

I took her advice immediately. I stopped looking for people to serve, and I started serving the people that God had already placed in front of me.

There is a lovely old Buddhist idiom that I like: before enlightenment, carrying water, chopping wood, after enlightenment, carrying water, chopping wood.

I'd had a wonderful, enlightening moment of clarity. I was different, but things still needed to be done. The difference now though, was that they would be done consciously, and always with service in mind.

I kept in mind always the words of my sage wife: serve the people that God has placed in front of you.

My mum and dad were right in front of me, immediately so, and they badly needed serving. Me and Sharon were doing well financially by now. Lots of book sales, full classes, busy courses every weekend, and the DVDs I was producing were great sellers; the money was coming in. My parents were still living on a council estate at the time, and my dad was at the very beginning of an illness that would eventually claim his life. The estate was nice if you were young and you had children. For the old, (my mum and dad were pensioners) it was not so good because the kids were loud and they liked to kick a football off the wall of my dad's end of terrace home.

His nerves were in the wind. He couldn't bear to be in the house with all the racket, so he spent most of his time walking the streets looking for quiet, and dreading going back home.

We decided to intervene.

We bought my mum and dad a beautiful detached house on a quiet lane, an idyll, just to get them off the estate, and settle my dad's nerves. I am grateful that his last years were lived out in that quiet abode. When we bought the house I remember saying to Sharon, *if this is the only thing we ever do in our lifetime, it will be enough.* My mum and dad were overwhelmed by their new home. My dad was happy-dissonant. He wasn't very well at the time, so he didn't completely understand how this posh house on the lane could be theirs. It was what they might have called *a lottery house*, the kind of home you talked about buying if you ever won the lottery, even though they sort of knew that it would never happen, it certainly never happened in all their years of gambling with the numbers, not to them, and not to anyone they knew. He sat in the front room of this spacious property, my beautiful dad, a confused look on his face, and he said to me 'so this is ours then?'

'Yes, Dad, it's yours.'

'So...how is it ours?'

'Me and Sharon brought it for you dad. It's a gift.'

A beat.

A squint of the eyebrows.

He looked around the room, to make sure that it was still there, to assure himself that he was not dreaming.

He looked at me again.

'So it's ours then?'

'Yes Dad, it's yours.'

I loved my dad. I loved his very bones. If he needed them, I'd have given him the clothes off my back and the shoes off my feet; he could have it all, *I just loved him.*

My mum told me that for the rest of his life, the joy of living in that house never wore off for him. He'd be sitting in the front room, looking out the window daydreaming, then suddenly, randomly turn to my mum and say, 'I can't believe this is ours.'

In due course, my dad died. It was heart-breaking. Of course. When you lose your dad, you lose part of yourself, that's to be expected. My only solace was that he'd spent his last days in this quiet nirvana.

I was spiritually awake.

I floated in this holy bubble for two years. In esoteric parlance the period, post epiphany, is known as the honeymoon period. I didn't know this at the time, I didn't know either that post honeymoon would be the most difficult, the most challenging and frightening of my whole life; a time I look back on now as my 'atonement years'.

You can't fill thirty years (since I was sexually abused at the age of eleven) with lies, self-abuse, division and then ten years of heinous violence, criminality, deception and dishonour on the doors and then just expect all that sin to be wiped clean because you had a moment of clarity.

The shit, as they say, is still stuck in the plumbing.

All of that karma was still alive in me, it was a community, a force, one that I had fed and watered on the glut of pornographic living. I had unconsciously created a covenant with dark forces and this stain had moved into the tabernacle of my muscles, nerves and sinews, it permeated me.

Now that I had awoken, now that I could see true, I had to sever those old covenants and instead break bread with a clean energy, the divine force. This was not going to come without a fight.

The Holy Prophet was right. The spit, blood and death of external war (what he called 'the lesser jihad') was a mere scuffle when compared to the greater jihad, the war we wage not with the self, but for the self.

This was all to come.

Let me not rush too fast towards those experiences. They were difficult to endure, and they will be difficult again to retell, so for now, let me stay for a time with the joy, and I will come to the purgation in due course.

For now, I was blissful. I was being granted a two year sojourn in the kingdom. Twenty four months of pure equanimity, where nothing bothered me. Criticism? I forgave my critics. *They knew not what they were doing.* Money? It would be provided for me. Everything I needed would be supplied. Love? What are you talking about you crazy fool, can't you see that our human nature is made up of nothing but pure love? *I am pure love.* I'm swimming in the stuff; I am up to my neck veins in bliss. Relationships? My relationship was with God, everything else was subsidiary, the exponential effect of my marriage to the divine. Purpose? My purpose was so simple it was almost offensive: serve, serve, serve.

I understood things I never understood before. I became aware. The observer - the witness who was now viewing the world clearly through my eyes - was the real me. That might sound obvious, of course it was me, who else would it be? Well, to be brutally honest, it could be any number of strangers. It might have been any number of sub-personalities: internal demigods, the Freudian shadows, those Tollien pain-bodies holed up in my heart, the rising impressions of my class, the hungry ghosts of my ancestry, the devils of dogmatic scripture, the voice of learned scarcity, historical wounds, societal mores, the tabloid lie, televisual half-truths, mis-directions and blatant lies, the teacher's voice at school - 'get back onto the playground like the scum you are Thompson', the drunken slight of my drunken dad when he still liked a pint 'you slimy little cunt'.

I could go on.

So many impressions that live in us as a community of personalities.

The voices in me were myriad. The eyes looking out, legion. The angry eyes, the hopeful eyes, the eyes of rage, the eyes of self-pity and hopelessness. So many eyes peering through the same two sockets, so many sub-vocal voices rattling through the same noisy voice box, dripping off the same forked-tongue. But now, post Vegas the eyes looking out were from a singular source and the voice was from a dedicated Self and I was aware of it. I was aware of the real 'I'. It was who I am.

I could sense the hoards, the other voices, *they* were still there, somewhere, in quarantine *for now* but I knew that they were not me, and I knew that unless I allowed them, unless I gave the vampires explicit permission to cross the threshold of my mind-door, they could not joyride this fleshy vehicle and they could not view the world through the eyes of the personality called Geoff Thompson.

I can distinctly remember what I kept saying joyfully to my friends and family, 'I am the only person who is looking through these eyes, just me.'

I didn't fully realise what I was saying at the time. I couldn't clearly articulate my feelings, but I can see now that what I was trying to say was, 'I have found the true 'I', he is looking through these eyes and no-one else.'

Books read differently through the perspective of the real 'I'. When I read them, I knew what they meant, in their sub-text. I knew that the Art of War by Sun Tzu was not a book just about the external rules for military combat, it was a book about the greater jihad, the inner battle with the false ego. When it detailed the relationship between the generals and the soldiers, I knew it was talking about the relationship between the higher self and the lower self, the controlling ego and the army of the senses. The sub-text read so simply to me that I was amazed that others could not see it.

The Bible too, the Pentateuch, the revelations of God. I knew that Sinai, the mountain Moses climbed in order to receive the commandments was no doubt a real place, it was literal, but sub-textually it was his mind that had to ascend in order to receive the instruction of God. The five books of refuge did not just record the journey of the Israelites after their deliverance from Egyptian slavery, rather it is a didactic on the plight of the lower soul, the possessed ego, tricked into servitude by the Pharaoh of dark forces, Al Shaytan (materiality, the world) and sent into the desert on a forty year search for the Promised Land, the kingdom within.

I read the Bhagavad-Gita. Prince Arjuna and his family (the Pandavas) are tricked out of their kingdom by their corrupt cousins (the Kuravas) and Arjuna wages war at Kurukshetra to win it back. I am sure that Arjuna existed and I know that Kurukshetra is a real city situated in the north Indian state of Haryana, but when I read the Gita, I saw again that it had an allegorical subtext about the battle to win back control of human perception.*

---

* I have written about this process extensively in my book The Divine CEO.

People in the world were like open books to me. Suddenly I could discern them at a deeper level. I could see beyond the cover, even when I didn't intend to. They started to look like x-rays to me. I could observe my martial arts students and know exactly where their techniques could be improved. I could read their strengths and their weaknesses, and through this I could predict where the strengths and weaknesses lay in their broader life. One man would not fully commit his punch on a bag or pad for fear of injury or exhaustion and I knew immediately that, in his business life and in his family life, he would be playing out the same unconscious restrictions. Until he fixed this fear he would always throw half a punch and he would always live half a life.

Another student always came to the class a little late and always found a reason to leave a little early. I knew what this meant: he was afraid to be there. The beginning and the end of my sessions were the times I delivered my own Gita, a spiritual discourse that would pull defilement out of people like a claw-hammer dragging nails from wood. This told me that he was afraid to hear the truth and if he was afraid to hear the truth in my class, he would be afraid to hear the truth in his relationships, in his employment, in his life.

Another woman would literally manifest road blocks in her home town that would stop her from travelling to my class.* She'd ring me, post training, to tell me that she really wanted to attend, *but it was impossible*, because she'd been hemmed in by roadworks. She wasn't lying. There really were road works, and they did curtail her ability to travel, but I knew that she was the one creating the blocks, she was so afraid to attend my class and see what she might see, hear what she might hear, or feel what she might feel that she'd literally created traffic to stop her from attending. This demonstrated to me the power of unconscious intent: that she could affect traffic was a potent and miraculous power, one that could be positively harnessed if she was able to recognise and re-direct it. On one occasion the same woman broke a bone in a freak biking accident that forced her to cancel a whole six month course of training that she had paid for in advance.

These distractions were real, no doubt, that is not the issue here. That the student in question was in denial of her self-sabotaging, that it was her who'd caused the blips in the matrix, was the most revelatory and the most disturbing and inspiring

---

* If you are a former student and you think I might be writing about you, don't worry, I am; you and hundreds of others just like you, who manifested the exact same blocks. And me. I have observed all of these phenomena in my own life too.

observation. It immediately told me two things: she was in denial and her potential (beyond the obvious material success) was immense. When the forces resisting you create injury and accident, when they affect the movement of traffic and break bones, you know they are concealing something very big.

After the Vegas epiphany I also knew that my touch could affect people in a powerful and healing way. I knew that my voice could do the same. Why this was such a revelation to me I don't know. I'd already used my touch and my voice to harm people on the doors of Coventry nightclubs, I had been witness to its destructive power, so why I thought the opposite would not also be true, is difficult to fathom.

I found too that I was able to pull people out of a depression with an inspirational talk. I could release shadows by recognising where they existed in the person before me and covertly create an opening in their heart to release them.

Please bear in mind that all this was happening to me, it was coming through me rather than from me. It was not Geoff Thompson the person who was able to suddenly affect these Siddhas, it was the Holy Spirit awakened in me, the Tao or the Flow and it was using me as a vessel.

The healing gift and the other miracles I was experiencing were not the product of some delusional Christ complex. It was the simple realisation of a human potential that is innate in us all. What blocks us from acknowledging this gift, developing it and making the body a cleaner conduit for its use, is fear. We are afraid, because to fully realise the gifts, means to surrender to their Benefactor and this is a terrifying prospect to our lower elements. The false ego is always fighting for control, vying for power and searching for the Holy Grail of longevity, if not immortality, so the idea of giving up its autonomy is anathema, it is literally life threatening to it.

I was shown also that the ego is not lost, dissolved or killed when it surrenders to the Higher Good, it merely sheds its false impressions, gives up its pseudo sovereignty and exchanges them for freedom under the authority of divine nature.

'Less and less me', as Paul of Tarsus said, 'more and more Christ'.

At the time of all this massive internal change, I was running a very small, non-commercial Thursday morning class for my closest students, probably ten in all. A beautiful group of world class players who were so physically competent that their natures had softened to an attractive and gentle glow. This class became an impromptu healing room for the next few years, for me and for others. I would create the time and space and invite the right atmosphere to both enact the healings, and also come to terms with who I had become. That small, back room, in the AT7 Sports Centre in a small suburb of Coventry was the anvil and forge that would shape my new inner life and temper me into a keen vessel. Over the next few years, we would greet many visitors in this room, people that had been sent for specific instruction and for particular healing. They would arrive, these lovely strangers, from myriad disparate places, and they would always alight when and where I least expected.

My job was to make sure I only let the right ones in.

I also started to heal on the go. When I was out and about, teaching or promoting my books and DVDs, I would be introduced to people who were sick, people who were depressed, and some people who were just plain lost. Everywhere I went, every city I visited, every small town and village I entered I knew that someone would be placed before me, and the right word, the right gesture or mudra or simply my presence in the room as an aligned energy (perhaps a combination of them all) would bring them instant balm if not spontaneous healing. Sometimes, my presence or my word or touch might act as a catalyst, to trigger the beginning of healing. I knew I would be divinely introduced to specific people and there would be a connection made between us. I didn't know who they might be in advance, and I had no idea how or when or even why it would play out, but I was certain that a meeting would occur, and an intercession would ensue. Every time I appeared in public - a talk, a class, a book signing - I would say to Sharon, 'I wonder who will be placed before us today'.

I realise now of course, looking back, that I was living in the third level of yaqeen - certainty of experience. I was certain I could heal people. It was as simple as that. There were no grand proclamations. I did not don an orange robe, and change my name to OB1 and announce myself as the second coming or the last of the Jedi knights, I just went about my usual business in the world, and when people were placed before me for healing, I followed my intuition and let it happen. It felt so obvious to me and so normal that I wasn't even conscious of what I was doing, there was no sense that it was in any way out of the ordinary.

This was the gift I was now carrying.*

---

* I have written comprehensively about these healings in The Divine CEO.

This whole period was a full-on, foot-down, high-speed, kick-bollock-scramble of learning on the bleeding edge. The big thing I learned was that certainty - or the lack thereof - is what stands between man and his potential, between scarcity and wealth, between sickness and health, between happiness and misery, between the boiling rivers of blood-and-fire of Dante's seventh circle and the land of cool water. But certainty has to be revealed. It is ours already, but it is hidden, it is obscured by a field of nescience, the ignorance of conditioning and fear.

Not everything I was *seeing* pleased me.

My clarity enabled me to see who I really was and who I patently was not. But what was revealed about me was also revealed about others. I could see who they were too, at their core, and I could also see the masks they were wearing, the disguises that obscured their true being.

It did not always make wholesome viewing.

I think at some level I could always see this, but pre-Vegas I had never consciously articulated or even admitted it. To acknowledge what you see (that others are wearing masks) is frightening, not least because amongst the population of *others*, you will find your nearest and dearest: friends, family, lovers. It is hard to admit that the person you wake up with every morning is sometimes not herself, not himself. You also start to notice the disturbing incongruence in your own nature. How can you not? If you see truth in the general, you will be forced to see truth in the particular.

How many dishonest masks to do we each pull on and peel off over a single day, during a calendar month, across a year or a lifetime?

Perhaps the most bizarre and disturbing aspect of my revelation is not that we are all wearing masks, rather, it is that we all know that we are wearing masks, but no one wants to be the first to announce it. And anyway, I doubt you'd be thanked for your honesty. If you offered your seeing unadulterated, people would be cut to the quick, they'd be falling over themselves in offence and denial, each reaching for the defence mechanism of their choice.

People will attack you when you tell them the truth you know!

Before I only sensed this, now I could see it, very consciously. I could clearly see people's demons, their divides, their alternate-selves and it was incredible. It was incredible but it was not nice.

It is not a comfortable experience, sitting with one person, someone you know very well, perhaps a significant other, and then moments later watching them as they literally morph into another person, a stranger, often a personality that is completely at odds to the one you know, completely antagonistic to the one you love. And, because they are unaware of the change, it means they don't know themselves, they don't know who they are below the wardrobe of elaborate disguises. This also means that they can't trust themselves, which by proxy indicates that you can't trust them either, not really, not fully. Any of the myriad unconscious personalities could take them over at any time and act through them - often inappropriately, sometimes immorally, occasionally outrageously or illegally – and create a karmic debt that at some point, someone has to pick up.

This can be heart-rending if it is someone you love or someone you work with, maybe it's your husband, perhaps it's your best friend or business partner.

I could see masks.

I could observe people, and watch the gear change between different personas, a shift that was often so subtle and so smooth that only the keenest eye would catch it. Because I could see masks, I could also see lies. I could see agendas. I could see contrivance and conniving, even in people I admired. But, very occasionally, I met people or I talked with people who were not wearing masks and when I did, it was stilling and beautiful and I would become lost in the void of their pauses. I learned to cherish these rare moments as much as I learned to endure the times where authenticity was not present.

I learned too not to judge.

It is very dangerous to judge. It is not my job to judge. It is not my business to judge. There is an allegorical scratch drawn in the sand, and unless I have not sinned at all, I am in no position to step across it and cast the first stone. And if I do, I shouldn't be surprised when the stone rebounds and hits me with twice the force it was thrown.

The lovely Byron Katie says it best, 'there are three kinds of business: your business, someone else's business and God's business. You have no right being in anything other than your own business.'

How could I judge anyway, when I was still so full of demons myself?

The world became a hall of fairground mirrors for me. Every ugly image I judged *out there* was a reflection of my own inner grotesque. If judgment ever rose in me my newly awakened conscience would quietly (sometimes loudly) remind me that it was unwise to throw stones whilst I was still living in a house made of glass.

Instead of judgment I reached for compassion, especially for those who never removed their make-up. Many of my old friends, people from my past life as a bouncer, had either gone insane, got killed in criminal pursuits, or were living hideously violent lives in prison where they were surrounded twenty-four hours a day by monsters of their own design.

My protection against this was to stay completely centred in my newly revealed, true self: the awakened person no longer wears a mask.

I found that when I was compassionate with others, they were compassionate with me.

I was compassionate with me.

I had always been the most severe and unkind self-critic, but the compassion I proffered to others had a beautiful and unexpected healing effect on me.

There were moments when my eyewall cracked and the stormy chaos of the world rushed in and caught me and I drew detritus towards me like a shit magnet, but these *accidents* became less frequent as I tightened my game.

Because of the expanded awareness, my teaching changed radically. I found myself suddenly and immediately out of step with the story I'd been telling and selling just a few months before.

I'd been flogging ignorance to the ill-informed, the philosophy of *greater violence to control violence*. And I was teaching this to some of the most physically violent people on the planet. But now I had a new teaching for them… love.

Love!

Yes, you heard right.

No more smashing teeth in, love was now my weapon of choice.

The message did not land well.

It went down like a dripping hamburger at a vegan picnic.

It was received by some with ridicule and scepticism even great revile. In my defence, at that time, I was not just teaching and preaching love, I was love.

Someone, years later, accused me of 'thinking you are God'. I almost laughed, 'I don't think I'm God' I said, knowing even as the words left my mouth how heretical I must have sounded, 'I don't think I'm God, I know I'm God'.

Of course I was, just as we all are, just as everything is. If God is omniscient and omnipotent and omnipresent, of course God is everything.

I knew I'd connected myself to the substratum of all that is, to true power. People thought that I had become the liberal left, a softy, that I'd lost my bottle, that I had gone all 'socks and sandals' on them. I'd shifted from being a respected fighter to a 'fucking tree hugger'.

You hug one tree!

I was a tree hugger, it's true.

I was so aligned that there was nothing, there was nowhere, there was no one and no thing, sentient or senseless, spiritually conscious or materially comatose, man of God or madman in the psychiatric ward that was not my immediate brother, who was not my blood sister, or my beautiful mum, or my adoring aunt - I loved everything, I loved everyone.

Even Peter Consterdine, my closest friend, my business partner, my erstwhile mentor pulled me to one side worriedly and said (in paraphrase), 'what the fuck Geoff! Don't forget what we are selling here'.

He was right of course. I had transcended, and I was expecting the people who'd come to me for tuition in the hard arts, to automatically and unquestioningly follow me inside, to the internal arts.

And my private class too, my non-commercial, experimental Thursday mornings, where we wrestled like Apollo and drank tea like Lao Tzu and engaged in exhilarating Socratic dialogues, even they, my most devoted students, viewed me like I was an imposter in their midst. They looked at me like I was a ghost in their works, certainly they did not recognise or understand the new me. I felt like Odysseus returning home to Ithaca after many years of fighting the Trojan Wars, only to find that no one in his household recognised him anymore. My devoted Thursday group vacated my class like they were running from a burning building.

Peter was right.

What I'd been gifted had to be introduced slowly, covertly, piece-by-piece.

You can't just walk into a class of broken noses and cauliflower ears, a room full of hardy warriors and say 'yeah, yeah, I know we were learning to kill people last week and I know I told you that that was *the way*, but everything has changed now, I was wrong, no more killing please, it's all about love now...come on, gather round, let's hug'.

It had taken me decades of acid-bath exposure before I tipped into this new frequency; I couldn't expect people to just accept what I was saying overnight.

I still had the residue of that killer in me too. I could feel him bubbling away, not many fathoms beneath the new order, the spiritual governance that had usurped his reign. At some point, he would have to be encountered again, this man of violence, and I'd be forced to evict, dissolve or convert that snarling menace before I could expect my students to do the same.

So, I *wound my neck in* (as they say around these parts). And I used the gift of hard-fighting martial arts as a Trojan horse to sneak the higher game through the gates. It got me inside people's heart space. Once I was inside, once my audience was captive, I would drip-feed the new truth, the true truth.

But this method of covert teaching could not last forever. Eventually I would be forced to eschew the blood-and-snot of physical scrimmage, and work exclusively on my inner game. Intuitively I was led away (with much wailing and gnashing of teeth) from exoteric martial arts, and directed instead towards the esoteric, where the battles are won or lost at the doorway of the heart and not at the entrance of a seedy night club. My schooling would come from invisible densities, beyond the material realm - known in theology as *the teacher-less teaching* - and my guides too, would be mostly incorporeal.

More about this later in the book.

Inevitably my transition from the external to the internal battle ground was not without its casualties.

As I worked increasingly inwards - non-violence, charity, correct palate (light eating/veganism), meditation, fasting, prayer - my proximity to God drew closer and closer. As I have already mentioned, divine proximity acts as a spiritual poultice, and this has a duel and oxymoronic quality: being around you allows people a clear view of their own divinity, but simultaneously it can draw out their shadows or weaknesses if they remain in your atmosphere for any length of time. When I started teaching love as the ultimate defence against the adverse forces, I witnessed this anomaly first-hand: devoted students became ardent critics. Loyal friends, people I love, fashioned me into a reviled enemy, they made a metaphoric voodoo doll in my image, and used Facebook posts and twitter feeds and internet blogs to stick me full of pins. Lifelong friends and family members joined internet hate campaigns to try and attack and discredit me.

No complaints.

No one grows without opposition. And there can be no better opposition than that of a trusted friend or a blood relative, who turncoats. If you can survive the betrayal of a friend, a brother or your most loyal student, everyone else is going to be a walk in the park by comparison. And anyway, who better to strengthen your inner-wrastle, than those who know exactly where your vulnerabilities lie? What better way to perfect your blade, than to sharpen it on the whetstone of Satan's master swordsmen? They are, after all, sent to teach you how to seal your fractures and perfect your arsenal.

I loved these people. I still love these people now. I am grateful to them, they led me towards love, even when everything inside me wanted to hate.

And, as I may have already mentioned somewhere else in the book, I was no better than them: hadn't I betrayed people? My first wife, my children, my friends, my students, my morality, my integrity, my God?

When the boomerang of betrayal returns and whacks you in the gob, you can't complain, and you can't deny that it was you that threw it in the first place.

Enough to say, that over the next decade, I bled out of martial arts as a warring discipline and eased into the practice of Budo, where perfection of the world through perfection of the self became my raison d'être.

Many good flowers became weeds in my life.

That is to be expected.

The good seed and the tare often grow together in the same field, but they are separated in the harvest, and the weed is burned in the fire.

Spiritual altitude demands corresponding lungs, and these can only be developed in the thin air of a holy mountain.

Running simultaneously and alongside my martial arts and spiritual evolution was the writing.

I mentioned this in chapter eight and promised to come back to it.

I can never remember a time when I did not want to write.

Even when I had nothing to put to the page, no experiences to share, and no idea how to articulate them even if I did, the quill still called me, and the molten ink still burned inside.

The moment I received my letter from Summersdale offering me a book deal for *Watch My Back*, I knew for the very first time that this was now a real possibility.

A Memoir

The Writing

Back to the year 1992, and the publication of Watch My Back.

I promised I would return to the writing arc, and soon as I had exhausted the martial arts.

I was thirty-two years old.

My first book was finally in print.

I was still working the doors.

It was like being in a human fish bowl and I could no longer bear to swim around in circles looking out at the same voyeuristic faces staring in, so I left my job as a bouncer. I had to. I left that bastard trade for good.

My personal living situation improved in line with my growing platform. I moved from the shitty beautiful bedsit to a small damp but delightful flat. Eventually we bought a tiny detached house about two hundred yards from where Sharon used to live with her mum and dad. They accepted me into their family by piecemeal, but with some reluctance in the beginning. I understood this. I never allowed myself to take it personally. I had done nothing to demonstrate that I had any honour at all, so the fact that they even spoke to me, was a bonus in my eyes. I think they knew that if they couldn't be at least civil to me, it would have threatened their relationship with Sharon, and they loved her too much to let that happen. They are both beautiful people, and over the following years, when they were able to see how dedicated Sharon and I were to each other, they came to love me. This was greatly helped by Sharon's lovely brother Alan, who fought our corner all the way, and convinced his parents that I was good for Sharon.

It was strange but beautiful living with Sharon after being married for eleven years to someone else. All the restrictions and embargos that were associated with my first marriage were lifted and I was suddenly a caged bird set free. I don't think I was ever fully conscious of the caveats in my first marriage, those unhappy enforcements, until they were lifted. At my old place I was divided, I was half a man, living in two dimensions, like a fading cardboard cut-out, a paper thin template of the real me. Before emancipation I was a half-living automaton, following a predestined set of social rules that dictated how I was expected to live, act, work, socialise, dream, procreate, age and die in the arc of conditioned life. I said what I was supposed to say. I ate what I was conditioned to eat. And I aged in the exact order I'd been programmed to age. I even dressed how I was supposed to dress for a man of my class and age, like a tired, drab, fuck-boring facsimile of everyone else. In my new life everything changed. I was Dorothy in the Technicolor city of Emeralds; I was not in Kansas anymore. In my new life I was allowed to express myself in three and four dimensions. Sometimes I wasn't sure what dimension I was in, only that I was expanding like an un-gripped sponge and I was blissfully happy.

Martial arts were never spoken of in my first marriage. The mere mention was explicitly forbidden. I didn't really register this restriction as being unhealthy, unkind or even unreasonable at the time, it was just the way we lived and I never questioned it. I should have rebelled, of course, and sometimes now, looking back, I wish I had stood up for myself sooner, but the regime was never fully conscious, certainly not enough for me to kick up a fuss. It was just a throbbing background ache that I thought all normal married people suffered. How can you fight for freedom, when you are not even aware that you are incarcerated? MA was a foreign religion in our house, so we just didn't (or I didn't) speak about it. I was not allowed to have martial arts magazines either, or more specifically, I was forbidden from buying them. I did of course, buy them, and I consumed every page like a beggar at a rice bowl. I just couldn't get enough of the inspirational manna. I went from the front page to the back page reading everything. I could easily glut a whole publication in one sitting, but I never allowed myself to do that, instead I savoured the pages. I read an article at a time, maybe two if I was particularly ravenous. I tried to make the read last as long as I could, so that the gap between drinks was not too long. I even read the adverts, pored over the blurb selling books on exotic arts in the back pages. I dreamed of one day having enough money (and my wife's permission) to actually order one of those books from the magazine and wait in excited anticipation for it to drop on my doorstep, like a gift from the gods. As soon as I'd finished reading, I'd flip back to the front of the magazine and start all over again. Because I wasn't allowed MA mags in the house, I tucked them away in secret places. I hid them like most men hide porn.

Living with Sharon, this was no longer an issue. There were no caveats in our relationship, so I was able to catch up on lost time. In fact, I could do anything I wanted to, and she encouraged it. I filled my mind with reading and writing, with training, with excited late-night conversations about our collective obsession with martial arts. Do you know how intoxicating it is to spend all your time with the person you love, fully immersed in the art that you have made your life? In the biblical lexicon, it is the land of milk and honey. It was exhilarating.

Sharon too was a black belt and just as enthused as me. So, we were either talking about training or we were reading about training or we were out somewhere, actually doing the training. Add to this, the protein-rich diet of magazines and books (that I was now able to buy) about every exotic martial art under the sun, and it was no surprise that my level of skill, knowledge, vision and experience literally went through the firmament.

My martial arts and my teaching took off like a rocket from a milk bottle. It was at this time, *Watch My Back* in hand, confidence in abundance that I decided to give up the day job. This had been a dream of mine for as long as I could remember but, up until now, it had remained in the land of wild imagination. I had neither the means nor the wherewithal to give up conventional employment before. But now, with certainties installed, skills improved and my products and services selling like summer lollipops, I decided to set out my stall and go it alone.

I have to admit, the break from paid employment was not clean. It is a little embarrassing to admit but, I didn't really know how *not* to go to work. The forty hour week was ingrained in me. I was thirty-two at the time. I'd worked part time since I was twelve years old (in Coventry market on a clothes stall, and in pubs as a glass collector), and full time since I was sixteen. Conventional work was all I knew. So, although I gave up my job as a floor sweeper at the factory and officially left work, I kept going back to it, like an addict returning to the phial. Even though I wasn't actively looking for *real* work, real work kept finding me, people kept offering me *the shift*, and I kept taking it. I didn't want to do it, but I was scared not to. I was afraid (I think) of not making the mortgage. This was my conditioning kicking in, and it was strong. It was thousands, perhaps tens of thousands of years old, my genetic inheritance, so of course it was strong, and I felt its weighty resistance every time I tried to release myself from the minimum wage. But I knew that if I kept taking conventional work, I was never going to emancipate myself from it, I was never going to matriculate into self-employment as a teacher and writer. Eventually, recognising the negative pattern and the infecting nature of what's perceived as a *proper* job, I embraced my innate fear of being free, stopped accepting *real* work and started earning my crust as a full-time teacher and writer. It was a revelation. I couldn't actually believe I was doing it. I could not understand how I was able to actually get away with not working. Was this allowed? I'd spent my whole life on the tools. Everyone I knew worked, and we never once questioned why we stayed in jobs we hated and for a wage that was not commensurate with our labour.

I didn't know a single person in my own world that did not do a proper job. Everyone worked. You were seen as a malingerer if you didn't. I personally didn't know anyone who had given up the day job in the pursuit of happiness, even though, morally and constitutionally, it was everyone's right.

It was unheard of.

It was not understood. Around our way, it was simply not done.

And yet, here I was, doing it. An ordinary man, embarking on an extraordinary odyssey. I can't really say why more people didn't do it, all I knew was, I did and I loved every minute of my new found freedom.

I relished my new life. I didn't waste a single moment. I knew intuitively that what had been found could easily be lost again if I did not capitalise on it. Now that training was my job, I treated it as such. I respected the opportunity I had been given, and I filled my every hour with new learning. I became a tireless autodidact. Everything I did now was based on learning and personal development - in fact *learn and develop* was all I did. I even took up a speed-reading course so that I could get through more books and expand my education. Not only was I studying the arts intellectually, I was also training full time (three times a day) and always under escalating instruction. It was no surprise that I raced ahead of my peers, so far ahead that I couldn't see them for the dust kicking off my boot heels. I'm not bragging. This is a simple statement of fact. While everyone else was doing their ten hour day at the factory, I was training in a martial art discipline, and for extended periods of time I was training in several disciplines at the same time.

It was my job; it was what I did.

Watch My Back was selling pretty well all over the country.

The nature of my book and the subsequent profile I received brought me into close proximity with all sorts of characters, not just in the martial arts, as I mentioned earlier, but also wider afield, much wider afield. Some of the people I crossed paths with were criminals who felt an affinity with me and with what I was writing. At the time the hard man genre of books had not yet been inaugurated, so I was often seen as an unofficial voice for those residing in the underbelly of society, people without a voice, folk who felt they had not been heard before. Within a decade, bouncers and hard men would enjoy their very own section in the high street book shops, but for now there was only me, and (once again) this meant I was noticed. The doors and the world of organised crime are often uncomfortably close, cheek-by-jowl you might say, and many of the lads I worked with when I stood on nightclub doors, were either dabbling in crime (I know that I was) as a side-line, associated with the criminal fraternity, or would later enter into serious, organised crime as a life choice. So, it should have been no surprise that bouncers and criminals from around the country would read my book, feel an affinity with what I was saying, and connect with me, either serendipitously or by arrangement. Some of these men were infamous, certainly they were dangerous gangsters, and one or two were criminal icons.

My correspondence with Reggie Kray was probably the strangest of these encounters, and it came about after I featured on a BBC Radio 4 discussion programme called The Locker Room, hosted by the lovely Tom Robinson. I shared the mike that day with a Falklands war veteran who'd written a beautiful and acclaimed book about his experiences. He was a man who seemed ill at ease with his accidental celebrity and kept saying things like, 'I don't write very often, but when I do, they tell me I am very good'.

His incongruent character (which sat uncomfortably with the show's humble host) was completely at odds with the obvious power of his prose.

The other guest that shared the mike with me was a gay, tightly manicured, articulate, former cellmate of Reggie Kray's, who, on release from jail, had written a splendid book about his experiences, inside. Tom seemed to take a particular shine to me, and offered lots of advice on the publishing world, specifically about getting a literary agent, something I was struggling to do at the time.

During an off-air conversation, Reggie's former cellmate said to me, 'I think Reggie would love your book', and gave me his prison address. Not thinking too much about it, I sent Reggie a copy of *Watch My Back* with a note saying that I'd met his friend on a radio show and thought he might enjoy the read.

I received a reply from Reggie within weeks. It was written in his own distinct hand, thanking me for the gift and telling me how much he had enjoyed the book.

This one letter led to a casual correspondence between the two of us that lasted several years. I always knew if the letter on my doormat was from Reggie because the writing was very large, and the words were almost impossible to read. The letters themselves were written in the same unsteady manner; his handwriting was indecipherable, and he always only ever wrote on the extreme left of the page. The whole right hand side, from the centre out, was strangely blank, as though he was leaving space for an unseen hand to fill in the gaps - perhaps his estranged twin Ronnie?

As far as it went, I liked Reggie. His letters were polite, and he sounded like an old-fashioned gentleman. I can't say that I wasn't naive, forming a friendship with one of the most notorious gangsters in British history, I was, very. And I can't say either that I didn't feel a certain egocentric cachet in receiving letters from the cult that was Reggie Kray, I did feel flattered, absolutely. But I learned soon enough that this world, the world of organised crime, of gangsters and convicted killers was not a world you could flirt with. The letters from Reggie soon became calls from Reggie. My wife would pass me the phone, a quiet, worried look on her face and whisper, 'it's Reggie'. He was soft spoken, a little effeminate and very polite, but the oppressive weight of his dark legend always lay heavy on my receiver.

I had faced and spoken to a lot of fighters in my time, and I'd gone toe-to-toe with more than one killer on the doors of Coventry. I knew intent when I saw it and I knew when the intent was deadly.

With Reggie I could feel the presence of a probing energy that scanned me through the telephone line. I knew he was hunting for weaknesses; he was feeling for cracks that he might enter; he was searching for a fear that he might feed on and manipulate.

It started politely enough. He would ask me for small favours: could I send him this, could I fetch him that? Usually his requests were for unimportant things, a training vest, a weightlifting belt, a book that he couldn't source through the prison library. People of a criminal mindset are innate masters of the human psyche. They put the feelers out and test your depth. They start by asking very casually for small favours, things that seem almost insignificant at the time of asking. The small requests become big requests. Eventually, politeness is replaced by menace and the requests become demands. I innately knew this. These were the subtle grooming techniques used by people expert in the art of manipulation. I had dealt with violent men for over a decade, so I knew how it worked, although I must admit, I had never experienced a presence as mighty as his before. He politely requested favours, I politely and firmly declined. Not easy when the weight at the other end of the line almost compels you to acquiesce. In the end it got that, every time I received a letter from Reggie, I felt a rush of adrenalin. And each time I received a call, it left me feeling uneasy for hours afterwards. I knew enough about violent criminals to know that if they located even a hint of tremble in your voice, or fear in your manner, in your pauses and hesitations they would engineer it until it was a gaping hole, a doorway that a legion could enter through.

Later still, I started to receive unsolicited phone calls, at odd hours, from complete strangers, saying, 'we're friends of Reggie Kray's. We are in town. Reggie said you'd show us around'. As soon as this started to happen I carefully withdrew. I stopped writing to Reggie and I stopped being home when he called. I knew many people who had been flattered by the attentions of infamous criminals, people who'd been sucked into their dark realities and were never able to extract themselves.

I learned early that you can't flutter your eyelashes at people of this ilk, and not expect them to respond. I was tempted, I admit. I was attracted to Reggie's alluring and seductive energy and like lots of other fools, I held a vague notion that standing on his coat-tails might take me somewhere, it might help me to sell books if people knew that Reggie Kray had recommended them, it might help me to get connected (whatever that means). But I instinctively knew that this siren call from the bardo would take me into a hellish region and I knew that this was not for me.

I have been many things in my life, but I was never a gangster. I always knew deep down that the implicit and illicit promise of this nefarious world was illusory. Notorious criminals and gangsters have been lionised on screen ever since the medium was invented, and millions of column inches have been written about them, in newspapers and magazines, so you would not be foolish for thinking that they are respected people, admired even. I have been a violent man. Believe me, people do not respect you, they do not admire you, but they do fear you and it's not the same thing. It is an ugly way to express a life and I didn't want it.

In one of his final letters to me, Reggie asked if I'd be his personal bodyguard when he was released from prison. When I politely declined (I was no bodyguard), he found someone else to do the job: a very large Scottish gentleman from Glasgow whom I later met. He even came to Coventry and took a class under me. What was calling me was the word, I longed for writing that connected me to my bliss. This, the gangsters, the crime world, Reggie Kray et al, was not it.

If I needed further proof of this, it would be provided for me soon enough when I heard the tragic news about Reggie's bodyguard: he'd been gunned down and killed, not as you might imagine, by another gangster in an underworld shootout, or an organised contract killing, rather, he was killed by the estranged husband of a local girl he'd been dating. Incensed with jealousy, he got hold of a shotgun, killed his wife, killed the bodyguard, and then he turned both barrels on himself.

It was very tragic.

There but for the grace of God.

I met another notorious gangster when I was promoting *Watch My Back*, and in very similar circumstances. Ironically, Mad Frankie Fraser was a former henchman for the Kray twins, and I have to say he was equally menacing. I met Frankie when I was invited onto Talk Radio with Terry Christian. Terry had been very kind to me regarding Watch My Back. He'd read it and wrote me a lovely quote for the front cover, saying *this book is ten years overdue*. He invited me on several occasions to appear on his programme as a guest. He was a generous soul with his praise and his time, and also with his money. He paid for me out of his own pocket to stay in a posh London hotel so that I could guest on his show.

On this particular episode I was sharing the studio with Mad Frankie, his girlfriend (who was the daughter of one of the great train robbers), a beautiful former female New York cop who'd become a porn star and (on a telephone link from Rio de Janeiro) Ronnie Biggs, also of the infamous *great train robbery*. Ronnie had escaped from prison soon after being jailed for his part in the heist and was now living in exile in South America. The theme of the show was… you know what, I can't even remember what the theme was, only that I felt like I was sharing a weird dream with the salacious underbelly of the criminal elite. It was as though Beelzebub had thrown a party, and somehow I'd been sent an invite.

I can only imagine that Terry must have thought I was a part of society's sediment, otherwise why was I there? I didn't think too much about it at the time and didn't really care either. I wanted to promote my book, and Terry had offered me a national platform, and the chance to talk to millions of people, all in one go.

I was not the star of the show, neither was Ronnie or the deliciously stunning porn-cop. Mad Frankie was the highlight. Physically he was a small man, but he filled that room wall-to-wall with his personality. Never was his potency more evident than when I casually mentioned that his young girlfriend was very attractive. I meant it as a compliment. My own girl Sharon was beautiful. As a self-absorbed male I loved people to know that she was on my arm, that even though I was a throbbing lump who could fight (and with a face like ten boxers), I could still get the girl. Frankie did not receive my compliment with the spirit in which it was intended. He met it instead with a piercing, probing, staring silence, a paranoia that I could almost hear whispering in his ear, 'is this man taking the piss?'

Realising that he had taken my comment as a slight, and feeling his murder spreading to every corner of the room, I quickly added, 'but I'm not surprised Frankie, you're a very charismatic man'. There was a momentary pause when I thought the situation could go one way or the other, then he broke the impasse with a smile and whatever demon had entered him only a second before left again. Frankie shook my hand, we exited the station and I never saw him again.

It is easy to lionise criminals and gangsters and common to envision them as folk heroes, latter day Robin Hoods. The murder, the bullying and the intimidation are often romanticised, rationalised or simply relegated to something that criminals do, but only amongst themselves. Their crime is contained. They are bound by an unwritten honour-code that holds public safety sacrosanct. Innocent people are never caught up in their illegal, immoral and unethical activities; certainly they would never be harmed.

We all know that this is a comforting lie.

I'd believe in the tooth fairy, sooner than I would believe even a single word of this adulatory rhetoric. It's insulting nonsense and it has not been my experience. Believe me, anyone that chooses to compromise the security of their own family by engaging in a life of crime, will not give the safety of the public - perfect strangers - a second thought. As far as I can see, most criminals do not give a monkey's hoot who gets hurt. If anyone gets in their way, they become collateral damage. That's all. They will readily exploit any means - criminal or otherwise - to meet their own ends. So I don't want to lionise Reggie Kray or Mad Frankie. Criminals, those who choose violence as their way, are an aberration in a civilised society. But there are attributes in everyone, especially those who live in extremes, qualities that often get lost in the fire. Although it might not make me very popular amongst the liberal left, I want to record in these pages what I saw and felt and what 'madly' inspired me about Frankie and Reggie and many of the other mad and violent bastards I met on my travels across twentieth century planet earth. Like many men of his ilk, Frankie was charismatic, he was a gifted raconteur, and when he talked - on the radio or face-to-face - he held the room.

When he spoke, you listened.

When people rang into the show to ask Frankie a question, he was genuinely and tremendously kind and patient with them. I could absolutely see where the notion of folk hero came from. Many old friends from my days on the door (two men in particular, both currently serving life in prison for murder or drug dealing) were generous to a fault, incredibly brave, and unquestioningly attractive. These were friends who'd risk it all for you. And they'd have you rolling around the isle with laughter: they could fight like Ali but they were as funny as Keaton.

In Terry's Talk Radio studio, Frankie filled the airwaves. He absolutely owned the universe we occupied for those two short hours. Granted, he was a damaged force, he was corrupt and defiled, of that there can be no doubt. I knew this because I'd walked in similar shoes. I'd been filling rooms with volatile and unpredictable energy myself for the last decade.

Corrupt or not, the energy was powerful, it could control a room, a house or, as in the case of the Kray twins, our capital city. It could definitely take a life. But corrupt energy is an inferior force, and this was the revelation I was gifted. The fact that a lower energy could exert such a manifest effect, greatly intrigued me, it was definitely worthy of deeper investigation. I didn't want to dismiss Frankie as *just another criminal* and ignore the fact that I'd been greatly moved by him, at least I was moved by something essential that I felt through him.

I was inspired because I knew, even back then, that there was a bigger expression of this inferior energy. It had its source somewhere. I wanted to find out where it was, and study it. If possible, I aimed to become a vessel for it. I'd experienced Frankie's presence as a distracted but innately creative force. Its signature was there, I could feel it just below his molten insanity. In his case the force had been hijacked and maligned by an unstable host. If it could be managed and righteously directed, I knew that the same powerful energy could heal instead of hurt; it could inspire and awe, rather than terrify and harm. I wondered how many rooms, how many stadiums, how many realities this charismatic, unpredictable Obscurial might have filled if he'd cleaned his vessel and aligned to the source energy. What could this man have achieved had his covenant been made with the forces of good instead of being in league with the adverse forces of evil?

Frankie, for all his indefensible sin, inspired me to look for the undefiled source of his mucky-essence and intercourse with it.

I was nowhere near that place yet; I was still a throbbing young ego, a selfish little clod enjoying my sojourn in the animal realm.* I was still a hungry ghost, caught in the net of carnality: fighting, fucking, feeding and trying to sell my book.

Before I could even contemplate the higher stations of my potential, I would have to first raise the dead bodies from my past and let them speak their piece, qualify

---

* In Judaic mysticism the three levels of Man are recognised as the vegetable realm, the animal realm and the human realm. The vegetable is where the herded and sleeping masses reside; the animal is the domain of the money-makers, the entrepreneurs, the businessmen, and politicians; the highest level is the human realm, this is the echelon of the spiritual adept, someone who has mastered the lower realms and seeks only to serve God.

their actions and make good their folly. By necessity I would have to face and atone for my many indiscretions... but that is a story for later.

The London gangster and writer Dave Courtney very briefly entered my world around this time too. As I hawked my book and told my story in the media whorehouses that all hungry authors frequent, it was inevitable that we would meet. I felt the same charisma, the same dynamic energy from Dave, as I did Frankie. He possessed many of those outsider qualities that I so admired too, but with the same burred edges of a world that made me recoil. Although we were both in circumambulation of the same rings of Dante's inferno, I sensed that Dave knew where he wanted to go and was descending deliberately into the fiery grasp of the three headed Dis at the centre of hell. Myself, I was attempting to crawl out of the fire to meet my Beatrice, on the mountain of Purgatorio.

The infernal tunnel of crime with all its salacious associations was alluring and seductive. It was one of the many womb entrances that enticed me. I specifically and definitively knew that this was not the reality for me, so I eschewed all offers of interaction and opened myself up to other possibilities, higher potentials. The world of crime with all its fool's gold and its false promises emitted a light, but it was a dull and indistinct glimmer. I was looking for the glow of truth; a lamp that I felt sure would lead to inspiration.

This West End playwright, Jim Cartwright - a soft spoken Northerner with a brilliant and poetic voice - was definitely the kind of light-glow I was hoping for, and it was not long after the release of *Watch My Back* that Jim entered my life. He turned up at a demonstration I gave at a martial arts convention in Birmingham. Jim (as it turned out) had read Watch My Back and found something of note in the pages. After I'd finished the demonstration and was preparing to go home, Jim stopped me in the corridor and introduced himself. He was with another man, his business partner, a funky, deliciously quirky, middle class maniac of a film producer called Martin Carr. Jim congratulated me on *Watch My Back*. He said he loved the read and thought the poetry and truth in my writing would transfer very well to theatre and film. I wasn't really looking to get into film at the time, I didn't understand it and theatre was a distant and foreign land to me. I knew what theatre was of course. We had the splendid Belgrade Theatre just a few miles from where I lived, but I had never been, not once.

It seems strange now, looking back. How was it that I didn't understand this ancient and time-honoured province of storytelling? I suppose it was because we were brought up on a fast food diet of telly. We were weaned on the glitzy ostentation of popular cinema, and if we could afford to go to the pictures more than once a year it was a rare treat. Theatre was *over there* somewhere, proper posh, a hangout for the middle classes, the gentiles. It was plum-in-the-mouth as far as I was concerned, full of thespians wearing cravats using big words that made me (and my kind) feel marginalised and small and....well, thick. I felt unintelligent around educated people, and it made me squirm.

Ridiculous I know.

I'm embarrassed even in the remembering. But, back then, it was how I felt. I would no sooner have frequented a theatre, than I would fly to the moon. Now, these days, I love theatre, it is like home turf to me, it is my stadium of light, it's the medium I most love writing for and feel best suited to. It is so accessible; I think it's the pure concentrate from which telly stories and cinema films are taken.

Back then I was a reverse snob. I was proud of being common, certainly I was too proud to mention theatre without projected judgement. So, when Jim said he was a playwright, I have to admit, it went right over my head. And when Martin mentioned that he was a film producer, I hardly heard him. These were two lovely but ordinary men showing their appreciation for the demo I'd just performed, that's all.

Martin told me years later, when we got to know each other a little better that he never wanted to meet me. He'd been slightly horrified by Watch My Back. He thought I was a monster, a baby eater, a bona fide serial killer, some kind of strange throwback from the great Khan of the Mongol empire. Jim pretty much forced - or tricked him - into the meeting.

Martin was not unlike a lot of people at the time, who thought that by looking at the front cover image on *Watch My Back* and perusing the back cover blurb, they knew what kind of person I was. As soon as we became better acquainted, he realised that I was not the violent marauder he thought I was. I was not going to ransack his village any time soon or rape the women and frighten the horses. We became good, good friends me and Martin, lifelong friends. Over many years this delightful man selflessly, arduously and relentlessly helped me to evolve both as a person and as a writer.

Jim introduced himself. I thanked him for his kind words and offered to send him a book. That was what I always did back then, it was my default setting. I loved giving out free books to anyone and everyone. Gift giving was a perfect way to punctuate a meeting. Jim said he would reciprocate and send me a compilation of his work for theatre and we promised to stay in touch.

It wasn't until his gift arrived in the post and I looked a Jim's plays and the author biography that I realised what a prolific and accomplished writer this quiet, very funny northerner was. Olivier Award, Evening Standard Award, West End playwright, one of the best British theatre writers since the war. The list of acclaim was impressive.

It was Jim who encouraged me and helped me to adapt my writing to film and theatre. He and Martin sat with me for countless hours and over many years, helping me to find my voice for the stage, encouraging me to find my sound for the cinema. I had no idea what I was doing at the time. I didn't have the first clue. I was delightfully unaware. I was naive. Perhaps that's why *Watch My Back* had been so well received, it was without contrivance, it was raw no doubt, and brutally frank and visceral without question, but it was not aiming at a specific demographic, or trying to masturbate the current publishing curve, or satisfy the latest flavour. Back then I just thought writing was writing, and what worked in a book would automatically work on screen or on stage.

Not so.

Whilst I had accidentally stumbled upon my voice, my own specific sound for books, I would have to work equally hard, even harder and even longer to find my voice for stage and film.

My apprenticeship in film and stage was initiated directly after I met Jim and Martin.

I started to (try and) write an adaptation of Watch My Back for film, with their help. I thought I might be able to do this quickly, maybe write the first draft in a month, and get it out in the cinemas a year later. I am still laughing now at my naivety. I can't tell you how many times I wrote and re-wrote and scrapped and then re-wrote that script (eventually called *Clubbed*) over the next fifteen years (yes, honestly, fifteen years!). I can't and I won't. It's too painful. It was relentless. Like Milarepa's wall, it always promised to be completed tomorrow, but tomorrow always seemed to be extended to the day after, and the day after that ad infinitum. It seemed as though it would never be completed, and every time I thought it was finished, I'd receive more notes, more addendums, more cuts and I'd have to start all over again from the beginning.

No complaints.

I cut my teeth on that script.

The unrelenting nature of the work tempered me like a fired blade. I will always be grateful for it.

I started to read lots of screenplays just to give myself an idea about layout, style and form. With Watch My Back I didn't know anything at all. I only knew I had stories to tell and I wanted to tell them to as many people as possible. I didn't understand story arc or chapter set out, my grammar was not strong, my spelling poor, but I did know how to tell a story. Now, suddenly I needed to know how to use screenwriting programmes on computer (Movie Magic at the time, later Final Draft). I needed to know how to write loglines, short synopses, long synopses, step outlines, and character breakdowns. Man, I just wanted to write. Why did I need to know how to do a synopsis? I could just as quickly write a full-length film.

This was a whole new world of writing for me, and whilst I had to learn these new skills - and the learning was good for me - I fought hard not to lose the intuitive voice that had come through my words without any outside instruction.

Film companies, I was reliably informed, receive thousands of scripts every year from new and highly established writers. There is no way they are able to read them all. But they could read a three hundred word synopsis and from that get a feel for your idea, your style and measure your level of writing.

At the same time as venturing into film, and learning its ways, I was also looking at theatre. It intrigued me. Unlike film (which is heavily director centric) theatre was all about the writing. From the very outset I could see that film was unashamedly commercial. Even though it *blurbed* itself as edgy, original, dangerous and innovative, it was usually none of these things. It was largely safe and very conditioned and often contrived, and definitely London centric. Companies were investing millions in a film, so of course, they wanted assurances, they wanted certainties and guarantees. No complaints and no criticism intended. I understood. But we all quietly knew that in art - which was the huge elephant in the room - certainty will only ever guarantee one thing: that your film will be the same, or similar, or a poor facsimile of the next man's film, and that did not excite me at all. One or two mavericks managed to hack the system and sneak the art through the commerce but they were the rare anomalies and not the norm. They were all trying to second guess the perfect film, and predict the market trends. Everyone, from the producers, to the distributors, to the sales agents, right down to the kid making the tea on set, wanted a creative input into the script. It felt like film by committee, which didn't suit my bent at all, although it took me a few years to figure this out.

Jim's work in theatre was all the things that did excite me about writing. It was original, unique, impossible to generalise and it said something that no one other than Jim could have said. His work was as individual as a fingerprint; it was his own voice, which was different from every other voice in the world.

Jim was a normal man like me. He had a very similar working-class background. He'd excelled in theatre and had now moved into film. If it was possible for him, it must surely be possible for me.

I rushed in the beginning, with both theatre and with film. I openly admit that. I rushed and I was arrogant. I'd had a book published. It was in the shops. Great writers like Jim thought I had a voice. I was being asked to write a movie, anything was possible. And of course it is. Anything is possible but everything takes time. Everything has a season and a nature that will not be rushed.

Because I'd had *Watch My Back* published and I knew my way around the book world a little, I thought this qualified me to transfer my knowing into the foreign language of film and theatre and speed the whole process up. I didn't just want to learn every medium, I wanted to learn it now!

If you'd told me then that it would take fifteen years to produce my first full length film, I'd have probably sacked it as a bad job then and there. And if it wasn't for the fact that I was happily distracted during this time with writing more books, teaching martial arts around the world, doing national book signing tours, starting my own publishing business, pursuing theatre, trying to bring up my kids and continue my own martial arts development, I might well have.

I was so hungry to learn all of these new skills and I had so much energy that there was not a single day when I was not working on one creative project or another. My life was like a landing strip at Heathrow. There were always projects stacking and waiting to land. There were projects landing. And there was always a bevy of projects taking off and flying into new horizons.

I decided after reading Jim's plays that theatre was not only something I'd like to do it was something I could do. I knew I could. I had no doubt. The only thing I'd underestimated (again) was the amount of internal cleansing writing anything of any worth was going to involve.

I was on holiday (Center Parcs in Sherwood Forest) when I wrote the first of what would become many stage plays (One Sock, later re-titled as *Doorman*). I stayed close to my own experience and wrote a semi-autobiographical monologue about a bouncer in a police cell who is trying to rationalise his violent life and come to terms with the fact that he has just killed a man in a nightclub bust-up.

Jim read the play, liked it very much and encouraged me to send it to the Royal Court Theatre in London. If they thought I had a voice, he told me, they might invite me into their young writers group. A veritable pantheon of heroes had started at Royal Court: Jim, Sarah Kane, Beckett, Osborne, Mark Ravenhill, Debbie Tucker Green and Sue Townsend to name but a few. As I said, at the time I was so inspired and so full of belief and certainty that I doubted the possibility of nothing. If Jim had started at the court then I was going to do exactly the same.

I sent the play.

I waited for a reply.

And I waited.

During the same period I also wrote more books. Only now, instead of being published by Summerdale, I decided to start my own small print and, still under the Summerdale umbrella, self-publish my work. The rationale was simple enough: if I published myself, I could make more money. It wasn't quantum physics. I could make more money, not just by selling the books through the shops, but also by selling mail order to my growing list of readers, and direct to students at the many courses I was now holding all around the country.

I'd collected the names and addresses of people who'd contacted me for training classes and courses, an impromptu mailing list. I knew that if I could sell directly to these customers as well as through the usual shop route, I could make more money, and keep more control of my own work. My personal mail list began organically. I had two hundred people on my list. Eventually this swelled to over 10,000 individual customers, all of whom brought from me on a regular basis. I started writing and publishing martial arts books, motivational books and producing instructional DVDs. The moment they were produced, we wrote to our growing fan base and sold directly to them. In the shops I might make £1 or £2 profit from a £10 book after everyone -publishers, agents, salesmen, distributors, shops etc. - took their cut. If I sold directly to my own list, I could cut out all the middlemen and make £9 on a £10 book. If it was a DVD (or video when we first started) I might make £22 profit on a £25 DVD.

I didn't have to sell many of these to make the rent.

With the newly established publishing business I did what I did with everything else I was learning. I studied how my competitors worked, and then modelled them, adding my own little twist, just to stay unique. Over time I managed to improve the quality of all our products, reduce the production costs and supply them in greater quantity.

We ended up with forty five published books (some very specialised, some with a broader appeal) and forty five, one hour long instructional DVDs. And it was not local, eventually we were published in twenty one languages. One of our motivational books hit the top ten in Japan. I sold 150,000 copies of *Fear - The Friend of Exceptional People* to Men's Fitness Magazine who used an abridged version as a cover mount. And my seminal book *Dead or Alive* was voted the best self-defence book in the world by the prestigious Black Belt Magazine in the USA.

Sharon gave up her job at the Co-op at this time.

She had worked in the cash office for some years, but I was getting busy, I needed help, so she left her job to join me in the burgeoning business and between us we built Geoff Thompson Ltd. Ours was a steep and exciting and at times intimidating ascent. We had gone from working in normal day jobs (didn't even know anyone that owned a typewriter) to running our own business selling eighty products and holding training courses all over Britain. This did not happen in a vacuum. We had to learn a lot of new skills: how to organise and run MA courses; how to manage hundreds of souls who'd come to us for instruction; price and print books and register them with the British Library; get the books distributed to shops all around Britain; invoice; organise cash flow; keep our personal business accounts; design new books and get them typeset, formatted and edited; set up and run accounts with printing companies; set up, organise and run national book signing tours; contact media outlets and set up high profile interviews on television, on radio and in national newspapers and magazines. Eventually, as our business expanded, we had to negotiate the rapids of VAT registration, and set up a limited company. We also had to hire an accountant and keep strict business accounts, learn how to build websites, manage online retailing, and set up our office so we could accept credit card payments.

When we went Limited, I thought that Sharon was going to have a nervous breakdown. She is an intelligent woman. But the cavalcade of new learning was way beyond her usual remit. The responsibilities she felt running her own business, being accountable to HMRC, keeping detailed records of our myriad daily transactions, nearly tipped her. The learning curve for us both was as steep as Everest and just as intimidating. Later she would handle all of this and more with the ease of a circus juggler, whilst at the same time managing two properties in Coventry, and an apartment in Islington, London.

At the same time as all this (as I mentioned) I had written my first play, sent it off to the most prestigious theatre in the world for new writers, and was awaiting their response.

I will come back to theatre imminently.

I followed the publication of *Watch My Back* with a second anecdotal book about the further trials and tribulations of a nightclub doorman, ironically called *Bouncer*.

It was terrible. It was a dog's dinner of a book. It suffered from a malady known in music circles as *the second album syndrome*.

The first book was a happy accident. I didn't know what the FUCK I was doing. I didn't know what was right or wrong or what people would like or dislike. I just wrote what I wanted to write and people loved it. Now that I was a professional writer, I thought I knew what I was doing. I tried to second guess what people wanted and what they liked and filled my lines, paragraphs and pages with contrived shit. I wrote how I thought I should write, how a real writer writes. I was attempting prose that was unconvincingly poor, it was as though a monkey had snatched the pen off me and scribbled illegibly on the page, certainly it was not the raw voice that had torn through the parchment of my first book. It was full of pretension. I used words I'd read in the dictionary, words I would never use in my daily life, and I added ostentations in places where simplicity was all I needed. I threw in fortune cookie philosophy that I'd guessed at or copied or made up on the spot, it was definitely not qualified wisdom. I took myself off to posh cafés or beautiful public gardens to write. I was important now. I needed an artistic place to do my work, and a quality pen to bleed the words onto the pages of the most expensive pads I could find. I was a published author. I needed a pen and pad that reflected my new station. No more reliable Bics for me, no more chewed pen lids, cheap note pads and ink-blotched pages, *I was a writer*.

I'd forgotten what raw was.

I'd forgotten about the urgency I'd felt on my first outing, and the truths I'd wanted to share, and the need I felt to see my stories on the page. I was no longer honouring that urgency. Instead I was writing true stories but with corrupt ink. The voice that I'd accidentally found in a factory toilet with an innocent naivety was now drowning in pretension. I had found my voice and lost it again, all in the space of two books.

It happens.

I know that.

It happens to a lot of people, but it still hurt.

Terry Christian (the broadcaster) who'd been so kind about Watch My Back didn't recognise the voice in Bouncer and he didn't enjoy the book. He said I sounded like I was trying to be a philosopher. The first book was naturally, if naively, philosophical without even knowing what that even meant. Jamie, an old friend, another fan of *Watch My Back* read *Bouncer*, hated it and rang me with a question that was on the lips of many people I am sure: 'what the F have you done with my old friend the writer Geoff Thompson?'

Good question.

What had I done with him?

I wanted to know just as much as everyone else.

Where the fuck was Geoff Thompson?

Up his own A-hole, that's where he was.

Generally, I am of the consensus that we should never care too much what others think about us or our work. We should only write to tell the truth, to please ourselves, to connect to something vital, and fuck everyone else. But we should listen when what they have to say comes from a good place, especially when what they say is true. At first I rejected the criticism: *they didn't know what they were talking about. They didn't know the world I came from.* I was childish and reactionary. Eventually, when more and more *good* people observed the same incongruence in my writing, I started to listen. I did a hard drag edit through the pages of Bouncer. I went at it like a worried mother with a metal nit comb. I clawed out all of those *pretentious creatures*, the tare hidden amongst the wheat, the elements that were not me.

I left only what was real.

I was self-publishing by now so I could change a print in a heartbeat.

The second version of *Bouncer* was tight, and I learned much from the painful rewrite, and I was shown how easily a voice can be hijacked if we are not constantly vigilant.

As hard as all my many mistakes were, I learned a lot from them. I definitely learned things that could not have been earned in any other way. What can be found can be quickly lost again if we don't capitalise on it, if we fail to nourish and care for it. I learned too that honest, sometimes harsh critics are often our kindest teachers. They act as the third eye on a soul's output, unpaid quality controllers who can weed out a single lie hidden amongst a million truths. Most of all, I learned that in the game I was playing, anything peripheral to the truth was a lie.

In the wonderful David Mitchell novel, *Cloud Atlas*, Somni-451, a fabricant waitress turned anti-government rebel, is asked before her execution to proffer her version of the truth: 'truth is singular,' she tells the archivist, 'its versions are mistruths.'

A mistruth is an ugly bridge-troll in a world of beauty queens.

Quickly after *Bouncer* I wrote and released *On the Door*, the third book in my series of anecdotal tales from the world of nightclub security. This time I learned my lesson. When I sat down to write the last in the trilogy, I went back to the raw and direct language of *Watch My Back*. It wasn't as naively affective, but then how could it be? I wrote that first book while I was still doing frontline door work. It was poetry from the trenches. People were living large and dying violently right in front of me when those words found a corner to preach from. The seminal immediacy of *Watch My Back* was like essence from the well of wyrd, and it pretty much pumped through my pen unfiltered. It was almost spilling onto the page. And I wrote it in a bog for goodness sake, because I didn't care about comfort, I just cared about finding a quiet place where I could write undisturbed. I was unconcerned about anything other than the word and the rhythm of the word on the page.

Separated from the toe-to-toe immediacy of door life, it was inevitable that a certain amount of romance was going to creep in and replace the blood and snot of the original writing. And of course I was unconsciously going to filter certain stories, to protect myself, to protect the guilty, and to shield those I loved. I knew more now. I knew the effect the first book had had on me, on the people I wrote about, and the city I laid bare for the sake of context (not all Coventarians liked their city laundry being washed in public), I knew too much, and I was a lesser writer for it.

The moment you start to self-edit your work for fear of offence and to avoid reciprocity, you are lost.

Later I would return to the beginner's mind that all artists seek. I'd learn how to disengage the fear-censors that neuter and emasculate potent writing. I would come back to delivering raw content direct from the honest muse and not a sanitised abridgment censored by the false-ego; he was an unreliable and frightened proxy, he had too many concerns about the social mores to be trusted as an emissary of truth.

I heard back from The Royal Court Theatre, in London.

They called me on the phone, 'we have read your play. We enjoyed it very much. Are you in London often? We'd love to meet you and chat further.'

I had the temerity to send my first play to the best theatre in the world for new playwrights and they invited me into their young writers' programme.

Me!

Invited to join the great pantheon of dramatists that had gone before me.

I made hasty plans to visit London as soon as was humanely possible.

The news from the Court landed at a busy time. I'd just been invited to Vegas by Chuck Norris. I was working on a feature film (based on *Watch My Back*) for Jim Cartwright and Martin Carr. I was planning a compendium version of my three bouncer books, and a British tour to promote it. I was juggling these projects - on top of teaching MA courses – all at the same time, but my energy seemed infinite, it was boundless, I felt that there was no challenge beyond me.

12

Invitation to The Royal Court Theatre

I have to say that being offered a place in the Royal Court's Young Writers' Group felt like being invited to play for England when Gordon Banks kept goal and Bobby Moore wore the captain's armband. I was elated. At my first meeting with the Court's associate directors, Graham Highbrow and Dominic Hill I nearly burst into tears. Part of me was so indentured in the slavish ideology of my upbringing and my class that any validation, let alone validation from the theatre that had discovered and nurtured some of the best playwrights in the world, filled me to overwhelm. But it was also strangely and profoundly liberating. I wanted to run around London announcing my new position to the world. Later of course, validation from an outside source would be less enticing, in fact it would become unnecessary, even limiting. I'd learn to know my own worth. What other people thought about me, how others judged my work would be of small significance.

An artist should never be a member of anyone's club.

But, now, at this time, as an emerging talent, validation was vital. I didn't really know what I was doing still. I couldn't tell if I was writing a powerful BAFTA-winning script or an illegible scribble for the milkman. I needed some kind of guidance. I hadn't yet been introduced to my inner tutor, who would later become the only corroboration I'd need. For now, a nod from the establishment acted as both steer and rudder for me and for my writing.

Mere association with the Royal Court woke something vital in me, something urgent and real, and I was visited by the strangest elations. I had fleeting desires to paint my toenails black, like the great Boehme's of antiquity, to buy loose clothing and wear canvas shoes without socks and drape wrinkled cheesecloth shirts over my shoulders, and coil oversized scarves around my neck and don a natty hat that I could doff at the ladies. In flights of wild fancy I would see myself writing in late night cafés, or New York loft apartments on Moleskin notepads with a Mont Blanc pen. I would stare achingly into the foreground, and ponder and bemoan, between paragraphs, the burden of my gift.

I felt, yet again, another part of the real me had emerged. The despicable, unworthy elemental, drummed into me at school, was defeated and disproved by my latest validation. It was forced to pack its bags, this unwanted house guest, and asked to vacate the premises.

At the same time my old friend *cognitive dissonance* visited again, only this time the confusion felt clinical. For a while there I thought I was going mad. The new information - that I was being accepted into a prestigious writing circle because I could actually write - clashed violently with the established order, the sleeping belief that deep down I couldn't write shit. Seeing myself as a real writer, working at the court, was at complete odds with everything I'd ever been taught; actually it went tusk-to-tusk with everything I'd ever known. I thought that getting *Watch My Back* into print had earned me enough certainty to erase this dichotomy, and whilst I could publish a book now as easy as I could write a letter, the certainty did not extend itself to theatre, definitely not at the level I was entering. It is very hard to explain, but I couldn't reconcile the warring parts of my psyche. Deep down I didn't believe I was good enough to be taken seriously as a writer, and it would not sink in that I was. I even wondered whether the Court had made a mistake, or if they were humouring me in some cruel and underhand way. I kept saying to Sharon, 'what does it mean? I don't know what it means'.

Recognising my mania, she said calmly, 'it means they think you are a good writer Geoff; you have a voice. It means they want to help you to develop your voice'.

'Yes, yes, I see that,' I said grasping the sanity of her words for a second before spinning back into madness, 'but what does it actually really mean?'

I'd ask the same question over and again. Sharon would repeat the same answer over and again, and around I went, like a bullock strapped to a water wheel, always heading towards the place I had just left. I was struggling to reconcile the fact that I was being invited into the same writers' group that had nurtured many of my literary heroes, not acknowledging that they too were once unknown aspirants, that they too had their moments of elation juxtaposed with abject terror.

Most of the greats had started out just like me, *trying* to become a writer. No one arrives at a destination without a journey. Yet still the confusion bounced around my swede like a half-brick in a cement mixer, until one morning, waking to the same weary voice of irrationality, a bigger voice spoke to me, and it spoke loud and firm and clear inside my head, 'you asked for this' it said 'now shut the fuck up and get on with it'. I sensed that this must have been the voice of a lower angel, not God himself. I am sure that the Redeemer would not be in the habit of using expletives, when he had an infinite vocabulary at his disposal, even if I was driving Him to distraction. Either way, it worked and I was grateful. I snapped out of the dissonance and I did as I was told; I got the fuck on with it.

Sharon came with me to my first session with the writers' group. I was so nervous that I asked Ian Rickson (the current artistic director), if she could tag along. I can see now how inappropriate my request was and that Ian had agreed more out of embarrassment than kindness or understanding.

'She can stay', he insisted, 'but she will have to do some work'.

Why did I ask for Sharon to stay with me?

I was a grown man. I was in my thirties. I was not an eleven-year-old boy on his first day at big school.

Why did I ask?

I was nervous I suppose. I didn't want to go on my own. And Sharon was nervous too. We didn't know London. And she didn't want to be left to wander the city streets while I worked with the Court.

'What am I going to do for four hours on my own?' she asked.

The simple solution would have been for me to leave her in Coventry while I visited

London once a month.

But that wasn't what I wanted to do.

These days I'd just go on my own or Sharon would come with me and have a day out in London by herself. We'd meet afterwards for a meal, maybe book into a nice hotel and then head back home the next day, job done. Back then, I was scared, Sharon was scared. As ridiculous as it sounds we were still cleaving to each other, post-storm, like bits of shipwreck in a choppy sea, and we were still clinging onto our small-town fear of big city life.

I felt as though she was all I had in the world. And she had given everything up for me, everything. So, London felt threatening, in a naive way; it felt foreign and exciting but full of danger. Not the kind of visible danger I was used to - if anyone had picked a fight with me in London town or anywhere else, I'd have tipped them on their head and emptied their pocket change onto the pavement. I understood the physical domain to a frightening degree. But place me in a higher frequency where the air was thin and the rules were changed and I was like a terrier on lino: big bark, no bite, and unsteady of foot. You adjust of course. You adapt. But that takes time and time (if it actually exists at all) is a stubborn mule that will not be pushed or hurried. There was also a throbbing ache rising in me that I knew I would be forced to look at very soon: deep seated insecurity: psychotic jealousy. The fragility I felt with my writing, the innate sense of being dirty and unworthy, extended itself to all areas of my life, especially with Sharon.

Like a man bequeathed a kingdom, I lived in constant fear of it being snatched away from me. If I didn't keep a close eye on Sharon, someone would sneak in and snaffle her away. This was my story. It was only a story but man it was a powerful tale that had me guarding all my treasures like the Balrog in the mines of Moria. It made my life unbearably painful. And sad. At times I felt I couldn't move for fear that moving would spoil and unsettle my situation.

When you feel as though you are unworthy of everything, and I do mean everything, you have to know that the problem is not in the world of people, the problem is in the world of you. The first thing the London trips did was make me recognise this. It drew my shadow to the surface. I was not ready to evict it yet. I was not wise enough or strong enough. But I saw it, and I noted it for future reference, and for now that was enough.

The Royal Court were very gracious.

They even paid me to attend the writers' group. I was so grateful for the opportunity I'd have paid them ten times more just to be in the company. Like publishing my first book, the Court opened doors in me that would otherwise have stayed shut. I am very aware of this. I was also aware that none of this happened by accident. I had to play my part. I had to do the work. I had to engage my will to sit down and write the play, and re-write the play, and then re-write it again, before I could send it to the theatre and bid for their attention.

It's the best kept secret in esoteric practice: **first we do, then we hear.**

The Chuck Norris experience would never have happened had I not written a brave book, that told a bold truth, that travelled the wide word, and caught the individual attention of a movie legend, triggering an opportunity that demanded more courage than I knew I had.

Let's rewind a bit here: if I'd not embraced depression by writing the fear pyramid in the first place, I would not have been directed to working nightclub doors. If I'd not worked the doors, I could not have written Watch My Back. Without *Watch My Back*, no book, no book deal. I would have remained unnoticed. Not just by the higher influences in the world but by the higher densities in me.

I absolutely loved all the sessions at the Court. I didn't learn much about the process of writing from these classes, but I learned everything about my own voice, and that was all I needed to know. That's why I was there. The Court and their tutors were very subtle. I'm pretty sure they knew that you can't teach someone a voice, you cannot give them their own specific sound. All you can do is spot it, highlight it and place people in an environment where it can be brought forth and nurtured. I will be always and eternally grateful to them. In the classes I attended we (there were probably ten of us) were exposed to seasoned writers and directors, who spoke with us about the art of the dramatist, and they had us do spontaneous writing exercises to help tease out, encourage and nurture the voice they had identified. On my first meeting with the lovely Graham and Dominic, in a small office at the theatre, Graham had said as much. He indicated the shelves full of manuscripts all around the room. He told me that they received hundreds even thousands of submissions every year but only a small handful, a dozen from the last year had a specific voice, a talent that they thought they could work with. Mine was one of them.

Their job, he was quietly inferring was not to teach people how to write a play - the formatting of acts and scenes etc. could be learned in any local writers' group or college course. Rather, their purpose at the Royal Court was to use the weight of their platform and experience to simply recognise and acknowledge a voice. The acknowledgement alone, from such an esteemed body, was usually enough to inspire the new writer to develop his or her specific sound.

I was inspired.

Actually, I was bouncing off the walls like a kid full of E numbers. This was all I'd ever wanted to do my whole life and now I was here in London doing it. The only problem was, after I'd finished my six months sojourn with the writers' group, I didn't know where to go next. Although they loved my play, they felt it wasn't quite right to put on at the Court. But they encouraged me to pursue a professional production which they felt sure I'd secure.

I was out in the cold.

I didn't know what to do or where to go next.

Looking back, I can see the hand of fate at work here, and how guided my path was. For now, I was being steered away from the Court and directed instead towards other stations of development. If the Court had staged my play at that time, I am sure that theatre would have completely enveloped me. I would have nestled down in that delightful space and turned myself into a dedicated dramatist. Which means I would never have explored film, or written for Ray Winstone, or wrestled on a film set with Paddy Considine, or walked the red carpet at the BAFTAs (twice), or sat in a pub listening to Pete Postlethwaite read lines from one of my scripts, or sculpt a career defining role for Orlando Bloom, and I would definitely have missed out on and all the other spectacular delights that were waiting just around the next few corners for me.

Life has a funny way of taking you on a winding road that can only make sense with the wider perspective of hindsight. When you look back you can slot all the pieces in place and see that everything happens just as it is meant to happen. And if you listen to your inner direction you will rarely go wrong.

The Court must have known that over-nurturing can spoil a voice just as quickly as neglect can kill it. Ultimately, I have found, those with the will to strive, will always be favoured by the muse.

Very soon after I left the Royal Court, synchronicity placed me before a theatre producer called Paul Crewes and director and designer Michael Vale. They were very taken with my play; they found a home for it at the Plymouth Theatre Royal and the playwright was born.

The playwright *was* born, but something else was dying, something inside me. When my play was staged and toured nationally, it initiated the beginning of a very painful and challenging period for me. I later came to see these as my atonement years.

However, this was to come. Theatre takes time. They have schedules and programmes to meet. Even though we had secured a space at Plymouth, it would still be another year before my work was staged.

In the meantime I had other projects to consider, one of which was combining and re-publishing my trilogy of bouncer books as a compendium and taking it on the road.

I was about to embark on a thirty-two city book tour.

13

A Thirty-Two City Book Tour

Recognising that there was a burgeoning market for this new genre of storytelling, I decided to join all three of my bouncer releases together into one large book, collectively called *Watch My Back*. I filtered out all the episodes in the books that felt weak or disparate, re-ordered the stories into a biographical chronology and then re-released it as a 552 page, 120,000 word epic that sported a provocative, full-colour front cover image - me dressed in a tuxedo, in boxer pose, knuckle duster in hand - and included two plates of historical photos in the middle pages.

The first books were honest, but they were also ignorant. I told my stories of daring-do and I justified the violence that splattered blood-red across every page with a romantic tinge and weak rationalisation. But now, post Vegas, the dove of spiritual epiphany firmly established in my heart, I could no longer sanctify violence. The new Watch My Back reflected my growing consciousness. This time, when I released the trilogy as a compendium, I also knew a lot more about publishing. I understood the industry. I'd completed quite a few successful book signing events by now, and had established relationships with shops, magazines, newspapers and TV. I knew how to get my book into Waterstones and I knew how to draw a crowd.

Instead of printing 1500 copies - which was the print run on the original book - I now decided to go for broke and ordered 10,000, in hardback. This presented me with a diarrhoea-inducing £20k print bill, which I had 12 weeks to find from the day of delivery. There is nothing like a large debt to inspire fast action. I was extremely worried about my ability to sell the books and meet the invoice, and this 'healthy' fear put me to work like a stallion at the plough. I knew that in order for the book to meet its own costs (not least turn a profit), for it to sell, people had to know that the book was available, they had to be told where they could find it, and be convinced that it was worth the £16.99 asking price. For all this information to stick the public had to be exposed to it at least five separate times. This meant a lot of persistent and repeated publicity.

There was a bookselling machine out there, and I knew how to kick-start its engine.

I loved the new version of *Watch My Back*. It was congruent with who I had now become, rather than who I was back then. However, whilst *Watch My Back* had undergone a fierce edit, I refused to remove any of the rawness of the early writing, or tone down my naive rationalisations about violence. Instead I allowed the book to naturally evolve from the first page to the last. It started off the same as the original version, talking about the microcosmic wars, the local violence that occurred in small cities and towns around the country, with me attempting to justify greater violence as a legitimate controlling force. The book concluded in honest reflection: the naive and ignorant Geoff was usurped and replaced by a quieter, more cogitative man, steeped in experience, sickened by brutality, certain that there was a redeeming force, and that it was unequivocally not violence.

I annotated this new theology with quotes from the likes of Gurdjieff and Krishna and Dante Alighieri, but the true qualification bled from the remorse, the sadness and the pain evident in every bloody remembrance.

One of the times that this remorse hit me hardest was when I saw a review of the new *Watch My Back* by the popular FHM magazine. When I read the first two lines, my heart leapt for joy. I thought (and probably they thought too) that their words would please me and that I'd use them as a front cover quote, but the last line knocked me over. 'Lenny McLean has the brawn,' it started off, 'Dave Courtney has the brain, but Geoff Thompson is in a league of his own…. when it comes to knocking out front teeth.'

I was wounded.

Not because the critique was harsh or unkind, I was depressed because it was true.

Not just the fact that they'd written or noticed such a heinous detail in my book (which was full of heinous detail) but that they thought I would be delighted about their noticing.

Maybe at one time, to my shame, I might have revelled in such notoriety. Now I felt as though I'd peered into a fairground mirror expecting to see a beauty in reflection but found instead a beast gurning back at me.

As I said, critics can be good teachers. They see what you don't want to see and tell you what they see, even when you don't want to see it. They can strike the knell of truth, these tabloid seers, and call out your corruption like societal whistle blowers. They tell you and they tell everyone else. It's painful. It is thorn and crown and cruel lashes on the station of growth.

But it's a good hurt and if you are brave, a good hurt can lead to honest reflection which must always precede inner healing.

I was not quite ready for that yet.

There were a few more stations before I was ready for that level of honesty. Actually, I say there were a few more stations, there was in fact one major step to take before I could hold my own gaze in the honest mirror, before I could use the reflection to pick out, clean out and kick out the sin that was still wearing me like an ugly suit. I'd had the epiphany, yes. I'd had a moment of clarity, surely, and I'd been floating in the ether of first love fumes for nearly two years since Vegas, that is for definite, but I was being called, imminently in fact, to do the real work, the inner work. The catalyst would be the Plymouth Royal Theatre, where my first play would stage like a purgatorial life review.

It is only now, in hindsight, that I can see how placing my work in front of critics was an unconscious provocation. I was daring them to see, highlight and expose failings that I was unable or unwilling to clearly see myself. The public and the press, those reading or watching my work, those who were attacking my words and exposing my many failings were the lay priests of reciprocity, forcing me to face what I was hiding from. I was using my published writing as a personal exorcism, outing demons with my prayer-pen and crucifying them on the broken hill of public criticism.

They were like an army of pins, these critics, picking the crab-shell of my inner being for the last juicy remnants, the salty meat and fat of my sin.

The play and its karmic *gifts* were still to come, and I will tell of that imminently. In the meantime, *Watch My Back* (the compendium) needed to be sold. I had a big print bill to pay, and I worked tirelessly to meet it. I hit the publicity from every angle; TV, newspapers, radio, and articles. I let everyone on my growing mailing list know about the new book and invited them to come and meet me *at a book shop near you*. With the tireless help of Stuart and Alistair at Summersdale and of course the relentless labour of Sharon who organised our travel and accommodation, we set up a thirty-two city tour of book shops from Southampton right up to Edinburgh, Scotland. We printed large posters promoting every event on my whistle-stop tour. In every city I did talks and Q&As. I signed books. I posed for photos. I shook hands. I offered personal advice. I hugged troubled men (some of whom cried - they had never been hugged by another man before). I was so busy and so diligent (and so afraid) in the pre-release promotion that the first 10,000 books were sold as pre-orders, even before I had a copy of the book in my hand. Before even embarking on the tour proper, I had to order another 10,000 copies. They all sold too.

Lest we forget, I self-published this book, and the retail price was £16.99, so there was a very healthy margin in ever sale. 32 cities, 60 shops, 20,000 copies sold in hardback and I hit No.21 in the Sunday Times Bestseller list. Not No.1, I grant you, but I hit the list as a self-published author, and that was good enough for now.

The following year we hit the bestseller list again with the paperback version.

I drove myself hard on that tour.

I drove too hard perhaps and the pressures were not just mine. Sharon was my business partner. She was quiet, a shy person, naturally reserved and generally risk averse. She didn't like being around people very much and yet here she was, caught up in the tail-spin of my whirlwind, churning up the sod, the length and breadth of Britain, having to deal with a burden of unwanted human contact: hugs, handshakes, cheek-kisses, all from well-meaning, overwhelmed and often overfamiliar strangers. Sharon was also a trained worrier. Her mum had been a worrier, and her nan before her, and she had inherited the ancestral curse. She was weaned on the need for financial security, and the guaranteed income of a nine-to-five, the working wage. Now she was risking house and home and the shirt on her back on this crazy entrepreneurial enterprise. She never ever once complained, but I knew that it was anathema to her. It was so challenging that towards the end of our tour she fell ill with a mystery virus in an anonymous hotel room in a drab suburb of Stratford, East London. In that dank hotel room, she was disorientated, she was sick and dizzy, and she was afraid. We ended up in an A&E corridor at the Stratford Hospital, waiting for medical assistance that took a whole night to arrive. After an excruciating five hour wait, she was eventually promoted from a chair in the hallway to a bed behind a curtain in a makeshift ward. If I thought the hotel was cold and anonymous, the hospital was a barren wasteland by comparison.

I'd had an amazing time on the tour, staying in hotels, eating out, sitting with friends over dinner in lovely restaurants in distant cities, driving along coastlines en route, travelling through the countryside in first class trains. I'd loved every minute, it had stretched my muscle, bone and sinew, but now, sitting in this shithole hospital, Sharon unconscious, not a nurse or a doctor in sight, *not one*, people all around us (other patients) ill, dying, insane, sad, calling out repetitively for help that was repeatedly ignored, I sat on the floor and unashamedly wept. My girl was suffering. She was ill, though we didn't know yet what her malady was. I sat on the floor, behind that cubicle curtain and thought to myself, 'what the fuck are we doing here? Is it all worth it?'

I felt responsible for Sharon's condition. I *was* responsible. I had a wild energy raging through me at the time, the gift of my epiphany, but I was not controlling it very well, if at all. It was spurting out of me - mid tour - with a gush of ideas for more books, more DVDs, more films and more plays. I even wanted to produce a range of soft toys and T-shirts, and martial arts training equipment. I had so many ideas my head was swimming with them. And that's OK, as far as it goes, but Sharon's head was spinning too, by proxy, and that was not good, in fact this is what had made her ill. My reservoir had spilled creatively, and yes, it had manifested lots of nice 'things' (money, books, material success) but it had also lashed the one person in my life who I lived for and that made me sad beyond measure. Even though we were expanding our world exponentially, pioneering new landscapes, and colonising unmapped terrains, it was still never enough for me, *it was never enough*. I always wanted more. It would have been fine if I'd kept my flood of new ideas contained, or if I'd revealed them to Sharon by piecemeal, as and when the time was right, but I didn't do that. I shared all the 10,000 things with my sensitive girl all at once and as a result I completely blew her bulb.

To be brutally honest, I just did not know when to shut-the-fuck-up.

My secrets were spilling everywhere, and like a burst dam people in close proximity were getting swept away in the swell, Sharon most of all.

I can still see that dank hospital now, like some kind of post-apocalyptic dustbowl full of disembodied, tumbleweed spirits.

I am not talking about the NHS, which, as we know is a wonderful gift to us all. This was nothing to do with the NHS or the beautiful staff who hold it together with plasters and string and field bandages. What I witnessed in Stratford was metaphysical. It was a long dark night of the soul. No doubt. And what I was shown was not a hospital, rather, I was granted a Siddha, a spiritual vision. It was both painfully instructive and hellishly real. It was a message from beyond, one that I was warned to heed. It was intuited to me that I'd been given gifts, and they were the exponential effect of my Vegas epiphany. As a result, my energy levels were disproportionate and I was creating at a prolific but unstable and unsustainable rate in the manifest world. I was not respecting my energy or the effect it was having on those close to me. Looking back at it now, I don't think I knew what was happening to me. I couldn't yet see that this new source of energy was a Siddha. I was so caught up in the effulgence that I failed to take stock of its potency or its source. The signs were there. I could feel how overwhelmed people would often get if I spoke to them for too long. Sharon used to advise me, 'too much Geoff, pace your talks, say less, people aren't ready for it yet'.

Did I listen?

I did not listen.

I just kept talking, talking, talking, like a puppet with its voice-string jammed on pull.

Just before her illness in Stratford, I remember walking back from the book shop, still high from the event, rattling away like a demented summer cricket, telling Sharon about the hundred new ideas I'd had that day, and her looking pale, her saying to me quietly, 'Geoff you need to let me rest now, I'm just about coping as it is.'

Did I listen?

Ask me the question, 'Geoff did you listen?'

Let me answer you: No, I did not listen.

In this cold, desolate hospital ward, unattended by nurse or doctor for the whole night, *through* the whole night, twelve hours without medical attention, I sat down, I wept at my own ignorance and my own folly and I listened. Perhaps for the first time since my Vegas clarity I really listened. This long dark night was created, this misery was crafted just for me, just so that I would listen to words that entered my consciousness like a divine audio download: *Listen now, man of the world. Your energy is your gift. It is also your secret. Do not waste your energy needlessly. Do not share your secret without cause. Do not speak your words, where speaking will cause harm. And lest you forget, it is your gift this energy. But it is not **your** energy this gift.*

I was being warned that divine energy can be dangerous. It demands Persil-clean interiors to contain it, an iron will to control it, and kid gloves to handle it. .

The moment I heeded this message, the moment the clarity alighted in my thick skull, help was forthcoming. The hospital that had seemed like the Badlands for a whole night suddenly came back to life and Sharon received the treatment she needed. The medical diagnosis was Labyrinthitis, a balance affecting virus. The stress of the book promotion knocked out her equilibrium. My own diagnosis was overexposure to my poorly managed divine energy. It was my ignorance of spiritual decorum that stunned her homeostasis and forced a mandatory eight count. I wound my neck in. I calmed myself and contained the energy that was coursing through my veins, and my girl soon recovered.

I thought I was on tour to sell books. As it turned out I was there to learn lessons infinitely more valuable than an inflating bank balance and a ranking on the Times Best Seller List. This was a lesson I was to forget and remember a few more times before it finally sank in.

We returned home to Coventry. Sharon took some prescribed bed rest and a course of medication ('take three Geoff-free-breaks a day'), and I finished the final dates of the tour alone.

Amidst the rush of my life-on-fast-forward, I was about to experience another unexpected, but delicious quirk of fate. Towards the end of the book tour I met a young guy called Ben Carlish. Our synchronistic encounter would lead to my first film (Bouncer), my collaboration and friendship with Ray Winstone and Paddy Considine, and a BAFTA nomination.

14

Bouncer: My First Film

Ben Carlish was working at Manchester Waterstones as an assistant, when I visited to hold a signing there and give a talk. After the event Ben approached me and asked if I'd consider meeting him for a chat. He was as aspiring writer, and wanted to interview me, with a view to publishing his article in The Big Issue. By now I had become a keen advocate of divine networking* and I intuitively felt the right connection with this lovely man, so I agreed to meet him the following week, when I was holding a similar event in nearby Huddersfield.

Ben was so lifted by the morning we spent together that he told his sister, Natasha Carlish, about me and about my story. Subsequently, Natasha contacted me to relay her gratitude. Ben had been feeling a little down, she confessed, and the meeting had lifted him, it had inspired him. As it turned out, Natasha was a television producer, and my unusual ascent from bouncer to bestseller had greatly intrigued her; she asked if I'd be interested in having a documentary made about me.

I was already starting to explore TV and film, so it felt like an ordained fit. We arranged to meet in nearby Birmingham. Natasha brought Michael Baig-Clifford with her, a director she'd worked with on numerous award-winning documentaries. We hit it off immediately. I loved Natasha. I loved her incredible drive and her can-do attitude. Michael was quiet and reflective, he might pause for a whole minute

---

* See my book The Divine CEO for more detail on divine networking.

before answering a simple question, but I liked him. I could read him. I could feel his gentleness, his sensitivity.

At the end of the meeting, Natasha mentioned that, primarily, she and Michael were documentary makers, but they were starting to explore narrative drama (movies). She asked casually if I'd be interested in writing a short film for them. She felt that with the right script, Screen West Midlands (our regional film agency) might fund the project. I'd already started working on a feature length film for Jim Cartwright and Martin Carr so this felt like a natural extension of what I was already doing. I asked what they'd like me to write for them, did they have a story idea in mind? Michael mentioned that, whilst training at the local weights gym, he really enjoyed listening to local bouncers talking about their experiences; seeing as I'd worked the doors myself, could I write something about that?

Yes of course I could.

Somewhere between our meeting in Birmingham, and me sitting down to write back home in Coventry, I completely forgot what Michael had requested and instead wrote a film about psychotic jealousy. This was a subject matter close to my heart, it was a personal ghost that had haunted me since my youth. I thought that a film on the subject might help me to explore, perhaps even expel it.

I wrote a first draft, sent it to Michael and Natasha and waited for their assessment of my script. There is a lot of *waiting* in the film world. Over the next two decades of sending out scripts, I sometimes got a good response, I sometimes got a bad response and often I got no response at all. Some people offer their assessment of your work by simply never getting back to you. The only constant in film is that the response will always be slow... which means learning to be patient, specifically it means learning to wait. But there is a sage idiom in film that warns, *if you are waiting, you are not working.*

Natasha and Michael finally got back to me. They couldn't relate to my film at all, not cinematically anyway. I was perplexed to say the least. I relayed my confusion to Sharon telling her that I loved the script (what the hell is their problem?), I thought it was potent and relevant, jealousy was rarely tackled in film and TV.

'Yes', said Sharon (the sage) 'but is it what they asked for?'

I hesitated and I ummed and ahed.

'No, not exactly,' I said.

'What exactly did they ask for?'

'Well,' I said, remembering my conversation with Michael, 'the director said he loves listening to bouncers in gyms talking about their experiences.'

'So, why did you give them a script about psychotic jealousy?'

No answer.

'Geoff...why don't you just give them what they asked for?'

Why indeed!

I'd been so busy trying to suit my own agenda, I missed the subtle voice of spirit directing me to a more immediate logos, and whilst I may have listened to Michael, I definitely had not heard him.

I wrote my first short film. I called it *Bouncer*.

In the beginning the script pretty much consisted of just one scene, with two burly bouncers in a gym remembering a bloody encounter they'd been involved in. At this early stage what I'd delivered was little more than a monologue, and although the words were strong, it needed developing if it was going to work as a film. Michael and Natasha pretty much held my hand through the whole process, encouraging me to break the monologue into scenes, with a voice-over narration. When I'd finished the final re-write, everyone was happy with it. Natasha sent it to Screen West Midlands, who kindly awarded us a bursary of £10k to make it into film.

We were on our way.

All we needed now was a lead actor.

When we sat around the casting table, I was asked who I had in mind as lead when I wrote the script,

'Ray Winstone,' I said, without so much as a second thought.

I'd had Ray in mind from the very beginning. In those days I wrote everything with Ray in mind. I loved him. I felt he was the ideal actor for the genre I was writing in.

There was more than one chuckle in the room.

'Ray Winstone?' Someone guffawed. 'We haven't got enough money to pay for Ray Winstone's lunch. He's Hollywood; he's on Hollywood fees.'

I was of the belief that anything was possible. If Ray liked the script I felt sure that money would not be an issue for him.

I suggested that we approach Ray with the script, and let him decide for himself if he wanted to do it or not?

The divine economy has a way of irresistibly drawing people towards an aligned project, and spitting out those it does not favour, irrespective of mundane concerns like money.

And so it was; Ray read the script, loved it, and came on board.

Yes, really, it was that simple.

This had a desired effect because it drew together a dream team of British actors - Paddy Considine, Sean Parkes, Ronnie Fox - some of the best talent around, all working on a ten minute film, and all working pretty much for free (expenses only).

I think the film actually cost Ray money in the end, but he was there because he felt compelled to be there.

I can't even begin to tell you how incredible it was to stand on location outside a Coventry nightclub (a place called Scholars, owned by my friends Gus and Tracy) watching Ray et al. lift the lines I'd written from the page and blast them through the firmament. It was a three-day shoot and I learned more about film making in that very tight window than I could from any how-to book, or step-by-step guide or fast track, high calibre film making course.

I remember being on set, watching the magic unfold and thinking, 'ah, so that's how it works'. It's one thing reading dry words from a blank page, thinking 'that should work all right', it's quite another to watch a British acting legend take it from the page and put a rocket up its arse. Ray was immense. And he was a beautiful man on set. He was kind and considerate and even when the nervous Michael wanted to do 'one more take, just for luck', he was patient and understanding. Paddy Considine was equally kind. He kept himself to himself, and didn't say much, even in the rehearsals. But when the director called 'action' he rose up like ten demons and he owned the screen. His power on set was impressive. In one of the fight scenes, towards the end of the shoot I also got to do a cameo (Ray insisted). I stood in for Ray and wrestled with Paddy down a midnight alleyway outside the club.

Sean Parkes was poetically mesmerizing too; the lines rolled from his tongue like he'd riffed them on the spot. Ronnie Fox too, impressed me with his natural timing and his infectious laugh and the little mudras he threw in to make the lines sing.

I have to say that the whole experience was overwhelming but completely inspirational. It was beautiful to be on the shoot with Sharon and my kids and say to them, 'I know I told you it was possible, but now you can see for yourselves, all things are possible.'

We all had an idea that Bouncer was something special, from the very first draft of the script, and on set our instincts were definitely encouraged. The finished film - dark, poetic, beautifully shot in natural light, superbly acted - was like a ten minute bombshell. I knew we had a gem on our hands, and that we needed to get the film out there, into the world: people needed to see our work. If you are going to tell a story that has something important to say - ours was about the folly of violence, the power of karma, and the love shared between conflicted men - you need to make every last effort to put it in front of as many eyes as possible.

Screen West Midlands were brilliant. They awarded us the bursary to make the film, and they supported us throughout the shooting process, but they were not really set up to promote Bouncer after it was completed. Michael (our director) was concerned, 'what do you think we should do Geoff?'

For me the answer was simple: 'Get it out everywhere. Make it a full-time job getting the film to as many festivals as possible. The film doesn't exist if people don't know the film exists'.

Michael and Natasha took my advice on board and did just that. They applied for every notable festival going. Once it had been accepted into some of the elite, A and B class film events, and had gained some traction and built up a reputation as a film of note, our little gem of a movie got picked up by the British Council, who promote acclaimed British Film.

We ended up screening at thirty-two international festivals.

Then we heard the amazing news.

Bouncer had been nominated for a BAFTA award for best short live action film.

I can't say that BAFTA had ever been on my radar. I didn't really understand film at the time. I didn't know my way through its innards yet, nor did I fully appreciate the significance of acclaim in the awards festivals. I only knew that our nomination elicited a considerable amount of excitement. One minute I'm sweeping floors in the factory, the next, I'm walking down red carpets and presenting my art to large appreciative audiences, all over the world.

As is often the way when the door to inspiration opens, lots of other ideas flood in. That's why it is worth every one of your last pennies to get yourself inspired. I was so inspired I thought I might pop.

I kept the ideas contained this time. I'd learned my lesson from the book tour.

While we were on the set shooting Bouncer, Ray kept asking Ronnie (who is a beautiful raconteur) to 'tell Geoff that story, the one when we were in Scotland and that drunken harridan kept saying 'get me a wee drinkie will ya?'

Ronnie recounted the experience in his own unique and inimitable way and had us all laughing from the belly. He punctuated his story by telling me that *this was way back, this was when I liked a little tipple, when I liked the odd line or two.* Ronnie talked openly about his alcohol and drug addiction and the time he spent in AA and NA. I knew this story. It resonated deeply within me. My brother Ray had died from alcoholism. I was with him when he was violently ripped from his mortal coil at the obscene age of forty-two. I'd long wanted to talk about Ray's drinking and the tragedy of his young death. More specifically I felt the urge to write about it. I was still carrying a lot of dissonance about the hideous nature of his premature departure, about the family shame concerning his addiction, the pandemic lure of alcohol and the craic that keeps addicts going back to their death-tipple time and again.

I said to Ronnie, regarding his story, 'I could write you a film based around that.'

Ronnie confided in me many years later that he thought I was probably full of horse shit. He wasn't being disingenuous. People in film are always promising you the earth and then failing even to remember your name, let alone return your call.

I put Ronnie's film to paper right after finishing the shoot on Bouncer, and I loved it, I loved it the moment I finished the last line of the script. I loved it because, although it had been inspired by Ronnie, this story was about my big brother Ray, who I loved and adored.

I called the film Brown Paper Bag, because everyone associated alcoholics with rough sleepers and winos, sitting on a park bench, *having it large from a brown paper bag*. My brother was not that man. This was not how it went down for him, although he was a chronic alcoholic. He was a sensitive man. He was a broken poet, a lost scribe, a divorced depressive who drank himself to death from a tall kitchen stool in the unwashed clutter of a high rise flat. He learned to drink himself into oblivion from home, my brother, and in quiet denial, while his children tip-toed around his scattered and spent life and suffered their daddy's addiction by proximity.

I wanted to write about this.

Ronnie was my catalyst, he gave me permission.

Some ideas are so urgent that they gush onto the page fast and need very little encouragement or edit. All you need to do is hold a pen and stand in the way of the muse as she rushes by. Other scripts are elusive, they hide from you like timid spirits, you have to practically climb Jacob's ladder and wrestle with the angel before she'll suffer you even a line. Digging into other stories can feel like mining for granite in the dark by hand with a blunt spoon in a bleak mid-winter.

Brown Paper Bag came easily. It came through me and not from me, and for that I was grateful. I offered the script to Natasha and Michael and told them I'd written it exclusively for Ronnie. They loved it, and vowed to raise the money, and get the script to film as soon as possible.

While the team applied for funding (for Brown Paper Bag), Bouncer was doing the rounds at festivals, and private screenings. It was receiving great acclaim. Excited about my first BAFTA nomination, I decided to give the process a little metaphysical assistance, by meditating on a win. I thought if I could visualise myself at the awards ceremony, picking up the coveted BAFTA mask, I might be able to increase the odds in our favour. I sat in a lotus position (I had seen it done before), and I tried to visualise winning the award. The image would not come to me. Every time I tried to picture the statue in my mind's eye, audio, visual and sensory defilements rose up in me like internet trolls; doubts about my eligibility, fears about not being good enough, and confusion about what it all meant, too much confusion. The path between subject and object was littered with shadows that told me I was greedy, undeserving, being too materialistic, charging that I did not deserve to win, and that other people were more worthy than me, more deserving and more talented.

At this time in my development - the honeymoon period of the Vegas epiphany now behind me - I was fluctuating between a spiritual adept and the village idiot. Some days it was the true 'I' observing the world singularly through my eyes, other days I was seeing reality through the filters of a stranger, an old fear or a conditioned script. One minute I'd be acting falsely humble and renouncing legitimate gifts, the exponential effects of honest work, and the next I'd be posturing like a righteously indignant braggart, claiming the whole world as my own.

This is where I was now, nominated for acclaim that would open doors to my inner kingdom, but unable to believe I was deserving of it.

I figured much later that the nomination itself was a potent gift. The bronze and granite mask was a wound dressing, divinely administered to draw out my hidden poison, the doubts and secret fears and uncertainties of the false ego.

It was definitely doing its job; I was all over the place.

I practiced as hard as I could to clear the doubts and fears that arose in me but to little avail. All I could muster were fleeting internal images of me holding the BAFTA statue, that quickly dissipated, or were swallowed up by negativity. Then, during one particularly strong meditation, I had a breakthrough... of sorts. For the first time I was able to clearly visualise the BAFTA and hold it steady in my imagination. *Good*, I thought, *I'm getting there*. Then, when I was finally able to see the statue, crystal clear, the strangest thing happened. Where the name of the winning film is supposed to be etched onto the brass plaque, I did not see the word Bouncer, as I had expected, instead I saw the words Brown Paper Bag.

Brown Paper Bag!

That was the short film I'd just written for Ronnie Fox. I'd written it but we'd not even raised the money, let alone put the script to film.

I rang Natasha, our producer, 'I've just had a vision' I said, 'a vision that we won a BAFTA for Brown Paper Bag.'

'But we haven't even made Brown Paper Bag yet.'

'I know'.

'Perhaps it means we'll win for Bouncer,' she said.

'Perhaps...' I agreed, but I was not convinced.

As it turned out, we went to the BAFTAs. We had the most extraordinary time, marinating in the juices of the best storytelling talent in the world but we did not win a BAFTA for our short film *Bouncer*.

The goody bag was amazing though.

A £500 watch (my son had that), a beautiful bespoke Parker pen (my best friend Peter had that) and thousands of pounds worth of goodies that brought us the greatest joy when we gave them away to friends and family.

It was a great goody bag, but we did not win a BAFTA.

It was worth not winning just to be able to flush out the incongruences in me that would not have been exposed otherwise.

You might think that a BAFTA nominated team would be able to raise money for their second venture together with ease, the math just works. We couldn't raise a bean, despite applying to every fund available to new film makers. We got very close with Film 4: Cinema Extreme, but in the end we were unlucky. They were offering two bursaries of £60k for short film makers. We managed to get onto a short list of four candidates, but we failed to make the final two, and left the meeting without even our bus fare home. We sat in front of a board of experts, who heard our heartfelt pitch, and in their wisdom decided that the director (Michael) was *in their words* 'not ready'. Natasha was brilliant and not unkindly abrupt; she is delightfully straight this lady. If you ever needed someone to fight your corner in a pitched battle, Tash was your girl, she was a superhuman powerhouse.*

After the rebuttal, Natasha shook hands with the judging panel, thanked them for their time and consideration, and told them flatly they were wrong.

'We'll make the film ourselves,' she said.

Michael was very unhappy about the board singling him out. He took it as a personal affront and vowed to contact (by letter) each individual member of the panel and let them have an unwholesome piece of his mind. I told him he should write to them, absolutely, 'but if you do,' I advised, 'make it a kind letter, send them a box of chocolates, and thank them for their notes, guidance and time.'

The panel were just doing their job. It was not personal. As far as I was concerned, if they'd closed the door on us, it clearly wasn't the right door anyway. There would be other doors that would better suit our project. Also, it doesn't take an Oxford graduate with a double first to work out that, in a world as small as film, there is a fair chance that you are going to bump into the same characters more than once during your career. You'll be facing the same funding panel (or individual members of it) in the near future. You'll be asking them for money, and they'll be assessing whether or not they want to give it you.

You can be sure of one thing: they will remember how gracious you were the last time. Especially if your 'grace' was articulated in a stinging letter, sent through the post on the wings of two second class stamps.

---

* Some years later, when a close friend of ours suffered badly at the hands of a corporate bully, a harridan in local film circles, Natasha stood back-to-back with him throughout the whole process, risking her own position and livelihood in the process. I have never forgotten her courage. I am always inspired by her example.

Brown Paper Bag was eventually made, but only because of Natasha Carlish.

I have absolutely no doubt about that.

She was solely responsible for our story making it to film. Unable to raise the money through traditional funding, she re-mortgaged her home to the sum of £3,500 and we made the film for that princely amount. I paid for the food, so that the actors and crew could eat, and Mark Leveson, a co-producer who came on board to support us, paid for accommodation and travel.

A year after our BAFTA nomination for *Bouncer*, almost to the day, *Brown Paper Bag* was in the can. It was the most beautifully realised film, with heart-breaking performances from our lead actors Ronnie Fox and Jo McInnes.

And we were BAFTA nominated again, for a second consecutive year.

Natasha called me, intrigued, 'You saw us win this!' She said. 'In your vision. You saw it.'

I smiled, 'Yes, I did.'

This time around, when I meditated on the outcome of the awards ceremony, I saw us win the BAFTA. All of those old, negative obstructions that rose up in me the previous year, were routinely dismissed, they couldn't stop me from seeing true: we were worthy of this award, we were worthy of every accolade for *Brown Paper Bag*, a challenging and beautiful homage to my brother Ray.

The BAFTA ceremony was *again* a rare treat.

We received another expensive goody bag full of delights that were routinely given away, only days after the awards. I knew that some of our friends and family would probably never get the chance to enjoy this unusual experience, so as much as I loved receiving the gifts, I relished giving them away even more. And when we walked down the red carpet, we savoured every moment. First time around me and Sharon pretty much sprinted down the felt runway, snaking through gurning A-listers, and dodging the feeding frenzy of press flashbulbs. But now we were practically old-hands, so we sauntered, we strolled, we took in the sights and sounds and views and we smiled at each other, me and Sharon, we smiled knowingly when reporters lifted their cameras in a Pavlovian twitch to catch our image, only to drop them again just as keenly, when they realised that *we were no one*, we were not famous.

'Who the fuck are they?' We could see them mouthing to each other.

Well, who the fuck is anyone, that's the question.

None of it was real of course. None of it meant anything, even though at the time I thought it meant everything in the world. It was just lines of uncomfortable men, camera-shy in dress-code tuxedo, shadowing fetishized women, oven-ready in shiny silk wrappers. If I'd taken a minute, if I'd looked beyond the veil of popping bulbs, and the blurring of celebrity glare, I'd have seen that the soft cinema carpet was all that segregated us from the hard London pavement, concrete bedding for the hungry homeless. We were separated by a smokescreen of security fencing, conditioned perception and a cluster of eager fans, hoping to catch a fleeting squint of a passing celebrity. We were being fattened foie gras geese at the Odeon cinema, while only feet away, our forgotten sons and daughters were clawing through rubbish bins looking for a scrap-supper in Leicester Square.

Perspective is a wonderful thing.

At the time I had none. All I could see through my dilated pupils was the glamour of the illusory. Later I would also learn to appreciate the ephemeral nature of celebrity, and how easily and how quickly the nurturing protein of intuitive art can be crushed under foot, in the stampede towards carb-heavy industry acclaim.

I think Sharon had spotted this from the very beginning, it took me a bit longer to open my eyes and see behind the curtain.

For now I was not only in it, I was of it, and I clambered after the unreal as fast as all the other fools for fancy.

I spotted the beautiful Emma Thompson in the crowd and I followed her down the carpet like a lemming, hoping to blend in by staying close to movie royalty. She'd been there many times before, so she knew exactly how to work the red. It was a strange thing: the first time we attended a BAFTA ceremony, we didn't know what we were doing, we didn't know what to expect and it was over before it had really begun. Suddenly we were back at home in Coventry thinking *what the fuck just happened?* At one point Sharon got so nervous she even contemplated not attending the ceremony at all. She'd been offered free dress fittings in London, we were wined and dined and treated regally, the phone never stopped ringing with congratulations, and the email was a constant *ping ping* of invites for meetings, industry events, and requests for interviews. She was dissonant. Where were all these people before the nomination? And why were they suddenly so interested in us now, just because an anonymous voting panel had added our name to a selection list? She absolutely felt out of her depth, it was just not for her. I on the other hand, felt as though I'd arrived. I felt validated by the nomination. My ego was dining out on the notice. Second time around I was determined to savour every moment. I didn't want it to rush past like fields of blur from a fast train window. After the second nomination in as many years the attention was heaped on us again, and the same invites and the same notice came our way, but already, within just one season, we were handling it better.

This time we won the BAFTA for *Brown Paper Bag*.

I jumped up and down on the stage like a football manager holding the FA cup at Wembley. I got my picture taken with Renée Zellweger, and Scarlett Johansson, and just about every other celebrity that would stand with me now that I was holding a BAFTA statue. And when I arrived back home in Coventry, I carried my bronze validation around with me everywhere I went. I was the ugly duckling who'd just been told he was a swan, and I wanted to let everyone know about it. I showed it to all my friends and family. I encouraged them to take it off me and hold it, *feel how heavy it is*, I said, I even took it up to bed with me, and sat it on the bedside table. It clearly sated something in me that was hungry, starving perhaps. It meant way more to me than it should have, I know that much. But that's where I was. I'd been conditioned all my life to believe I was less-than, and this award, this hunk of shiny metal, disproved it all. It expanded my self-belief and proved to me that I was worthy of anything, we are all worthy of everything.

This was a very important award.

It really meant something.

It was prestigious.

Only…it wasn't important really; it didn't mean anything and it was not prestigious.

Later... much later, later than I would have liked, I'd eventually lift my foot off the wobbly stepping stone of acclaim, the station of interim truth, and place it instead on something more stable, something solid and internal. Eradicating social conditioning - the belief that the world must validate us before we can feel worthy - is a common problem, but it is also time honoured, it is perennial. It is said that Saint Paul, after his moment of clarity on the road to Damascus, struggled ever afterwards to transcend the very same barriers.

For now I saw no barriers.

I was just like everyone else. I was happy-asleep in the belief that the world was noticing me and that was all that mattered.

But what the world gives, it can easily take away again, and that is the whole of the problem right there.

15

The Atonement Years

It had been a heady, exciting and expanding few years.

As well as the play coming on at the Plymouth Royal and the BAFTAs and Las Vegas with Chuck Norris, I was still working on a feature length script for Martin and Jim based on Watch My Back and I'd picked up a lovely agent called Debi Allen. Debi was fiercely loyal, brutally honest and the hardest working person I had ever met. All the other agents I came across - the BAFTA win attracted a lot of agent attention - were asking me to sell myself to them as a potential client. Debi was different. She sold herself to me, and I was impressed by that. There was humility in her approach, and I admired her for it. She loved my work and said she'd do everything in her power to sell me, in what is a very challenging industry.

Sharon loved her too, which helped a lot.

Debi managed to arrange a meeting for me at the BBC where I pitched an original series idea. A BAFTA win opens doors, of that there is no doubt, it acts like a guarantee of quality, and assures people that you are a serious writer and have a voice. I'd long nurtured the idea of doing a six-part drama, based around the life of a team of bouncers. It was unique, what I knew, had never been seen on the TV before, and we'd managed to get Ray Winstone and Paddy Considine to work on the short version (Bouncer). My pitch obviously convinced the BBC because they commissioned a treatment and a first episode script. I was on my way.

One minute I'm on a red carpet in Leicester Square, the next I am working at the BBC. I was teamed up with a brilliant producer called Sue Hogg and a beautiful soul of a script editor, Esther Springer. Both of them were meticulous when it came to a script and in the year I worked with them, I learned things about diving-deep and *doing the work* that have never left me. Esther told me that what I had (which she felt other writers lacked) over and above the ability to write, was the courage to delve into those hidden folds, the dark places that very few writers were prepared to go. I always went deep. I innately knew why: writing was my way of cleansing, and you don't deep-cleanse if you only polish the veneer. I had shadows in me still. I harboured secrets, fears, shames and an ancient rage that needed to be located and brought to the surface to be processed. Carl Jung called this process, individuation; we re-integrate and incorporate the unconscious shadows into the conscious world. To do this successfully demands great awareness both of the technique and more importantly, of the self.

I use writing to mine for shadows, those debilitating sub-personalities that quietly orchestrate our lives from within, without us ever consciously knowing it. This demands an awareness of shadow as it rises, and the ability to resist identifying or engaging emotionally with the pain-body that represents. Reality, I have found, exists at the level of engagement and demands considerable moral effort. It can be dangerous - the conscious mind is liable to be submerged into the unconscious at any moment if it identifies too deeply with a false notion.

I can see now that the books, the teaching, Vegas, the short films, the stage play, the feature film and now the potential TV series were all asking the same thing of me. Something inside, my higher self, must have known that in order to make room for the new, I must first reconcile with the old. Everything connected with my violent past had to be recognised, processed, atoned and ultimately renounced. The residual karma - following behind me like a funeral procession - had to be met.

In order to do this, I had to dig up my dead, process them, and in the same practice of individuation, integrate them into consciousness.

I had many years of depression as both man and child, followed by a decade of extreme violence on the doors before my Vegas clarity. This was followed by the aforementioned honeymoon period, the years of spiritual bliss and magical Siddhas. But now that the bliss had subsided, the reality of my unfinished business - the violence of my past - made itself evident.

God may delay, but He never forgets.

The message was very clear: I was being called to account for my actions in *the dark years* (as my mum calls them). I was being invoiced to pay my debt.

Before I could enter the gates of earthly Paradiso, I had to stand before the master of the scales; that master was my own conscience.

Atonement was on the agenda and there was no way of avoiding it.

Writing about the doors in such visceral detail, especially with experienced editors like Esther and Sue, there could be no escaping my mistakes. At this level of scrutiny, pressure and heat, even your own skin speaks a testimony against you. In yet another period of spiritual kenosis - *guided from beyond* - I was *clearing out a crowd of sorrows from my human guest house to make room for some new delight.**

There is an old but very true saying: each of us can have as much of God as we choose, but we have to make room for Him first.

This was me consciously, deliberately, willingly making room and I thought it might kill me.

I felt the first stirrings of my cleansing at the BBC.

It was a dream job. I had always wanted to write for television, but now that I had been given the opportunity I struggled. *Be careful what you ask for,* the old idiom goes, *you might just get it*. I never knew what that meant until now. I'd been given my dream, and it felt too big for me. I was like a dog that chases a fire engine and doesn't know what to do when he catches it. Writing for the BBC brought up a disproportionate amount of terror in me, such fear and I didn't know why at the time, adding to the confusion. Now of course, I can see why I was so afraid. They wanted me to write about the door days, where I dabbled and dealt in violence and vice, when I was up to my hairy nuts in all sorts of heinous depravity. They wanted to know all the seedy detail, they probed for it, prodded me until it splurged out onto the page, they scraped my innards until the tripe of my past found the page of a script *and it was not nice*. It was not nice.

---

* Taken from the Rumi poem, The Guest House.

I'd done with all that.

I had renounced violence.

I had eschewed my brutal ways.

I was not a violent man anymore. I was a writer. I was an artist for fuck sake. I was working at the BBC. That shit was behind me. I felt like I was stuck between the pages of some shocking graphic novel, where the reputable and honourable gentleman Dr Jekyll, was being blackmailed, and forced to pay the debts of the unscrupulous and scandalous Mr Hyde. I no longer associated myself with the *shockingly evil* Geoff of old, but as much as I'd tried to separate myself from past deeds, with geography, and job title, and professed philosophy, I could not. As unfortunate and as uncomfortable as he was, he was still a part of me, and his debt was my responsibility. No amount of distance would erase that.

The only way to clear the account was to pay the arrears.

At the BBC, every time I recalled *this story and that story*, every time I shared a vignette that *I couldn't publish for legal reasons* or sanitised for moral reasons, I had to shame and crawl and grope through the same slime again and again with each telling. I cringed and shrunk like a troll from the Lord of the Rings being brought before the dawning light.

I didn't realise that this was the beginning of atonement. I had no way of knowing that this was what spiritual atonement felt like. I thought I was trying to write a TV show and wondered why it was so hard. Why I was in so much pain. Each script session lasted somewhere between four hours and four lifetimes, they were amongst the most painful eons of my whole life. I dreaded them the moment they were booked into my diary and hated every minute I spent in anticipation.

As it turned out, I worked with Esther and Sue for a year on my drama (pun intended) but the finished script - as good as we all felt it was - went *upstairs* and came back down again without a commission. It was a blow. I'd allowed myself the luxury of thinking that this was my big break. My series would air to great acclaim. I'd be commissioned to do a second series maybe a third, and in a matter of no time at all Hollywood would slap me in the face with its fat wad and I'd be rich, rich, rich.

This did not happen.

Esther and Sue called me to London for a meeting, generally a good sign. Bad news is usually delivered by email, or text, or, when the commissioners are very brave, you might get a personal phone call. They asked me to lunch. Good sign number two. I anticipated congratulations. At lunch - posh restaurant, bottled water, hoity waiter and food you can't pronounce on the menu or recognise on the plate - they dropped me for an eight count with their commiserations; the boss upstairs didn't get it, and the big boss upstairs still did not get it and did not want it.

I told myself (unconvincingly) that the BBC boss was a posh, middle-class know-it-all, and I was trying to sell her a rough working class drama, so it was never going to work out in my favour anyway. I was basically accusing them of classism. And at the time I probably even believed it.

Later the same day I sat in a London café with Sharon, feeling like it was the end of the world.

She said, 'What now?'

My head sunk into my shoulders like a beaten dog. 'I don't know what now.'

'What you have to ask yourself Geoff is this, are you prepared to keep writing, even if you're not getting paid?'

It was a bit like asking me, *are you prepared to keep breathing...*

Yes, I was.

Of course I was (wasn't I?).

It would be easy to look at the BBC year as wasted time, but that would be to miss the obvious; I was not really there to write a six-part series, I was there to prepare the way for bigger things, and the BBC was there to help me. I am thankful now for that amazing, challenging, excruciating year. My plumbing was clogged with the fatbergs of past karma, and I am grateful to have had my pipes so thoroughly jet-sprayed by two such discerning and careful angels.

As I said, I didn't know I was being purged by God for my time in the criminal class, I thought I was being punished by the BBC for being born into the working class, so I had to suffer my psychic-surgery in quiet ignorance.

The BBC was only the first round of my spiritual chemo.

The next course of treatment was to take place in Plymouth, at the Royal Theatre who were about to stage my first play *Doorman* (formerly called One Sock).

Again, I was disproportionately anxious all the way through the rehearsal process, and as the opening night approached things only got worse. I was going to the toilet every five minutes. I constantly needed to urinate, even when I didn't. It was so uncomfortable. I was up several times, every night. Pissing, pissing, pissing. I put it down to stress, *I'm just stressed*, I told myself, *its first night nerves*. But why? I didn't understand. I'd faced killers on the door, murderers, maniacs and crazy women trying to stab me with the heel of their stilettos or their nail scissors or pointy combs from their very tiny clutch bags. What was I facing here? A middle-class audience and a murder of critics who might crow that they did not like my work?

Then it hit me.

I finally, consciously realised what was unfolding. I was not afraid of the audience, not really. I was not worried about the literary critics, hardly. What I was actually afraid of was standing with an audience in front of my own violence, going nose-to-nose with my own depravity, my own shame, depicted by an actor on a stage. I did not want to stand before my shadow, my sin, and kiss that heinous part of me.

Doorman was an autobiographically inspired monologue about a man (called Tony in the play) who kills another man in a brutal and bloody encounter on the pavement arena outside a night club. While he is in a prison cell awaiting charge, he tries to rationalise his violence by trying to deny the intent of his own actions. As the story unfolds, Tony reveals more, he has left his wife, abandoned his children, sold his integrity to the two highest bidders... greed and lust.

On stage, I was watching my own confession, live, in 3D.

It was so painful that, in the end, I had to close my eyes, hold Sharon's hand and pray for it all to be over. I kept my eyes shut for the full play, sat in the audience with my own children. They had travelled down to the coast to watch their dad's first play, only to find themselves witnessing instead their dad's first confession. I thought I was afraid of judgment, from my peers, and from significant others. That was part of it, but it was not the whole. I was not afraid of their opprobrium. It was truth that brought the tremble to my limbs, truth for which I would have to judge myself. Sat in the auditorium, with the discerning eyes of myriad witnesses, there was no way I could hide behind rationalisation, or any other dodgy Freudian defence mechanism. There could be no defence, only divine retribution. Fear rose in me. Shame rose in me. Regret rose in me closely followed by disgust and self-hatred, they all rose in me. It was hard to forgive myself; *I couldn't forgive myself.* Denial was no longer an option; the truth was right in front of me. I had beaten men up in bar fights. It was all there on the stage. I had written it. Now I was observing my past crimes, like some gruesome karmic reckoning in an afterlife bardo, at the Royal Plymouth Theatre on the West Coast of England. The single thing I can offer in my defence was that I was *willingly* (if reluctantly) re-living it, the pain I inflicted on others. It was gruesome. Blow by blow, I could literally feel the pain, the anguish, the humiliation they must have felt as I gave them lashes. The play was originally called *One Sock*, the word *sock* a colloquialism for punch: to *sock* someone in the mouth. In the story it is revealed that the title has a dual meaning: in a fight outside a bar that Tony (the lead character) is guarding, he knocks a man unconscious, and then kicks him so hard in the face while he is out, that he ends up with blood splattered all up the front of his sock, and his victim's broken tooth stuck to the cotton. To hide it from the police, Tony, thinking he is clever, bragging that he is always one step ahead of the law (in reality he is always two steps behind karmic law) takes the sock off hiding the evidence. At the end of the play the police find the sock and use the forensics to separate him from his children and send him to prison for life. The play was as close to my own life, my own violence and my own nightmarish fears about killing a man and losing my liberty as it possibly could be without writing a verbatim biography. In that old life, I was a savage and unrelenting fighter. I was always coming home from pubs and clubs at three in the morning, with blood splashed up my sock, and there were several men that I very nearly killed. That they did not die was not for want of trying on my part. I was saved from murder only by the grace of God. I once spent a week in hospital having bits of teeth removed from a gash in my knuckles an inch long. The scar remains with me to this day. Thirty years later, as I commit these words to the page, the ugly wound is a constant reminder of my heinous fall.

People have a tendency to lionise fighters and villains. I mentioned this earlier when I spoke about Reggie, Frankie and Dave. Violence is romanticised, even by men intelligent enough to know better. The sow's ear of brutality is fashioned into the silk purse of clever narrative and sold to the public as some kind of twisted virtue. It is no virtue. Even well-intentioned violence always rebounds on itself.

Please don't make the same mistake with me.

It would do me the greatest disservice, and it would be an offence against all goodness if you were to find any honour at all in my violence.

I suffered proportionately for my sins during this time.

I felt like I had entered the hell regions (I had). I deserved it all. No pity please, pity would wipe me out. I deserved everything I got. If you deny my position on violence, if you remain unconvinced, and it finds even a spark of justification in your mind, perhaps Dante will help snuff your doubt with his terrifying cantos on the inferno that awaits all mercenaries. Of the nine circles on the poet's descent into hell, the first ring of the seventh circle is reserved specifically for men of violence. It is separated from Satan himself, on the ninth circle only by fraud and treachery towards God (and I am sure I have been guilty of both).

Brutality against one's neighbour can never be sanctified.

On the first ring of the seventh circle of hell, the murderers, the warmongers, the plunderers and tyrants are immersed, each according to the degree of guilt, into *rivers of boiling blood and fire and held there for all eternity.*

There is a reason I was about to experience two years in the seventh circle.

I was Tony.

Tony was me.

I had knocked men unconscious. I had punched them so hard that I snapped the teeth clean out of their mouths. I'd often find them afterwards, the disembodied teeth, floating like white tombstones in a gravy of sticky red on the grey pavement slabs. More than once I was left with shards of bone in my knuckles from the violent contact. I stamped on their heads. I stabbed the heel of my shoe into their ribs as hard as I could and relished in my torture. If I punched a man unconscious and I judged him to be a future danger to me, I'd wait for him to regain consciousness and then savagely punch him out again, leaving enough injury to discourage him from coming back for more.

At the Plymouth Royal Theatre I was not viewing a great piece of theatrical art; I was watching my own life review over and over and over, every night, twice on matinee days. In my internal tumult, Rumi spoke in my ear. He told me that birds made great sky circles with their freedom. How do they learn it? They fall, and in falling they are given wings.

I was falling and spinning in painful circles, waiting, waiting, waiting for wings.

I had gone onto the doors thinking that I was hunting monsters, only to realise in the darkness of this theatre that somewhere along the path I'd lost my way, I had become a monster myself.

The Nietzschean void I was looking into was looking right back at me.

Every blacked eye, every broken nose, every smashed face and broken mouth, every cracked rib and fractured bone was on full display and I was sickened by it. The weeping women whose men I had savaged, every girl who's beau I had beaten, crying in confusion, trying to stem the spill of their man's blood with a pitifully inadequate pocket hanky, the wives, the brothers, the sisters, the fathers and the mothers of my victims screaming at me 'why?'... they all stood before me with their complaint, lament, their damning testimony and their painful limbo of dissonance and pain. A clanging brass band of ugly crimes marched past me in a parade that seemed without end. The affairs I'd had, the lusts, the flirts in bars; a blowjob in a stranger's car; dirty, vacuous fucking in a filthy, rotting caravan at three in the morning; soiled and urgent copulation in the back garden of a young woman's home, her parents unaware of the debauchery only a few feet from their bedroom window; my loyal wife back home oblivious to the betrayal, my kids asleep in their beds: 'Dad's at work. Dad's working dangerous clubs to put honest cornflakes in our clean, clean breakfast bowls'. While the world was asleep, I was up to my greedy nuts in bad sex. The liar-machine - busy back then - was firing off fibs like bullets from a semi-automatic, concocting false stories to hide dirty sin. A shot a second, lies to whisper as I slipped into the marital bed, greedy-cock washed under the soapy tap of guilt, just in case she notices, just in case she whiffs the cheesy-stink of penile deceit. She wakes, I guilt and babble and equivocate about how *I'm really sorry I'm late home, there was a fight: a young girl was hurt; the police kept us back; the manager wanted a debrief; my fucking car fucking stalled again on the fucking, fucking ring road* LIES!

Lies! Lies! Lies!

There was no end of lies, and I was hearing them all, spoken back to me one at a time by an actor on the stage. It was all there, every detail, acted out in front of me, to an audience, to Sharon, to my beautiful, beautiful children.

I heard no complaint from them.

Not one.

And not a single solitary word of condemnation or judgement either. I realised that they were not there to magistrate or protest, they were neither my judge nor my jury, they were simply there to witness, and perhaps in their witnessing, assist in my healing. Sin at the level I had committed, needed many kind eyes to affect redemption. I sensed no avenging deity in that theatre either, or the jealous God of scripture; that fiction was not present at the court of my atonement. I was my own judge and jury. I was my conscience, my accuser, and I was my only defence. The scales before me, weighted down with the black pebbles of misdeed were placed there by my own hand, willingly, consciously, because I was ready to look at my crime. I was ready to stand before the work of my own hands. And if there was a punisher, it was me, punishing myself, only my own remorse was present in that place, accompanied by an ever loving, overseeing Redeemer, holding the hair away from my face as I vomited the fat and the glut and putrid accumulation of my poor-choice-living.

I wept at my own play.

Not just because I'd violated so many people, I wept because, at some unconscious level, I knew that in hurting others, I had tortured my living soul. It would be some years before I fully understood what this meant. It would take time and an expanded awareness before this made any real sense to me. At this moment in time all I was dealing with was the agony of existential guilt, and remorse at the pain I had caused others.

The play had a successful run at Plymouth, and shortly thereafter toured repertory theatres all around the country. Having to watch *Doorman* again and again as it went from city to city, was like walking the endless corridors of Dante's purgatorio, relentlessly doing my life review over and again until my sin was cleansed.

The play wiped me out.

I was exhausted. I was stressed. I was on my knees some days in physical pain that wracked my body. In the end my pissy bladder was so bad that, when I turned up at the Warwick Arts Centre in Coventry to watch *Doorman* being performed (yet again) I literally could not piss. My bladder had called a strike. It was so locked in spasm that no liquid would vacate. My shadow had risen. It had claimed me, and I was locked in a perpetual state of fight or flight.

My dad had taken ill at this exact time.

He had prostate cancer, and the prognosis was not good.

The irony was not lost on me.

I was sad beyond belief. Watching my dad suffer added to my own suffering. I am sure you must already have guessed what happened next. I was an empty husk, physically vulnerable, emotionally and mentally too. I had no defence at all, it had been broken down by the relentless purge that I was going through. The gates, my conscious filters were non-existent. I felt like a crustacean, shedding its shell in order to grow. I was without armour, vulnerable to all prey. The suggestion of a life-changing disease jumped on me, it climbed inside my heart and said, 'you've got prostate cancer too'. I tried not to listen, but it whispered in my ear all day, every day until I was worn down by it. I read the symptoms online, to see if I could disqualify the thoughts, but it didn't help, in fact it made things worse. I was so suggestible by this point that any symptoms I didn't already have I automatically got. I mean automatically. Wow! I read the symptoms of prostate cancer, and I felt them manifest in my body instantaneously. It showed me how powerful the imagination can be when, by simply engaging and identifying with its negative suggestions, it can have an instant physiological effect on your body. I was frightened but at the same time I felt perversely inspired. If the mind was able to change physiology so quickly and so dramatically in a negative way, then surely the same potential must also be true, with the same thoughts reversed.

This inspiration was something that I would return to later.

For now, it didn't help. I had lost control of the ability to direct my thoughts towards the positive, my shields were down, and my mind-door lay gaping and unprotected. The unconscious shadow that I was attempting to single out into consciousness was defeating me, and I was being dragged down into a dark abyss.

I was assailed night and day by fears, suggestions and supposed proofs that I had a terminal illness until, eventually, I was convinced that I actually did have cancer. My mind was so overtaken with fear that at one point I even developed blood in my urine, which was one of the cancer symptoms I had read about online. I didn't want to go to the doctor. I was scared to go to the doctor. In my distorted thinking, I feared that if I went to see my GP, it meant I'd failed. The shadow would have claimed me, and I would be lost.

'Prostate cancer is in the family,' my mum insisted, 'you must get yourself checked out. It's hereditary.' She was insinuating that I would definitely get cancer, if not immediately, certainly eventually. I would die of cancer and there was nothing I could do about it.

This was such bullshit!

I didn't believe it, not even for a second. I would not allow myself to be determined by my mum's frightened and conditioned rhetoric, and I would certainly not be allowing ancestral inheritance to edit the story of my life. I didn't know how I knew but I was sure that no reality could be forced upon me if I did not accept it. I could not prove this at the time, but I felt its truth in my bones.

Reality existed at the level of engagement.

I refused to engage.

All this time, in pain, in fear, some days so tired that I would burst into tears for no apparent reason, I still turned up, I still trained, I still taught my classes, I still toured the play, I still continued to write my film script for Jim and Martin, and even started working on new scripts for TV and film. I can vividly remember a producer visiting me in Coventry for a script meeting. I was in such acute discomfort in my bladder that I could hardly talk. She didn't know what I was going through, this lovely lady, the cleansing, the fight for my own mind, the atonement of old sin. I have no idea what she must have thought about me at the time. I only know that she was with me for four hours and it felt like she was there for four fucking days. All I kept thinking, all I kept thinking, all I kept thinking was please go, please go, please, please go now and leave me alone. I just wanted to lie down and sleep.

As much as I suffered and as much as I pained, I did not give up.

The shadow of my past had its foot on my neck. It was poking words at me, playing with my mind, threatening me and telling me how I had cancer, that I would lose my ability to have sex, I would be emasculated, and Sharon would fuck off and leave me for some other man.

One day, sitting at the computer, still in pain, steeped in depression, reaching into the well of words only to find it bone dry, knowing that I must write, but unable to face what I must face on the page, I heard its voice in my head, and it was not a good voice, nor was it a kind voice, this was the voice of the whisperer. A shadow was talking to me, the adverse forces: 'If you had cancer,' it said with the hiss of a cartoon snake, 'people would understand why you can't finish this script.'

The lower part of me was so afraid of releasing even more past indiscretions to the page, bringing them to the light, and completing my atonement that it was offering me cancer as a good alternative, a worthy excuse, a valid reason why I could not write.

I still would not go to the doctor.

I resisted seeking medical advice because I feared that the influence of a white coat whilst I was in such an open and vulnerable state would literally talk me into a disease that my heart was telling me I did not have. I knew that what I was experiencing was psychosomatic, but I also knew that once I bought the lie, once I'd fallen for the lie, I would be incarnated into that lie and end up as just another NHS pinball being bounced from doctor to doctor, from consulting room to consulting room, and operating theatre to operating theatre. In short, I feared that I was so malleable at this point that I would not be able to defend myself against suggestion.

I knew that people fell into the suggestion of illness and disease all the time because they didn't know how to guard the doorway of their heart. I had watched people talk themselves into scarcity, into bad luck, and I had lost count of the friends who had talked themselves into clinical depression. I had personally witnessed friends talk themselves into addiction and homelessness, marriage splits and nervous breakdowns. I had even been witness to people talking themselves into suicide. I did not doubt the power of negative association and the spiralling circles of hell that awaited anyone who listened to the devil on their left shoulder instead of heeding the angel on their right.

I was sure that my fears were a lie.

I was certain I was being duped.

And yet.... and yet the nagging voice of fear was playing on repeat like a stuck record in my head. I knew, I absolutely knew that I needed help. I could not get out of this spiralling whirlpool of negative doubt on my own. Eventually, recognising that my reluctance to seek medical help had become a catalyst for fear in itself, I decided to face my fears, go to the doctors, and get a blood test in the hope that I could arm myself with some external proof that I was not ill (only dying).

I have had people try and kill me. I've mentioned this. Someone trying to kill you is no walk in the park let me tell you, it is a frightening thing to behold. But it was not as frightening to me as walking into that doctor's surgery and placing my heart in the hands of a practicing GP.

The doctor was kind.

That's the first thing.

She was kind, and the adverse forces, who desperately did not want me to find a healthy validation, had suggested otherwise. I told the doctor about my symptoms. I told her that I knew they were psychosomatic, but a collusion of circumstance had left me impaired and I needed to undergo blood tests in order to wipe out the terrorist in my head. I didn't mention my books, films, the Vegas epiphany, my dirty sin, the cleansing play, the Plymouth atonement, the adverse forces who were assailing me night and fucking day, or the quicksand of Jungian unconsciousness that was trying to drag me below the earth. I did not mention angels or demons or Dante or Rumi - all of whom had spoken to me in their own subtle way. I did not mention my metaphysical awareness. As real as I knew it was, voicing otherworldly concerns in a worldly doctor's surgery would guarantee me nothing but a canvas straitjacket, a chemical cosh and my own corner in a padded cell. It would have also removed me from my God-given opportunity to repent, and I did not want that. Whatever was happening to me, I innately knew that it was my own fault, and for my own benefit, and that when I came out of this furnace I would be, if not a tempered blade, definitely a better man.

Are you aware of how many people there are out there who experience a spiritual awakening, and mistake the initiating symptoms of epiphany for the first signs of madness?

More that you can shake a stick at. So many newly awakened souls are misdiagnosed by general practitioners and end up being treated for psychosis.

So, I did not talk metaphysics with my doctor. I told her of my physical symptoms and she concurred that in all likelihood they were psychosomatic. She felt it would be wise to have the blood tests anyway, just to clear away any lingering doubt.

I was terrified of this test.

My fear was disproportionate and wild, and it took exerted and conscious effort to stop myself from falling into the gnashing teeth of my monster projections. I knew that this final trial would remove any lingering defilement, but I worried that I might not be strong enough to stay the course.

I took responsibility for my own karma.

I did not project.

I did not blame.

I did not look to my God and accuse Him of forsaking me, even when my roaming imagination suggested He had. I knew that, through this hell, a new man would be born. In my most private thoughts, even when I felt sure I was dying, I spoke to God. I asked God more than once to take my pain away from me, and when the agony remained, I acquiesced and said, 'may thy will be done.'

Thy will not my will.

If that meant He took everything from me, then so be it.

I knew, despite my daily distractions, I was being helped to jettison the old in order to make room for the new. I had lost a lot of weight by this time, the clothes were baggy on my bones, and my trouser belt was as tight as a folk singer's fringe. Only God knew about the inner fight that I was going through. Only He knew that it was bringing me to my knees figuratively and literally. Sharon knew too, of course. She lay with me every night, she was there in my most vulnerable and emotional moments and she was strong, she was an immovable force. I was an emasculated male. I felt weak and tired and … I felt weak, let's stay with that shall we, there is no point in painting legs on snakes, it is what it is, there is no better word to describe how I felt; I was vulnerable, weakness personified. In desperation I turned inwards and took my pain to Paul - murderer turned saint - for perspective. He spoke to me through an epistle, as he had spoken to the Corinthians (Corinthians 12.9) some two millennia before. He told me that he himself had pleaded with God three times to remove his thorn, and was told by the Redeemer, 'my grace is sufficient for you, for my power is perfected in weakness.' After this, Paul told me, he 'delighted in weaknesses, in insults, in hardships, in persecutions, in difficulties, for when I am weak, then I am strong.'

I had to believe this was true.

Actually, belief was unnecessary, I knew what he said was true. Paul's arrows of truth cut through every layer of my consciousness and pierced me at the core.

My fears had lied to me.

They'd assured me that the moment my armour was down, and my weakness on full display, Sharon would leave me, I would be abandoned. She would find a vibrant young beau and I'd be left in the rubbish bin. This, I realised was my greatest fear, my girl leaving me, and it was grotesquely disproportionate. I mentioned this earlier, that the same fear arose before my Vegas trip, and I suggested that something might be revealed to me as a consequence of facing down my fear.

The revelation was here, it was now.

I knew this fear of abandonment must be a mask for some deeper angst that I was unable to immediately identify. All I knew was, the fear was blackmailing me, and

I had to face it, and in facing it, giving it over, I had to risk that Sharon might be removed from me by the hand of Grace. I went directly to God, I gave it all over to Him and said (with no caveats), 'if it is your will that I lose Sharon, may your will be done.'

Even saying the words was like lashes to me, but I said them anyway. I fully expected that this heartfelt prayer might sound the death knell for my marriage. My faith in God was so strong at this point, and so unquestioning, that I placed my greatest fear directly in His hands and prepared myself to accept whatever outcome He felt was optimal, even if it meant losing my girl.

Further down the line, I would be exposed to yet another layer of this fear, perhaps the final layer, one that I had not anticipated... but that is a story for later.

For now, I made my prayer, and I did not lose Sharon, as I had feared. In fact, the opposite happened.

The weaker I got the stronger Sharon became. The more I stumbled, the better she supported me and even when just living in the world seemed to pain me, she closed the doors, manned the helm and guarded me like a winged angel.

Everything I'd feared was an illusion, a lie.

She did not leave. She stayed closer than she had ever stayed. She did not abandon me, she embraced me.

I remember the quietness of her caring. I remember how unspoken it was, how rare. There were no announcements of what she was doing or how she would do it or why or for how long, no self-congratulatory acknowledgements of her own virtue. She stood silently at the doorway of my heart and held guard until I was able to return to my own duty.

Fear is a lie.

It lies.

It lies when it threatens us with illness and disease and loss and gain. It lies when it uses its greatest weapon against an unknowing immortal: that we can die.

The day before I was due to have my blood tests, I went for a walk in Coombe Abby, a beautiful country park close to my home. I was broken and emotionally spent. I do not ever remember feeling worse in my entire life, not before and not since. I hoped that a walk in nature might offer some balm. My bladder was still stuck in fight-or-flight mode, and I was in a constant state of unease. The pain did not leave me night or day, and the thought that I must definitely be dying sat like a jockey on the back of every unnatural urge to urinate. It was constant. Halfway into my walk, along a mud path that circled the park, I could take no more. I fell to my knees and I wept. I looked to the sky and said over and over again 'I can't do this, I can't do this, I can't do this.'

Stupid things were eating me, consuming me, claiming me. The idea of having a blood test was not the thing that weighed on me the most, it was the anticipation of sweating for hours at the hospital, sitting in a long queue waiting for the test, and then having to wait a month for the results. The very idea was killing me. If I could just get it over and done with, it would not be so bad.

A kindly voice in my head assured me that *all will be well*.

All I needed to do was turn up for the test, and I would be looked after. My job (I was told) was to not worry about anything else, 'just turn up. We'll do the rest'.

A divine vision I'd had some time before, dropped into my consciousness, like a coin falling through water. It was a reminder of a time when I was going through a lesser struggle, but one that had felt greater at the time. In the vision I saw myself walking down the street. Ahead of me stood a young boy. His skin was black. He was naked and dirty, snotty and covered in oil. He was weeping, this boy. There were other people in the same street, but they wouldn't look at him, neither would they approach him, or help him. They looked greatly perturbed by his presence and I realised they were all afraid of this boy, and each of them went out of their way to avoid him. They walked around him, crossed to the other side of the street, some of them turned and walked in the opposite direction rather than meet his pain, others just walked past, eyes to the right or to the floor or dead ahead, pretending they couldn't see him. No-one would help him. I felt the same reaction rise in me and I recoiled in disgust when he looked at me, vying for me to help him, tears streaming down his face. I too wanted to turn away, I was sorely tempted to run away, I definitely felt the urge to pretend I had not seen him.

A benevolent voice, a disembodied narrator in my dream instructed me to 'embrace the black child'. I did as I was guided, even though everything inside me wanted to turn away. I crouched down. I hugged the crying boy. I held him so closely to my breast that there was no separation between us. I picked him up, still tightly held in my embrace. He stopped crying. He became very still and all I felt for this poor boy was love. Then suddenly, and without notice, the boy turned into sand and fell through my arms into millions of granules that were picked up by the wind and carried away.

Afterwards, the next morning, I committed my dream to paper. I didn't want to forget the detail. It felt important that I not lose the essence of this biblical vision. The only difference when I recorded it to paper was a single comma, and it changed the whole context of my vision.

Instead of the narrating voice telling me to, 'embrace the black child' as it had in my vision, I was instructed instead to write, 'embrace the black, child'.

The comma between black and child transformed it from the general to the specific, from the impersonal to the deeply personal, from the social to the metaphysical. 'Embrace the black,' my God was telling me, 'child, embrace the black.'

The reminder encouraged me towards the hospital, where I had a date with my own personal demon. I intended to embrace that demon, and take it in under my care.

The next day, at the hospital, it was exactly as I had expected; rammed. More heads than I could count sat on chairs waiting for their appointment number to be displayed on a large wall clock. I noticed the number on the clock as I entered; number 81 was next in line. I pulled a number out of the machine, which would offer an indication of how long I would have to wait for my turn. Hours I suspected. Days even. Some people have entered waiting rooms like this never to be seen again. My fear was making cartoon exaggerations that even I had to laugh at. As I sat in the Disney-queue, I looked at my number. It was 81. I was confused. What is this sorcery? How can my number be 81? 81 had been called before I took my ticket. It'd been announced before I'd even arrived. I looked at the clock again to make sure that my tired mind was not playing cruel tricks on me, and again I looked at my own number, they were both the same: 81. It was definitely a match. I walked up to the counter where a nurse sat. I said curiously, 'The clock says number

81.' I showed her my matching number. 'Yes,' she said, as though it was the most usual thing in the world, 'you've been called.'

I'd been called.

It was an interesting turn of phrase.

My number had been called even before I'd arrived at the hospital.

I was being looked after.

And that was how the rest of this story unfolded.

My fear, my shadow was using every trick in the book to make me terrified of doctors and hospitals and blood tests, convincing me that even the NHS would lock me into an abyss of medical dogma and painful procedures and then spit me out the other end with vital body parts missing; an emasculated man, with a limp cock, and a broken spirit.

When I faced the fear, when I leaned into those sharp edges, when I challenged my demon-voice to step up, take what it wanted of my body *take all of my body, it's my enemy anyway*, it disappeared like the morning mist.

My bloods came back clean and healthy.

I had the constitution (they said in not so many words) of an elephant.

I had defeated my shadow, denied its existence. In order to capitalise on my victory, I went to see my doctor and asked for a rectal examination in order to doubly confirm what the blood test had robustly reported. The doctor did the examination, confirmed that my prostate was perfect in every aspect and I left elated.

I was never so happy to have a finger poked up my arse.

It doubly confirmed what I had known all along, that the threatened illness was illusory, and my symptoms psychosomatic, the result of a tired and unguarded mind.

I had once again broken through the firmament of an old world and I was floating in the stratosphere of a new frequency.

There would be more challenges to come of course, and in time this new room too would be outgrown, and I'd be invited to pioneer and explore and colonise other densities, and others still, always just one station beyond my current clarity.

This breakthrough, though it was galling and testing to a degree I had never before experienced, would become a powerful reference point for me in future trials. One that I would call on when I fell into another forgetting and another forgetting and yet one more forgetting.

I had fallen.

I was given wings.

Now all I had to do was make great sky circles with my freedom.

But not before I rebuilt my strength. After my hard fall, I was in poor shape. Physically, emotionally, and physiologically I was wasted. The internal war had used up nearly all my internal resources.

I was relieved to have survived my sojourn in the bardo but realised that I would now have to re-build myself. I would have to climb out of the ruins of my old self and re-muscle the physical and psychological infrastructure. There would be greater challenges ahead. I would need all the strength I could find.

In Lord of The Rings, the Tolkien classic, it was said that even Gandalf the Grey did everything he could to avoid a confrontation with his own Balrog, Durin's Bane, who lived deep in the mines of Moria. Eventually, when circumstance forced the Wizard to face his dragon, they met and pitched a ferocious life-and-death battle, might against might, staff against whip, the light magic of a wizard against the molten fire of the monster. The fight concluded with Gandalf and the Balrog, tangled in mortal scrimmage, tumbling over a cliff edge, into the depths of the mines below. Initially, they appeared to have both been killed by the fall.

For Gandalf there was a death, but it was only the demise of his former self, *Gandalf the Grey*. The forthcoming battle he undertook to kill the fire breathing Dis, deep in the mines, needed a new level of wizard, it demanded a metamorphosis, nothing less, a transformation into the more powerful magi, *Gandalf the White*. But Tolkien describes tellingly in the book (not in the film version) that it was not just our hero's fight and defeat of the Balrog that earned him his new station as the white wizard, rather it was the weeks and months it took him to literally crawl on his hands and knees out of the mines of Moria that completed his transition from grey to white. It was only then that Gandalf was able to unite his three armies (body, mind and soul) and take on the might of his enemy Sauron's Orc army. And with his united front, even the ghosts of the ancestors, those stuck in the bardo of broken vows, would fight by his side to win the freedom of Middle Earth.

This is where I was now. Weak, tired, crawling on my hands and knees after the war, building myself up again, and preparing myself for the work that lay ahead. Initially you come out of these very personal trials feeling weaker than when you went in. You think, 'well I got through that', but it doesn't feel as though anything has changed or that you have changed, not really, certainly not so as you would notice. But slowly, subtly, the spoils of your war - the new Siddhas - present themselves. You might be delivering a speech, holding a class or talking to a stranger on the phone, using the same words as you always used, delivering the same advice as before, but they are the same words and the same advice plus Yaqeen. Your delivery is infused with a certainty that is healing, that is stilling, your breath contains a magic that can only come from someone who is possessed of the Holy Spirit. It is too easy, when you're feeling weak to mistake how low you feel for how far you've come.

A spinning wheel appears to be going backwards when it is at its peak speed.

16

Clubbed

I was changed after my recovery. I was different, reborn perhaps, a new man. This newness manifested in many ways. First there was a rush of ideas; newer, broader, deeper, more profound and more abstract and meaningful than any I'd been gifted previously. Ideas were forming like crystals in my mind. The level of my writing changed dramatically too, with new books, new films, and new stage plays queuing for my engagement as far as the third eye could see. They stacked like jumbo jets waiting to land. It was no coincidence that my spiritual promotion coincided too with the final draft of my first feature film script for Jim and Martin (eventually called Clubbed). Martin teamed up with a workaholic director called Neil Thompson (he really did have an insanely strong work ethic), and after a labour-intensive rally around the country securing production funds, they eventually raised £2million and the film was officially financed. I was about to add that raising the money was incredibly demanding, but I suppose that should go without saying.

Trying to pluck £2m out of the economy for any project is a ball-breaking task, let alone trying to raise it for an investment as precarious as film. Most people with money won't give it up without at least some guarantees. Others won't release a penny or a pound unless the guarantee is cast in iron, and an unhealthy portion of them won't give it up at all. They value their fiscal health more than they protect their personal wellbeing. Even the health of their personal relationships often becomes diseased in the pursuit of profit. Many value the $ more than their actual life. I've seen many business-gannets sell their top soul to improve their bottom line. I have witnessed ordinary working men and women twisted spastic by the seductive allure of filthy lucre. I have witnessed it in myself.

We raised our finance, but not by conventional methods, or through traditional means. The general film bodies, set up to fund British film, did not favour our project. Perhaps that's because it was not a generalist film. We didn't tick boxes, and we refused to realign our film so that it concurred with their brief. We didn't receive the support we needed from them. No complainants. It is what it is. I never felt as though anyone ever knocked us back, I always imagined that they were simply nudging us in a different direction, a better direction. A lot of people in the arts are very bitter, they complain endlessly about what they perceive as *the lack of support*. I will not be that man. If I allowed myself to be aggrieved, I'd join a long queue of disempowered excuse-makers, forming lines to make complaints: working class writers, female directors, mature female actors, marginalised minorities all looking to use a social handicap to ensure a special handout. If you happened to be a mature working class female director, from a social minority you could tick all the boxes at once. The governing bodies will be clambering over each other to give you money.

I am exaggerating, but not much.

If I have a handicap, I will do my best to use it to empower the words on the page, not grease the wheels of association.

There's already a long queue of excuse makers, and I will not join it. If I allow myself to blame the world for not meeting my demands, in complaining - or more precisely, in believing my own complaint - I will become disempowered.

If one door closes, another presents itself to be opened by me. If there are no doors available to me, I'll become a carpenter, and I will craft my own bespoke entrance way.

If I really want to go BIG, I will let God be my doorman.

As with *Brown Paper Bag*, we raised the money to make our film privately, this time through independent business men and women, and through fans of *Watch My Back* (which the film was based on), who were either happy to take a punt on our film, or patronise us simply because they liked what we were about. There were many of the latter, and I have always been grateful to them.

Watching *Clubbed* come together was a strangely unreal metaphysical experience. I'd written words on the page, and suddenly here we were, in a large empty warehouse in East London watching a full-sized working nightclub (where the majority of the film is set) being built by carpenters to the exact specifications in my script. My ink was lifting from the page, it was coming to life. The characters I'd written, the scenes I'd described, the locations I'd specified suddenly appeared before me too, as if by some strange magic. There was one very surreal moment that really stood out for me. In the script there was a scene where the lead character Danny (played brilliantly by Mel Raido) was standing on the edge of a very busy dance floor. My description of the scene was very simple: 'Danny watches a scantily clad lady on the dance floor'. The next thing I know I am on set watching the scene being shot and there on the dance floor was the 'scantily clad lady' (portrayed by the beautiful Page 3 model Michelle Marsh) I'd written. She was dressed in little more than a spray tan. I remember stealing a glance and thinking, 'note to myself'.

Me and Sharon were on set every day, and when it was a night shoot, we stayed with the process until daybreak. After a night shoot, we would walk hand in hand through the waking city back to our hotel for breakfast and a well-earned sleep. This film was a long time in the coming, and I did not want to miss even a moment of it. Watching a film being shot is magical, and it is also fantastically instructive. There are lessons and certainties from observing the process that cannot be learned in any other way. I was grateful that our producer Martin understood this and made sure that I was welcome on set.

It eventually took us fifteen years to get Clubbed written, financed, cast and in the can. But what a small cost, if it is spent creating proof of certainty. Once you have made one feature length film, making the next is easier and the next easier still.

Clubbed had a cinema release (very unusual for an independent film), and we were blessed with three premieres: Birmingham, London's West End and Paris, France. I'd gone from a depressed young adult living a two-up-two-down existence in the suburbs of Coventry, to travelling through Paris by taxi looking at billboard-sized posters of '*Le Club*' (the French title of *Clubbed*). It was an incredible time, and though not all the critics appreciated our film, we found a vast post-cinema audience online. For me it was less about pushing the film across the finish line, and much more about the inner obstacles I had to remove en route.

From the outside looking in, film appears to be a fantastical world, a rare and unique reality, an employ that very few people get a chance to experience. Behind the curtain however, it is not always quite so glamorous. Like the martial arts I was concurrently exploring, appearance and reality are rarely in accord. Also, just like in the martial arts, narcissism in film is pandemic. There is a lot of desperation, too many film makers chasing too few bursaries, which produces ugly bulges of insecurity, in the artists, in the production, and in the distributors of funds. Film had always been a famine or feast affair, now it was more a case of *famine or small snack*. To mix metaphors, vows are handed out like candy, and broken like Greek wedding plates the moment a better opportunity presents itself. Rather than relying on their own God-given talent, coat-tails are sought in this industry, rode on, and then disembarked the second a new flavour-vehicle enters the traffic. On one job, I was encouraged by a prominent producer to 'drop the director' because 'someone better' had become available. I rang him up and said, 'look, everyone in this business is fucking everyone else, and I am not prepared to be that man.' My job on the film disappeared quicker than a politician's promise. On another film I wrote, the producers flat refused to pay many of the artists, who had to start legal action before their fees were honoured. I have watched very good people turn into insidious creatures, over the space of a six-week shoot. I have witnessed people lie, cheat, and connive, then deny they ever uttered a dishonest word, all in the space of a sixty-minute meeting. And for what? A film!

Other so-called professionals have just been unsavoury. They have been cruelly unkind to souls who deserved better, without cause or justification, and for me that is the greatest sin of all.

If they could feel even a fraction of the atonement that I'd had to go through in recompense for my own sins, they would never cast a slight again, of that I am sure.

Then there were other times, where this was not how it went down, and I had an altogether different experience, where I felt nothing but bliss, bliss, bliss. I can't even begin to describe how it felt to watch Ray Winstone (in *Bouncer*) still a whole film set when his character held a dying friend in his arms. Or to witness James Cosmo (in *The Pyramid Texts*) bring an audience of five hundred people to tears with a performance that was bone deep. Or to feel the chill that ran up and down my spine when Jo McInnis (in *Brown Paper Bag*) delivered one of the most harrowing scenes

I have ever seen in film. Observing the ovation of a tear-soaked audience as they watched Quinn Patrick (in *We'll Live and Die in These Towns*) enacting a dying man's lament for his lost poetry, will never leave me. And Craig Conway (in *Romans 12:20*) literally quaked my insides with his performance of a child abuse victim forgiving his attacker. This has only happened to me, without exception, when the project was not led by the pay cheque. The degree of moral corruption I have personally seen in film could usually be measured by the level of coin in the contracts.

I learned so much about who I was not in the process of making *Clubbed*, enabling me to get one step closer to who I actually was.

As *Clubbed* was coming to a close, and making its way from cinema to DVD, I was presented with another film that I (knew) I needed to write, a film at the next level of cleansing.

Romans 12:20 was a thirty minute script I wrote for two visionary directors, called the Shammasian brothers. Let me be very honest about this from the start: *Romans 12: 20* was a film I definitely did not want to write but it was a film I knew I must write. The Shammasian brothers had entered my life some years before. Paul was a budding filmmaker who'd made a documentary about my life. I loved his wanderlust, his boundless curiosity and the fact that he was actually making films whilst most people were sitting in cafés talking about making films and bemoaning the lack of resources available for them to do so. He was out there. He was pulling the funding he needed from out of the air, he was making it work. I loved him. Later his brother Ludwig, a man of immense integrity, joined him on his quest and they became a powerful directing partnership.

They invited me to a screening in London to see an impressive short film they'd made called *The Carriageway*. I loved what they did with it. The combination of script, performance, music and camerawork was very accomplished. I remember saying to Sharon, 'can you imagine what they'd do with one of my scripts?' Almost as soon as the words had left my lips the brothers approached me, 'Do you think you could write a film for us to direct, perhaps that handshake story?'

Handshake story?

I was confused: 'What handshake story?'

They were referring to a story I'd written in *Watch My Back* about how I'd forgiven the man who sexually abused me as a child. I'd crossed paths with him in a strange quirk of serendipity, some twenty years after the initial assault, and instead of killing him dead where he stood, I found a sudden and unexpected burst of compassion. I shook his hand, and I forgave him instead. The boys had been moved and surprised by the story and now they were asking me to write it into a short film.

The moment they mentioned the abuse story my heart sank.

I'd written about this incident - the abuse and the forgiveness - in my book and naively believed that this constituted a complete psychological cleansing of the incident. I'd forgiven the abuser. I shook his hand. I recorded my testimony in print, move on... *can't we move on from this, I've done it, I've written about it, it is done.*

I didn't want to look at this story again.

The very idea filled me with trepidation.

The fear, the foreboding, the reluctance and the emotion behind my reluctance were bubbles rising from a puncture in me that was so tiny I didn't even know it was still there. This invisible wound had determined and directed my whole life thus far.

But I'd forgiven him. It was over. Wasn't it?

Apparently not.

If we do not see a thing through to its end, Siddhartha warns us, we will have to keep repeating and keep re-living it over and over with all the associated pain and emotions until we do.

A thing is either completely dead or it is still alive; there is no in-between.

Forgiveness has layers. It has depths. And until they have all been fathomed, the cleansing will always remain incomplete.

I felt I had done sterling work when I met the man who'd betrayed me as a boy. It had taken all my courage to stand in front of this manifest demon and splash the holy water of forgiveness in his face. And yet, although I'd faced him down said kind words and shaken his hand - the bastard-children of his dark, dark work - the effects of his abuse on me, the unfolding consequence of his actions over one child-grooming year, stretched out and lived with me and lived in me and lived off me like invisible parasites, for all my childhood, and for much of my damaged adult life.

The inceptive cause has to be removed, yes. But what of the effects of that cause? The effects of abuse, if they are not met, if they are not healed at source, become their own cause, creating more effects and causes in a perpetual motion of distorted action and consequence. Left to their own devices they multiply like cancer cells, unless their momentum is stopped by some greater force. The abuse I was subjected to as a child, determined every decision I made from there on after, not least the choice I made as an adult to turn myself into a killing machine, in an hysterical and pathetic attempt to protect myself from a cruel and threatening world. Now that God had atoned the violence within me, I became acutely aware of its genesis, the initiating cause. I knew that the brutality I inflicted as a bouncer was a displaced reaction to the abuse I received as a child.

The abuser fractured and divided my perception as an eleven year old boy, forcing my vision of the world to project through distorted filters. He was not only the cause of my violence towards others but also the cause of my self-harm, the physical and sexual violence I had heaped upon my own body ever since I was a child. This was something that no-one else knew about. I had not shared my depravities with a single soul, not my mother, not my father, not my family or friends, not even my wife. Only I knew. It was my dirty little secret. And God of course. He knew everything about me, about my damage, and about the healing of my ugly lacerations. He knew, and now in an act of divine grace, He was saying, 'look at this Geoffrey, do not tarry, and do not turn away.'

I told Paul and Lud that I would write the film.

I had to. There was no choice. By this time I knew enough about spiritual ascension to understand that if I was met with opposition on my path, and filled with fear along the way, if a job made me feel like running in the opposite direction, it was something I needed to look at.

If there is opposition, you can be sure that there is opportunity.

And if there is great opposition, the opportunity presented will be proportionate to the challenge.

I also naively said yes to this film believing that it would definitely be the end of it. If I wrote this film, the full story would be out and, it would be cleansed and I would be free. Had I known that this film would precipitate the three most challenging projects of my entire life on the same topic - a stage play (*Fragile*) a feature film (*Romans*) and a TED Talk - I might well have stopped before I even started. I'm sure I would have complained to my God, as I had complained to Him so many times before, 'you ask too much of me Lord'. But if I'd done that, if I had refused to step up, I would have missed out not only on three beautiful projects and the souls I met while bringing them together, I would have missed out on the level of consciousness I experienced as a direct and immediate consequence of making more room for Him.

I wrote Romans 12:20.

It was a story based entirely on my own experience with abuse and forgiveness but I introduced - or I was intuited to include - artistic licence. This allowed the film to be bigger than just my story. It became an amalgamation of many true stories, weaved into a thirty minute narrative.

The writing of this very simple arc (so simple I wasn't even sure if it was any good) triggered a series of strange and mysterious occurrences and revelations.

The man who abused me was still walking the earth at the time of writing *Romans 12:20*. He was still in the world, which meant he was still a danger to people, he was still a living threat to young children. As an adult, some years before, when I'd grown hairs on my balls, and found a conscience, and a little moral courage I sought judicial retribution for this historical crime. I approached the police and I reported what had happened to me as a boy. I won't bore you with the detail only to say that the policeman taking my statement seemed more concerned about whether I was complicit in the abuse, than he did with hauling an active paedophile before a court of law.

I have to stipulate here, that the physical nature of the abuse in my case was not severe, I was not raped or physically damaged in any way, only touched sexually on that one night. It was the weight of the abuser and his dark and palpable intent that left me ungloved. It was the shock of waking in the dead of night, pitch black, to intruding fingers inside my underwear, waking up to a large hand clumsily unbuttoning my pyjama bottoms, my penis out, my genitals fully exposed, and the terror of eventually lifting that adult hand off my naked thigh and bottom, again and again and again. And that stark, urgent realisation that I had to remain in the highest possible state of alert for the rest of the night (for the rest of my life). It was as though I had woken into a real-life horror film where I was the victim, and the unseen monster was behind me in the same bed. The fact that he was unseen was what made it all the more frightening. If you can see the monster, if you can bring some light to the situation, there is at least a healthy chance of exposing it. But when it remains hidden in the dark, it incubates and the imagination projects your fear onto every future situation that falls outside of your control, every potential threat might be that invisible monster-hand looking to rape and pillage. My back was to him, lying asleep on my side. I can remember it vividly. Perhaps this is what made it all the worse, this is what caused the greatest alarm. I was not able to physically see my abuser. There was not a single point where I had the courage to turn and look at him. I was literally frozen to the spot. It was as though a disembodied hand, a hand with its own autonomy, a hand that pierced through the darkness, right out of a Hammer Horror movie was invading my body. Just a hand, but undoubtedly a heavy hand, the hand of a big man, the hand of a persistent and disturbed man. It was the stuff of nightmares, blind abuse, waking to a ghost hand on my body. It was not just what was happening to me in the present moment that left me in abject terror; it was the very fearful anticipation of what might happen next if I closed my eyes for even a second. It was the feeling of being completely out of control. I was eleven years old. I had no control whatsoever. I was at his mercy. And this I realised was my legacy; this is what he left me. This was the real abuse, a mind left in a constant state of fearful alert, always anticipating that something terrible might happen at any moment if I did not always, always, always stay in complete control of every situation, of every person, of every life event. This fear stayed with me for most of my adult life. I guess that's why I perfected so many martial skills in my early development. To stay in control. If people stepped across my threshold, I battered them. This is why I became a teacher. To stay in control. I can see now how I had carefully orchestrated my whole life from that moment on so that I was never exposed to situations where I was not the one in complete control. I remember once, when a director wrote over a film script I was working on. It is bad etiquette to do this of course, but my reaction to his clumsy oversight was unkind and completely off the scale. I was absolutely incensed and emotional and nearly crying with a cocktail of fear and rage and dissonance. I said to the producer emotionally, like I was a betrayed boy and he was a parental figure who had not protected me, 'I can't believe you let that cunt get inside my pants.'

The events I felt I couldn't control were the ones that triggered this disassociated anxiety the most, a fear completely disproportionate to the situations that triggered them. I experienced chronic insecurity because I knew that, in reality, deep down, below my bevy of impressive defence mechanisms and posturing bluster, I was still an adolescent child with no control over what happened to me. I feared that if I lost my grip of a situation, any situation, and my defences were broken, that hand would advance from the darkness and I would be eleven all over again, exposed to unknowable and unspeakable abuse. And the psychotic jealousy too, it always spiked when I felt I could not subtly, covertly (but unconsciously) control the partner I was with. This left me stuck in an existential limbo, a very tiring life of constant anxiety and painful confusion. The moment I tried to control the things and the people of the world in order to keep my anxiety at bay, I became the despotic horror-hand, the monster that I had been trying to run away from for all these years.

I couldn't control everything, in all honesty I was not really in control of anything at all other than myself, and even then I was flawed and my abilities limited. There are a million things that can happen to any one of us at any moment that we have no control over. I can't control the world and its people, I cannot, all I can realistically hope to do is choose the way I react to what does happen to me and perhaps that is control enough.

All of this was dismissed by the policeman taking my statement, as though the assault was not serious enough to consider, as though the year of insidious grooming, my night of absolute terror and the years of subsequent emotional disturbance were not relevant. I was eleven years old for fuck's sake. The abuse had greatly damaged my young psyche. As a teenager, I would find myself kissing a girl, and my abuser's face would suddenly morph over hers, literally, stubble and all, and I'd recoil in horror.

At that age there can be no such thing as complicity. At that age there is no such thing as casual abuse and serious abuse. To me there was no difference between physical damage and psychological damage. Damage is damage. It would take many years before I could mentally repair, many years of displaced self-harm and physical violence, and the torture of wildly distorted images and beliefs before

I would be able to face down my fears, and bring my mind back to any kind of balance. The negative conditioning left me perplexed and guilty too but because the psychological damage was not immediately on view, it was not considered a serious crime. I wrote fictionalised versions of my story – the play, the films etc. – where I used amalgams to both share the stories of other abuse victims and explore my own distorted perceptions. I did this as a way to try and heal their fractures at the same time as mine. The assault against me was psychological, it was definitely spiritual, but that does not mean it was not serious.

'Did you get aroused?' The policeman asked me, with a nervous smile, and a suspicious twitch. At the time I was so incensed that I could have ripped his head off and used his neck as a bedpan. I know that he was probably just doing his job, he was asking all the questions that needed to be asked but, in my head, in my mind, all I heard was, 'Did you enjoy it? Were you complicit?' Which was front-loaded with the same implicit assumption: that I led my attacker on. The single accusation that all victims of abuse dread and fear the most: 'It was all your fault'.

This was just the first of many revelations and hidden rages that the writing of the *Romans 12: 20* drew out of me and exposed. Themes that I would later hunt down, draw out and exorcise in ever greater detail, on the page, on the stage and on the screen.

'Did you lead him on?'

The question itself, asked or implied, exposes an astonishing level of ignorance concerning sexual crimes against children. It is the one question that should never be asked. It can stain the child for the rest of their life. It places the blame for this heinous affront firmly on the shoulders of the victims, most of whom never escape the shame that comes with the accusation, even if it is only suggested or hinted at.

I wrote the film. It was a very simple script. The best ones usually are. I felt a great reluctance to send it to Paul and Ludwig, our directors. I thought I was worried because they might not like it, perhaps they'd think it a poor excuse for a script. Really I was afraid that in sending my work I would not be able to stop the subsequent unfolding.

Opposition.

I felt the adverse forces of resistance.

Opposition is painful, but it is always a good sign.

Energies will show you the potential of you endeavour by the level of their oppose. It is proportionate. I felt a mighty fear with this film, and with its subject matter, so I knew I'd hit a rich vein. In my world, fear, opposition, are not the red stop sign of metaphor, for me they signal green for go, go, go.

I sent the script to the directors.

The next day, literally the next day, I was in the conservatory at home when Sharon shouted through from the front room; 'did you see this in the newspaper?' She walked into the room, looking a little pale, newspaper in hand, opened at the offending page. 'The man who abused you when you were a boy… the police have arrested him.'

I looked at the newspaper. I hurriedly scanned the article. He had been charged with several historical counts of sexual abuse from the 1970s, which was the same period he'd groomed and assaulted me. One of the many victims was his own disabled nephew.

A shiver ran through my body, not just the shiver of serendipity but the cold shake of confirmation. It was confirmed. It was true. I was not a liar as some people (who should have known better) had insinuated. It did happen, and not just to me. I had not lied about it or exaggerated it or imagined it in any way.

This was the second most powerful revelation that came from the writing of *Romans 12:20*. I was not a liar. He had abused more people, lots more people, not just me. Were they all lying? I found myself saying these lines over and over in my head. I was saying them to my mum, to my dad, to the police, to the whole fucking world. I was also saying it to myself. It did happen and you were not alone.

After the abuse, the night after, at breakfast in the boys' club where the assault had happened, I was red-eyed, broken, deeply afflicted, sad *and old*. I felt ancient, like an old man living in the skin of a young, young boy. I said to the teacher, 'someone was touching me in the night.' He smiled and winked reassuringly, 'Are you sure you didn't just imagine it?'

Sexual grooming is subtle, but it is potent; man it is so potent. It makes you doubt what occurred. It makes you question your own experience. It wants you to believe that what happened did not happen at all, it was a fantasy, the wild imaginings of an attention seeking child. What kind of a twisted mind could believe that a boy, never hardly kissed a girl yet, would be imagining abuse at the hands of an adult, or that he would even be capable of knowing what that means?

'It didn't happen, you only imagined it'.

Even now, at fifty-nine years of age, easing towards my seventh decade on this spinning planet, I can still hear the ghost of accusation in the distant recesses, 'you're getting a lot of mileage out of this; you're exaggerating this; this never happened'.

I write about it and I write about it and I continue to write about it in the hope that this writing or any of the multiple-genre versions of this writing will proffer unconditional love to someone, somewhere in the world who has been damaged and had their innocence and their peace of mind stolen by abuse. I pray that these words will reach those brave survivors and hold them in a comforting embrace.

Paul and Ludwig loved the first draft of the script.

We moved it around a bit, took scenes out here, added words there (they came up with some of the strongest imagery in the film); we tinkered and tweaked it for the next few weeks until we had what we all agreed was a final draft, the shooting script. Ludwig (who is a great producer as well as an acclaimed director) managed to secure some private equity (£30k) to make the film so we set a date to shoot and started the process of casting. Probably a month after finishing the script, I was on the phone talking to an old friend. His son was a young actor and we were considering him for a part in our film. My friend didn't know that my script was autobiographical, so it was completely innocent and strangely arbitrary when he asked if I'd heard the news about 'the teacher from the boys' club?' He was completely unaware that the man he was talking about was the one who'd sexually abused me as a boy.

'He's dead!' My friend exclaimed. 'He committed suicide. They found him hanged in a hotel room in London.'

My friend had no idea of the impact this news had on me. He could not have known. The fact that this man had committed suicide was shocking to me, not least because in *Romans 12:20*, the abuser also commits suicide after he is confronted with the historical abuse he enacted on boys.

I told Sharon the news.

'What do you feel?' she asked.

'Compassion', I said. 'I feel compassion.'

The film was ordained, of that I was sure.

Another sign of the film's righteous nature was our association with Oscar winning musician Lisa Gerrard. Ludwig managed to get a rough cut of the finished film to her, with samples of her music from *Inside Man* and *Gladiator* laid over certain, pivotal scenes. She watched the film, and said it was the best use of the music she had seen and allowed us to use the samples free of charge.

Yet one more blessing came from my friend Warner Stephens. He generously gifted directors Paul and Ludwig £15k so that they could screen *Romans 12:20* in Los Angeles, USA, which was a qualifying criterion for Oscar consideration. Although we never shortlisted on this occasion, the trip (and the film) did enough to secure Paul and Ludwig one of the biggest movie agents in the business.

The film won a glut of international awards.

One British festival actually created a brand new category as part of their programme just so that they could include our film.

When we screened to a stunned audience in London's West End, one man (I will call him P), a complete stranger to me, wept and held me so tightly afterwards that I feared he might never let me go. He too had been abused as a boy. He too had suffered the post assault cavalcade of unwanted and disturbing thoughts, images and beliefs that often affected his mental health. He stayed in touch with me, this lovely man, and told me some weeks later that watching the film had encouraged him to report his own historical abuse to the police. As a result of his brave actions, his attacker was arrested and charged. In a second twist of fate, unable to face the judicial consequences, P's abuser took his own life before the case ever reached a court room. There was an ironic sense of divine justice running through the veins of this whole film.

The process of making *Romans 12:20* was revelatory.

I uncovered aspects of myself that I realised had always been there but were hidden in plain sight. These were truths that I would never have uncovered without this film.

During the filming, I remember talking to the make-up girl one day about the lead character (Malky), about his scars and his tattoos. 'He needs them,' I said with emotional sincerity, 'he needs those, they are his protection.'

I told her that the character's facial scars, the broken nose, the cauliflower ear, they were important too. 'When (our lead character) Malky was a boy,' I told her, 'he had long hair and female features, he looked like a girl, in fact he was often mistaken for a girl. The scars are his mask. They are an unconscious attempt to make himself look physically ugly in case anyone else is attracted to him, in case anyone else tries to abuse him. And the tattoos, they're his war paint. They say to any would-be abuser, *fuck off! Stay away. Leave me be - I am fucking dangerous.* The layers of muscle all over Malky's body, that's his armour.' I went on to explain that the character's inch deep, yard wide back was his shield. As I spoke about the importance of Malky's armour, his war paint, his musculature, and his need for bodily protection I realised that I was talking about myself. I realised for the very first time the unconscious lengths I had gone to in order to never again be controlled and abused by anyone.

My whole life up until this one point had been dedicated to building myself into a walking armoury so that I could protect myself from this abuser and others of his ilk.

Layers and layers below my suit of armour that small frightened kid, little Geoffrey, was still there. In stasis. Eternally eleven. Forever pinned below the body mass and the probing and defiling fingers of a soul thief. The realisation hit me so hard that I broke down in the middle of a room full of film crew and I wept.

Someone rushed out and made tea.

So British; in a crisis, we do not hug, we do not console, we make tea.

The next time I looked in the mirror all I could see looking back at me were the scars the badges of battle, the throbbing bulk, the flag-waving, drum-beating tattoos. My life, I realised, had been an orchestrated campaign of fort building and armour collecting that I did not consciously know I was participating in. I couldn't lose the scars of course, or the tattoos, and neither did I wish to. The disfigurements, the ink, the deformed knuckles and the broken face, they were the evidence of my journey, the map of my path and I would learn to be perversely proud of them.

This new powerful realisation about the scars and the armoury led to a palpable energy shift in my body, in my mind and in my life. Something in me moved and the movement acted as the catalyst to another powerful vision. Post Plymouth (where we produced my play *Doorman*), I felt an energy block in my bladder. I detailed this earlier. Now, post *Romans 12:20*, there was a palpable bloat in my belly, that had nothing to do with the amount of mushroom curries I was eating. At the time I didn't associate it with *Romans 12:20* at all, I had yet to identify the link. It wasn't painful as such, it was just *present*, it was just *there*, and it was letting me know. I didn't understand its purpose, though I sensed the energy was personal, that it was conscious, that it was trapped and that it was looking for release. I felt as though a hidden energy had been loosened from its moorings and was now free-floating in my body, looking for a safe exit point. I spoke with an old friend of mine, Tony, a former student, now a skilled counsellor. I told him about the block and he recommended I see his friend Helen (Braithwaite). She was a seasoned counsellor and a shaman who used sound therapy (known as *sound baths*) to help shift blocked emotions. The use of sound as a healing force is not new. Indigenous tribes have always used it, to this day, but it is largely unheard of in the developed West. It is a potent tool, used to locate and dissolve inner constrictions. The Shaman (in my case Helen) employs an impressive array of instruments (gongs, rattles, horns, drums, the human voice etc.) in their work, to penetrate, free up and/or removed human fatbergs. The healing session and the sound-instruments used in each session are individual and bespoke, and they are wholly determined by the nature of your complaint. The shaman intuitively chooses specific sound-vibrations to meet personal needs.

I was always open to new therapies. During my atonement years I investigated every therapeutic method in order to heal, so the idea of a sound bath, though a little exotic, did not offend my sensibilities. Ready for a new experience, and in the hope of removing the constriction, I contacted Helen, asked if she could help, and we arranged a session.

On the day of my sound bath, I lay on a couch in the back room of Helen's house, specially converted for the purpose of healing and counselling. I had never had a sound bath before, so I didn't really know what to expect. Helen is a consummate professional, she told me as much as she could about what might occur, but she also told me that the bath was individually experiential; everyone experienced it in their own unique way.

I lay down on a consultation couch and put an eye mask on to block out the light. I closed my eyes. I waited. Helen started to play the sound instruments. At times (when she felt called) she even sang. I can remember a strong egocentric resistance rising in me almost immediately, a scared voice saying *this is a bit weird*. It was trying to convince me that the very idea of a sound bath was silly and that *nothing is happening*, and *nothing will happen*. I was patently aware of the ego-nature. If the ego was making a lot of noise, it was because I was in divine proximity and it was causing it to squirm. I quietened the voice. I clicked into the observer-self and immersed my conscious attention into the very heart of the sounds as they entered my body. Just when it felt as though I was not going to experience anything at all, I felt a physical movement in my lower spine. It was as real as if someone had placed their hand firmly on the small of my back, and moved it upwards, only this was on the inside of my body and not on the outside. It wasn't painful in any way, but it was substantial, and it moved up my body with its own autonomy. The energy had a healing signature. It was deeply caring. It was in me, but I knew that it was not of me. As the energy moved up my body, I had to physically adjust my position on the couch and arch my back to allow it a thoroughfare. I could feel that it was heading towards the energy that was stuck in my abdomen and as it reached the block, it sat behind it and slowly, gently pushed it up towards my chest. As the movement reached my sternum, several very large, translucent, almost formless beings appeared around and over me. Although they were largely featureless, their presence was as clear as it was certain. Mine was like a patient's point of view, looking up from an operating table, as doctors hover over and do their work. As soon as the energy reached my breastbone, my chest gaped open, and one of the beings reached deep inside my body with both arms and very gently, very lovingly lifted out a child.

He was a boy of about eleven years.

It didn't feel as though the boy was dead, but he was definitely not conscious. I innately knew that these beings would take the boy and care for him. They exuded so much compassion that I can't even begin to measure it.

The beings took the boy away in their arms and disappeared from my view.

It was only after the session, when I told Helen about my experience that the full emotion hit me. As soon as I mentioned the boy that was taken from my body, I broke down in tears.

I was eleven years old when I was sexually abused, the same age as this boy. I intuited that the night I was assaulted - most of which is completely lost from my memory - something innocent in me either died or was shocked into a suspended state. These beings were recovering - or helping me to recover and repair - the psychological schema that was left as a result of the assault. I suspect that this trapped child, this energy-form inside me, was like a breached baby, unable to pass through the womb entrance and the spirit beings, were conducting some kind of spiritual caesarean section.*

After the sound bath I expanded again.

Of course.

When you remove an obscuration, your view clears automatically and proportionately. This is standard form in the metaphysical milieu, so I shouldn't have been surprised. But of course, I was surprised, as I always am. I don't know whether this was just some kind of unconscious, psychological safety mechanism I'd put in place, or a divine system installed to improve me by degree but, for some reason, every time I took on a very difficult challenge, I always kidded myself that, *this will be the last one*. And naturally it never is, it always leads on to the next challenge and the next ad infinitum. Our potential to grow is boundless, and our rate of growth is entirely commensurate with our willingness to accept challenge.

Whatever was removed from me had made room and once again I was rewarded with a wider consciousness. Under Helen's sound care (forgive the pun) I was witness to something beautiful, undoubtedly it was supernatural, and it opened my eyes to worlds beyond the everyday. Fears that are exposed and removed

---

* I have fully detailed this and other sound bath visions in *The Divine CEO*.

reveal deeper fears that, in turn also need to be addressed, like a Russian Doll (or Matryoshka doll) containing ever decreasing versions of itself *within* itself, so each removed fear reveals a concentrated version of itself, deeper inside, which in turn, has another concentration deeper inside that, and so on. The deeper you go the denser the fear appears to be, and the more difficult it is to remove it.

It would take the surgeon's scalpel of my trusty pen to write my next shadow out. *Romans 12:20* was a powerful poultice. It drew to the surface disturbing emotions and addictions that I had not, until now, consciously acknowledged.

It was by entering this cauldron of *bubbling blood and fire*, that my next project was revealed. It was a stage play that would eventually be called Fragile, a story that would expose everything left inside me that I was mortally afraid to face, specifically the mother of all Balrogs, shame.

In the Tao Te Ching, the Taoist sage Lao Tzu advises us, when confounded by a seemingly unassailable problem, to 'identify the children, when you have identified the children, trace the children back to their mother. Once you have located the mother, you have found the cure'. My previous projects saw me facing the overt expressions of my blocks, nakedly, and without rationalisation or excuse. These were the children, and through honest, written dialectics I was able to identify them. Now, with Fragile I was being directed to trace the children back to their mother, with the assurance that when I located the matriarchal cause I would find my cure.

I was still shadow hunting, I was still facing fears, and I was still climbing after thirty years on the mountain. But this was no external pyramid. This was a peak, certainly, but it was inverted, and the climb was down and not up. I was being called to scale deep and fathom the terrors of my unconscious.

I had been avoiding this *willing descent* since I was a boy.

Writing Fragile and walking it through to production proved to be a whole other level of exorcism. I used this play as a way of casting out demons. I intuitively knew that the adverse forces actively opposing the play would be consumed in the act of committing it to the page and stage. Perhaps that's why they resisted me so violently; surely that is why they opposed me so steadfastly.

Making Fragile would take me to the very edge of my last nerve, and I would be forced to stand before, not only the lower demon, but also the higher echelons of my soul.

As I will detail later, I felt more fear when I was shown the Soul, than when I faced the Satan.

The inner deviants that I was now being called to remove had been there all along, I was just unable to see them before. I realised, as I sat down to write the first draft of Fragile, that certain sordid and depraved *behaviours* - and I will detail these shortly - had been a dominating constant in my life since I was exploited as a boy. This man groomed me, abused me and then disappeared. But, as I mentioned earlier, he left his parasite in me, a twisted perception, a divided belief, and in his absence I was abused again and again and once again for the next thirty years, by my own hands, under the command of his sickness, left inside me like malware.

They had always been there, but they were a shameful secret (and we are only ever as sick as our secrets), and the cause was hidden deep below the surface, so I was never fully conscious of it. The cause was so far removed from the effects, referred and triangulated many times over, that I had never been able to trace them back. Some of these were revealed in the writing of *Romans 12:20*, but evidently not all. To be honest, I didn't even know there was anything to trace back to. I would not even have understood the concept of causation. I thought the behaviours were my behaviours, and the habits *my* habits. I always believed too, that the crippling insecurity I'd always felt was mine and mine alone. And the depravities were not just mine, they were me, they were who I was. I wasn't to know that the backboard of my human nature was without blemish. It was hidden from me that my original view was perfectly clear, undefiled and the scales that had obscured my vision, were forced onto my young eyes by a hideously warped teacher.

Abuse often enters covertly. It seeds its tare of dark impression and then leaves like a thief in the night.

It leaves, but its stain does not.

Its stain remains - the parasite of effect. It leaves its print in you, it impresses its stamp on your psyche and that dark impression grows, it grows in you and alongside you, and because it grows at the same rate, you don't recognise that it is not you. It's like a secret, hidden sub-personality, a pain-body that can lie dormant for days, weeks or years, until a situation or a stimulus arouses it, then it rises from its slumber and acts inappropriately, in you and through you and as you. Then, afterwards, it descends back into the depths and leaves the real you befuddled, confused and disturbed by your own uncharacteristic behaviour.

The shadow consumes like a gannet in the restaurant of life and the self has to pick up the bill.

Post *Romans 12:20*, I was able to see this for the first time. I was able to see what I was unable, unwilling or unprepared to see before.

And what you can see you can clean.

So what was this aberration, this abhorrent behaviour and why had I not removed it?

Let me answer the last part of this question first: I had not tackled this issue before because of *fear* and because of *pleasure*.

Fear was the more powerful of the two emotions, but pleasure followed not far behind, and I will come to this shortly.

The fear felt like it was the most powerful I had encountered so far on my earthly sojourn. As I have already mentioned, up until this point in my life I had faced many very frightening situations, some of them encounters with aggressors who tried to end my existence. But in reality, all the fears I had embraced on my pilgrimage were proven on close inspection to be illusory. This one too was an elaborate hoax, but it felt real enough to bring me to the point of breakdown several times. It was the same exaggerated mind-projections - selling a spill as a flood and a flame as a towering inferno - that threatened to raze my life to the ground many times before.

And pleasure, I spoke of pleasure as a stumbling block to freedom. The behaviour that I was in a secret covenant with, filled me with fear, but it also brought (something in me) pleasure, and pleasure is as hard to surrender as one's life blood.

But what are the specifics of this behaviour that even now with all my learning I am still reluctant to commit to the page? Even as I write these words, I can hear my opposition, the enemy, screaming out from its murky void, 'Boring! You've written about this already, twenty times, why again? Your poor wife is going to have to read this shit. She'll be disgusted by you. She'll judge you. She will be ashamed of you. She will leave you.'

I had to write it again and once more because there would be elements in this next telling that were not included in the last, and if there is one thing I am certain of it is this: before we can at last enter the kingdom, we must first attend to our dead.

So, what was my dirty hidden secret?

Sexual self-harm.

This is the behaviour that I felt most afraid to write about in detail.

When this seedy shadow rose in me it was not the kind of arousal that I could sate with masturbation or intercourse with a loving partner. I had a beautiful, healthy and monogamous sexual relationship with my wife, and any other sexual expression outside of that should have been completely unnecessary. But when this darkness alighted in me it was so potent that it often took me over. I felt like a bystander in my own body, watching from the side lines as strange hands - not my own hands - ravaged my body. Lately this addiction had weakened, and the occurrences were less frequent. Sometimes I could go for months without feeling it, and then suddenly it would be stimulated and it would rise like fire and boom! I was taken over again.

In the throes of this vile possession I would rape myself.

Anything phallic would be used in a frantic lust for a promised pleasure that never came, just physical damage, sometimes blood, and then days and days of confusion and shame that fed my shadow just as readily as the porn I watched fed it. Looking at it now, post healing, (this shadow was evicted long ago) the pain-body felt like a lion devouring the meat and fat of its prey, and the leftovers were pickings for the smaller, scavenging creatures; the shame and self-loathing and confusion, that skulked in after the kill, and consumed what was left.

That's how it felt to me. And trying to remove this pain-body with willpower alone was not working for me. Even though I was generally well practiced in the art of self-control, this one enemy - what the mystic Gurdjieff called *the chief feature* – seemed unassailable, and that made me feel even worse. It emasculated me.

My wife knew about my problem with pornography, and she was supportive in helping me to eschew it, but she didn't know about the self-abuse. This was something I'd never shared with a living soul. Deep shame rose up in me every time I even contemplated exposing it, in my attempt at weakening its hold.

The very idea of anyone knowing that I had consistently abused myself sexually filled me with so much fear and shame that, until *Fragile*, I was unable to verbally share it with anyone, let alone write a letter of confession to the world. Just the thought made me feel dirty and disgusting. It was so secret that the fear of being exposed was used by the adverse forces to blackmail me into deep depressions. The thought of anyone knowing *what I was really like* was anathema. And now I was going to share it for the very first time with everyone, all at once.

Psychologists will confirm that, when the initiating cause of abuse is sexual, the pain-body (or schema) that grows in the victim often develops an unhealthy proclivity towards sex. This shadow is addictively drawn towards sexual extremes. In my own case, I never expressed the sexual abuse outwards, towards other people, the harm was always turned in, it was restricted to myself, to my own body (physical and sexual self-harm) and to my own mind (self-hatred and shame). I also had an unhealthy penchant for pornography, unhealthy because it fed the parasite that I needed to starve.

I've already mentioned the displaced physical violence I enacted on others as a bouncer. I described how I cleansed my errors through atonement and renunciation. Writing Fragile helped me to understand why this had been so vitally important: violence is a rich source of energy that the pain-body feeds on, it keeps it alive. It will feed off any human drama, especially where it occurs in extremes. Now, in this next confrontation, I was being asked to remove its subsidiary means of consumption, so that I could starve it out of me completely, and make my body, mind and soul inhospitable to all parasites. I recognised that my personal pain-body fed off pornographic sex, it fed off shame too, and blame, and judgment, and self-loathing. It also dined out on something else, something deeply hidden. This rich feast of shadow-manna would not reveal itself until the play hit the stage proper and the concentrated light of a captive audience exposed it.

I will come to this revelation shortly.

To stop the food supply, I would have to remove all forms of defilement from my life. This meant revealing my deepest shame in *Fragile*, exorcising it by exposing it to the light of consciousness, on the page, on the stage and on the screen. Blackmailers are immediately disempowered when you reveal willingly what they threaten to expose by force.

It also meant renouncing pornography.

When you starve a shadow, when you draw it into the light and name it, when you challenge its actual reality it weakens it, and that gives you the upper hand.

This was my task, and it vexed me greatly.

I sat down, trembling with anticipation and I wrote Fragile, the stage play. I wrote it in two short sessions. It took only two days to write, but it had taken me over three decades to muster up the courage. Then the fear again: *your wife is going to read this; she will hate you. She will think that you are a depraved monster. Your children will watch this when it makes it to the stage and they'll be embarrassed, they'll be ashamed and will disown you. Your agent will sack you the moment this shit arrives in her inbox. Everyone will despise you. Don't you know that some things are just not meant to be unleashed on the public?*

Then the pleading rhetoric from an internal voice that I was able to clearly observe, a voice that was trying to convince me to sack *Fragile* as a bad job: 'Look, Geoff, you've done well, this is brave what you're writing here, very brave, but you don't need to show it to anyone. The writing is enough. You got it out of you. It is out. It is enough!'

I took on board the threats, the potential public shaming, the humiliation that shared insight often incurs and I accepted it. I accepted it all. I placed it on my inverted pyramid, as yet another fear I needed to face. And the sycophantic rhetoric, I recognised it as the whine of a lion in winter, a beast weakened by the lack of sustenance and cornered by a greater force.

I sent the play to my agent, Debi.

That was first.

Then I sent it to a West End director that I'd recently started working with called Nick Bagnall. He'd directed work by the outrageously brilliant *Joe Orton*, so he was not going to be easily shocked. My only caveat with *Fragile* was that I didn't want it to be staged in my home city of Coventry. I could almost hear God giggling when I revealed my stipulation. Caveat, I quickly realised, was just another fear that had to be trampled under the stampeding feet of the eager pilgrim. When you are in a covenant with God, there is no room for caveats.

My agent Debi thought the play was my best work to date, but confessed she had to read it in three parts, with a break between each session, because she found it so disturbing. She assured me that I had her full backing, but she was not so sure that it would ever get produced.

I didn't hear from Nick Bagnall for two months, and when I finally did hear back he told me that the play had greatly disturbed him too, and for that reason he definitely wanted to direct it.

Unfortunately, no theatre in the country would stage *Fragile*, even with a West End director attached.

With the exception of the Belgrade Theatre.

In Coventry.

The only theatre that I did not want to stage my play was the only theatre that would. *Fragile* was clearly a story that wanted to come home.

In fact, it absolutely refused to go anywhere but home. It was intuited that I needed to put my work on in my birth city, in front of a home crowd - my family, my friends, my peers. The Belgrade - an impressive rep theatre - sat in the very heart of Coventry's city centre, only a few short miles from my house, a stone's throw from where I was born, and literally a five minute walk from the boys club, where I was abused as a child.

The Belgrade was also just three miles from my mum's house, *my mum's!*

Ah my mum, my mum, my lovely mum.

And there we have it.

The first of the many revelations that this play would trigger.

The reasons for not wanting to write this play, and stage it in my home city, seemed at first glance myriad and varied, but in truth there was only one reason: I was afraid of my mum seeing the play. I was afraid of my mum hating me and withdrawing her love...I was afraid of her abandoning me.

This was my greatest fear.

Or at least it was my greatest fear, for now.

There was another deeper angst awaiting me, one that I had never before even contemplated, and it would not present itself until I had popped each preceding fear-bubble above it.

The play was brutally honest and viscerally explicit. It was an exploration of the sexual abuse I had experienced as a boy and the subsequent self-abuse. But in the play, I was also examining in depth aspects of the abuse that I'd never wanted to look at before.

I was angry with my mum.

That was first.

Not angry, actually. Fucking *enraged*.

I had never looked at this before, never. I loved her so much that I could not have consciously accepted that I harboured anything for her other than unconditional love.

I was angry at my dad.

This was another unexpected revelation. It bubbled and spat and spilled onto the pages of my script. I had never acknowledged this before, not to anyone, not even to myself, but it was there, seething just below a thin veneer of patriarchal devotion. He too came under fire in the arc of the play. I was so angry at my dad that I wanted to accuse him of many things, not least of being a drunken bastard (which he was not), and in the fictionalised narrative of the play I did just that. I let my unholy rage rip out in torrents.

The play script also revealed that I was still so angry with my abuser that I had developed an arsenal of killing techniques so that one day I could stamp my boot-heel on his windpipe and put him in the grave, out of harm's way. I would give him a taste of the trauma he had inflicted on me as a boy.

I thought I had dealt with this.

I'd forgiven him, seventy times seven I had forgiven my enemy. I met him in a Coventry café. I shook his hand. I used kind words with him, and I walked away. I took my grudge to the inferno, and I set it alight with holy fire... but there was clearly still a residue of hatred in me that had survived the fire, and now I was being asked to remove it once and for all. I was being instructed to finish the job I had started.

And as it turned out I was also angry with God.

I thought I had surrendered my life to the Redeemer, and yet, here it was, a hissing demon, rearing its ugly head through layers of my writing and hypocritical fidelity. I was so angry with God that the play, in parts, was nothing less than blasphemous.

I was fucking very angry at God...who would have thought?

I was angry at the Redeemer, but I didn't know what to do with that.

Until Fragile, I didn't consciously know that I was angry with anyone, not least my mum. I didn't know I was angry, only that I was very guarded around her. Only that I clothed myself in metaphoric armour when I was in her company, that I squirmed in shame, deep, fathomless shame when I sat with her for breakfast, when I took her shopping every Thursday. Even buying her a house, and becoming successful, and winning a BAFTA statue for *her* was not enough to settle the squirm that sat in my belly like a disease.

Writing the play, sitting through weeks of rehearsals, watching it staged every night for two weeks before an audience, showed me for the very first time that part of me was so angry with them all that unconditional love would just not come through, and that was what I needed to attain real/absolute healing. Whilst I held onto the fear, the shame and the dissonance, all I could bring to the world would be crumbs; I would be incapable of loving a living soul, even myself, especially myself.

So why had I not seen all of this before?

Why had I not seen this anger, hatred and rage for my parents, for God before? Because I loved them.

I loved them so much that admitting that I was angry with them felt like the greatest betrayal. In *Fragile*, in the midst of abuse, One (the lead character) confesses that all he is worried about, all he cares about is 'my mum, my mum is going to be so upset with me'.

When I started writing the play the title presented itself to me as Fragile. I assumed this was because I felt fragile as a damaged human being. One of the later revelations of the play was that One is unable and unwilling to talk to his mother about the abuse because, 'she is old. She's a pensioner. She wouldn't cope with this. She is fragile'.

I loved my mum so much, and I was so afraid of losing her love, that all I cared about was what this would do to her, how my abuse would affect her, and how (in my frightened imagination) she might withdraw her love from me as a consequence. Now, on the cusp of staging my one-man play in my home city the same terror arose: 'If my mum sees this...'

This became my one and only fear, and I surrendered it to the Redeemer.

I prayed to God. I asked that my mum be protected.

I did not need to do this, of course. If I'd had more faith I would have simply trusted that she'd be cared for. God knows what I want and He knows what I need.

In divine law, the answer always precedes the question.

Let me stipulate very clearly here that none of what happened was my mum's fault. I was not angry with her. She could not have stopped what happened to me any more than you could stop the weather. But there was something in me that wanted to feed off this corrupted energy, it wanted to blame everyone who was even remotely connected to this tragedy, and staging the play was my way of removing this projected bullshit so that I could see the true truth.

It was no one's fault.

No one was to blame.

I'd experienced a life event that had never been processed, like millions of other damaged souls in the world. That's all. And now I was redressing the balance so that I could remove it once and for all.

The set was designed for the play. The actor - the wonderful Craig Conway - was cast and the date set. The play was very potent, I mentioned this. So much so, that the Belgrade were worried that it might be too much for the viewing public, so they called in some help. One of the critics later wrote that *Fragile* was the only play he'd ever been to where the Samaritans were stationed at the stage door every night. It was true. The Samaritans were enlisted by the theatre, in case the subject matter had any disturbing mental effect on patrons of a delicate nature. The play was advertised heavily in the local press, regional radio, flyers, posters and booklets. 'Believe all the hype you've heard about Geoff Thompson,' one radio ad proclaimed, 'watch *Fragile* at the Belgrade Theatre.'

You couldn't open a newspaper, switch on the radio, or walk down the street without seeing or hearing something about Fragile and this magnified my fear. There was no way that my mum and dad - who usually didn't get involved in my work, other than from a distance - would not hear about the play. What if they wandered into the Belgrade on a matinee, and sat down to watch One spill his pain and his anger in front of hundreds of people? One is very damaged. He can't trust a living soul, so he vents his angst into a tape recorder and through this inanimate machinery he tells his mother how he really feels, he tells his father how he really feels, he tells his teacher *the abuser* how he really feels.

If my parents were ever to see this play, I feared it might hurt them, and they would never speak to me again.

This is not true of course; this was merely the projection of an unqualified fear. There was no way anyone could predict how they might react. My shadow had painted the direst possibility and sold it to me as the inevitable, and this was what had stopped me from exorcising this damage before now. As it turned out, my mum did enquire about my play. 'What's it about?' She asked, in the most casual manner. I told her the truth, that it was about a man who'd been sexually abused when he was a boy, and he was using a tape recorder to make sense of and ultimately release his pain. 'Oh,' she said, as though I'd just read her the weather report from a newspaper, 'what would you like for breakfast son?'

All that worry. All that fear and none of it manifested.

Sharon was next to quiz me: 'So why are you so worried about this play?' She asked. 'You never usually get this bad.'

I told her that I was worried about this play in particular because I was revealing very personal things about myself that I had never shared with any one before, not even her.

'What things?' She asked, cautiously.

My mum didn't ask too much, because detail scared her. Sharon was not my mum: she wanted to know it all, even though the detail scared her just as much. She would be watching the play with an audience soon enough, and she wanted to be a little prepared. I shared with Sharon only the most gruesome detail, the one aspect that I was most ashamed of. I told her about the self-harm, the sexual self-harm, the self-rape that was viscerally and explicitly portrayed in the play.

There was a moment of genuine confusion from my wife.

'Yes but...' she hesitated, 'you didn't ever do that to yourself... did you?'

'Yes, I did,' I said quietly.

She was silent for a few seconds, eyes darting, as though trying to process this new information. Then she nodded very subtly. Her way of letting me know that she accepted what I had said. We never spoke about it again.

She knew me. She knew my path. She had seen the negative displacement of my damage when I worked the doors and she understood my philosophy on spiritual kenosis, the self-emptying that had been the mainstay of my evolution. She also knew that I was courageous and that sooner or later I always confronted my fears.

The energy that I was about to dissolve in my stage play did everything in its power to stop, if not the play itself, then me attending the first performance. On the morning of the press night, I broke my ribs training. During a teaching session they popped like hot corn and a burning rush of pain raced through my entire body.

I knew what this was. I knew that this was a last-ditch attempt to stop me from attending, or at least give me a good reason for not turning up. But I had not come this far to be distracted at the last minute by a mere rib break. If I had to crawl to the theatre I would be there; nothing was going to stop me.

So, this was it.

My nemesis.

I was about to reveal every dirty, shameful, depraved secret in front of a first night audience of two hundred people. Family, friends, press, and people I had grown up with. Everything that had ever bullied me, everything that had ever blackmailed me, every thought, word and deed that had held me to ransom for all these years would be acted out on the Belgrade stage. I had written my shame in ink, and the whole of Coventry would be my confessor.

This was me.

This was me, *embracing the black* in front of a paying audience.

As it turned out, I had spent all that energy on worrying for nothing. Every terrible thing I feared might happen as a consequence of writing and producing this play turned out to be a big fat lie. I thought I was afraid of shame. Once the first night was over and the audience were on their feet giving what would become a nightly ovation, all of my shame died. It died on that stage and was never resuscitated. Actually, it did not die. How could it die, when it never really existed in the first place, other than as a twisted perception. The only thing that died was a false idea in my head, poked and bloated by that fear *whisperer*.

After the show, in the foyer, audience members were emotional. They wanted to hug me. They wanted to kiss me and hold me in warm embrace. They wanted to thank me for saying the things that they too had felt but had been unable to voice. One woman offered me sex! Really. She was so taken by my writing that she offered to have sex with me, at my earliest convenience.

'Thank you,' I said, red-faced, dissonant, slightly bewildered and strangely flattered, 'thank you but no thank you. I am married to the girl of my dreams.'

Proclamations of love were poured upon me, and one offer of sex was proffered, but there was no shame in that space. I felt no shame.

No more blackmail either. What am I going to be blackmailed with? I've emptied all my sin onto the Belgrade stage, there was none left. No more being held to ransom. My accuser was gone.

As Rumi once said in a fitting verse, "fear knocked on the door, Love answered, there was no one there".

The reviews that followed matched the audience reaction; they were all 4 and 5 stars, and the critics were falling over themselves with superlatives.

Later I would tour the play, in selected venues around Britain, to the same beautiful response, and later at the Edinburgh International Festival, and later still Germany. Everywhere it went *Fragile* played to audiences who were startled by the honest beauty of this play and its performance.

By the time the play had completed its run, I was spent and empty but man I loved my mum and my dad so much. My love for them was unadulterated, it was pure and unconditional, and there was nothing, nothing, nothing blocking the clear view between me and them. I realised that none of the fears that had circled my consciousness like a murder of crows were mine. These were the fiction that fed the fiction that had been using me as a squat and a bed and a free meal for way too long. But no more. They had been evicted, once and for all. It was over...

Well, it should have been over, but it was not completely over, not yet.

Staging the play asked everything of me, and it took it.

I was left temporarily empty. I was so weak. I was vulnerable again. I was ready for a holiday, desperately ready. I had a Mediterranean cruise booked for me and Sharon, but the ship didn't sail for two weeks after Fragile had completed its run.

I could sense that something was going to happen. I should have surrounded myself with spiritual protection the moment the play finished but I didn't. It is standard practice to always, always tighten your helmet straps after the fight. I knew this, this knowledge is bread-and-butter for any warrior, whether his theatre of war is on a nightclub door, in the boardroom or the spiritual battlefields of inner space. Post kenosis there is always a period of stark vulnerability. You are an open door post misogi,* not unlike hospital patients who are susceptible to disease immediately after an operation.

As I mentioned, an intrinsic element of spiritual growth is to make the body inhospitable to shadow, and a vital aspect of this is to stop feeding the shadow of abuse with its food of choice, in my case violence and sexual pornography. And I had been true to my vow on both counts. But renunciation is not a one-time only affair. It is not something that you withdraw from or eschew as a temporary measure; it is a commitment for life. There is an old saying in the Christian canon: *be careful when you kick out one demon, because he will come back again with ten*. In a moment of weakness, I fell into forgetting. It was when I was vulnerable, right after the play had finished. I slipped. I was out in the city centre, Sharon was shopping, I was alone in a coffee shop and out of arrogance, out of sheer folly, I accessed a soft porn site on my mobile phone. I had never accessed porn on my phone before, ever. I had always been too wary of pocket technology to dabble with its unpredictable ways. I was literally on the site for four or five seconds, the images had not even downloaded when I caught myself and said out loud 'what the fuck are you doing!' I had made a vow to stop feeding demons, and to stop going to the places where demons go, and here I was, only weeks after I'd made the holy vow, desecrating it. I closed the page immediately and disengaged from the site, angry and disappointed at myself for succumbing so easily and so quickly.

Almost the second I closed the page I heard my phone *ping* out a message alert. I looked at my texts and was informed that the porn site I'd entered and left within seconds had charged me £5 for accessing their material (even though, technically I did not).

---

* The Japanese concept of spiritual cleansing.

A con I know. Illegal, I am pretty sure. Immoral, definitely. In the overall scope of things £5 was neither here nor there, it was nothing. And yet the ping of the incoming text filled me instantly with a paroxysm of fear - terror is a more accurate description of what I experienced. Certainly the fear was disproportionate to the stimulus. I had been baited at a susceptible moment, and now I was sinking into an emotional abyss. Beast and fowl were queuing at the doorway of my heart. The one demon of scripture that I'd so recently evicted with the staging of *Fragile* had not returned with ten of its kind, it had come back with a legion. I could feel that some of these adverse forces had already invaded my heart chamber, and the rush of anxiety I felt was the result of my insides being consumed.

This overwhelming fear and dread is known in esoteric practice as a *spiritual shock*.* It is the intruder-alert that all serious pilgrims receive when they break their connection with virtue, when they break their vow with Goodness, and vice rushes the borders.

Without fully realising it, I had made a covenant with God. An agreement to renounce vice and to court virtue. And the covenant is either absolute, or it doesn't exist. You cannot serve two masters, because a house that is divided against itself will fall.

I had broken that covenant, and what unfolded next was the direct result.

I later recognised the responsibility of keeping a covenant with the divine, and the absolute dangers inherent with breaking it. I didn't know this at the time. Not fully. In retrospect, if I am being brutally honest, I was still infrequently flirting with porn. It is important for me to admit this, because accepting the truth, looking it in the eye, is what enabled me to understand why the devil I had so routinely exorcised, was able to so easily re-enter my abode. I was flirting with porn, because I had yet to apprehend the danger of my dalliance. When you access pornography, you invite the vampire of legend across your threshold. *You* invite him. And once he is across, he consumes your essence, and let me tell you he is a bastard to remove again.

I was flirting, and I was about to be shown in the most visceral vision to date, the torture we inflict when we expose our living soul to dead things.

---

* I cover *the divine covenant* and spiritual shock comprehensively The Divine CEO.

The terror from the porn-text set me on fire. I was neck deep once again in the boiling rivers of blood and fire in the seventh circle. I left the city centre, agitated and anxious, emotions threatening to spill out at any moment. I went to my usual meditation spot, in my usual retreat, Coombe Abbey, to take stock and try and make sense of what was happening to me. The fear so overwhelmed me that I broke down. I broke down on a mud path and I wept and unashamedly begged God to remove this dread that had so possessed me. My mind was flooded and overrun by the ten demons. And they assailed me with threats and fears and dreads and shame. All the ills that I'd just spent a lifetime exposing and clearing out were back with a vengeance. The first thing I did to weaken the hold of this fear was find a confessor. One of the techniques I'd learned from my hero Gandhi was that the moment you broke your covenant and fell back into vice, was the exact moment you needed to confess it to someone you could trust. A willing confession stems the inner onslaught of the adverse forces, when they blackmail you with exposure. I knew this was an immediate necessity, because the whisperer was already threatening in my ear, telling me that Sharon would see the porn on my phone bill, she would worry that the dirty seedy website might illegally bill me every month, gambling that I would be too ashamed to contact my provider to complain. Images flashed before my mind of becoming a victim of the recent surge in sexploitation cases splashed all over the front pages of the tabloids, where people who access porn are blackmailed for large amounts of money. All nonsense of course, none of it logical, but there only needs to be the tiniest grain of possibility for the pain-body to *imagine* it into an odds-on probability. My logical mind told me the truth: I had been on the site for less than five seconds. The duration of my visit would be a matter of record, and it could not be denied. It was an erotica site; I don't think there was any hard content on there. But all the same, due to my gaping mind door I felt as susceptible to suggestion as a defenceless child. I found myself (in my mind's eye) trying to explain my defence to a policeman, to a judge, to my family and friends, and the same question kept coming back time and again: *why were you on the site in the first place, even if it was for only five seconds?*

I have to stipulate here, to anyone reading in and saying *come on, get a grip, it was only a porn site* this was not about one silly visit to a website. This was about me escaping from the inferno, and then willingly entering it again, naively looking for a light frolic. This would be akin to escaping a torturer, and then willingly placing yourself back in their hands, so that they could torture you all over again. This was about me finally winning my freedom, only to lose it again to a moment of madness. When you live your life in quiet servitude to the mores, when you trundle through the nine-to-five of your magnolia life, never challenging the status quo you go largely unnoticed by the forces of the world and by the adverse forces that roam the atmosphere. However, when you consciously break your bond with these collective forces, and make a divine covenant with God, you will be noticed, and you will come under attack, that is guaranteed. The reason my terror was so savage was because I had broken my link with the old ways landing me on the wanted list of every adverse force that would take advantage of any situation to bind me in the chains of vice and drag me back to the hell regions. By arrogantly wandering back into their lair, their frequency, I had effectively handed them my arse on a plate, and this assault was the result. Now I had to get myself back out again, and I knew I couldn't do that alone, I needed invisible support.

To kill the blackmail I told Sharon. Her look of disappointment and hurt was heartbreaking. I was so upset that I had failed again. I broke down, once more. I felt so weak, so utterly defenceless. She accepted my confession without judgment, and she supported me. I took a deep breath. I steadied myself. I was where I was because of my own folly. I looked to God. I accepted the consequences of my actions, whatever they might be. I would accept whatever happened. I knew that I was desperately tired and that my strength had been impaired greatly by the kenosis of staging my play and all that it had involved. My overreaction to what had happened was also a sign of my weakened state. I was vulnerable, and my wound was attracting attack. If I could hold out and not panic, I knew that the assault on my mind-door would strengthen my reserve - there is no centre-eye without an eyewall and an eyewall cannot be formed without a tornado.

I knew if I could hold my nerve I would soon rebuild.

I was plagued with fear still as Sharon and I climbed on the cruise liner for our two week holiday. The fear did not abate for a long, painful month. I knew what was happening. I was still cleansing. In writing and staging *Fragile* I had removed an angry block of energy and broken a dark covenant, but latent residues were still hanging around. It was as though an enemy general had been routed, but some of his quarrelsome soldiers still needed to be rounded up and removed.

I also recognised another anomaly, something that was at the very core of my angst, the final bubble before I reached the puncture wound in my psyche.

I was angry at God.

I mentioned this earlier, when I was talking about Fragile. I said that I didn't know how to reconcile these feelings. I couldn't fathom how to approach my dissonance with an Essence that I didn't even understand. Even though I'd had a plethora of mystical experiences on route to this station, there was clearly a hidden element in me that was still an angry atheist. This frightened apostate did not believe in God, because God had not protected him when he needed it most.

I thought that in staging *Fragile*, I'd sounded the death knell to all my angers, but I had not. One whole act in the play is dedicated to my anger at God. In a telling scene our character shakes his fist at the sky in a fit of rage and screams, 'Where the fuck were you God? Where were you?' He then goes on to slight every prophet that God placed on the earth as his emissary. When a group of angry Christians stormed out of the play during this scene and I smiled at their reaction, it should have alerted me to the depth of my feelings, but perhaps I was too close to the whole to see the particulars.

This foxhole I now found myself trapped in would afford me the perfect opportunity to not only lay my complaint before God, but also, if I was brave enough, surrender to his protection and care.

If you think it was hard for me to admit that I was angry with my parents, for fear of losing their love, you can perhaps understand how hard it was for me to speak my rage to God. As a man who had been weaned on the wrathful and jealous God of scripture, I was afraid to openly voice my anger. This is clearly why I had written a fictional character to speak it for me. What he expressed on stage is exactly what I wanted to say in person, but I had not, I could not. How could I? Until *Fragile* I didn't even know the anger was in me, let alone that it wanted to be heard. And it only came out then, because I had given it the revered safety of a theatre space, and a fictional character to hide behind.

I was not struck by lightning for placing my blasphemy onto the stage in Coventry, as I feared I might be. God wanted me to speak my discontent. He directed me to expose the full body of my protest to the light of consciousness, so that I could see it in the plain light of day. Once I gave it a dock, outside of my body, and stood it before the scrutiny of my own eyes, God knew that I would be forced to qualify my complaint.

Lying in quiet agony on a sunbed, on the deck of the cruise liner, I closed my eyes and descended into the deep ocean, below the waves of pain. In that quiet, still place I found a lost question, suspended in nothingness. It was the question I had burned to ask as an isolated eleven-year-old but had been too frightened and too inarticulate to do so. Somewhere, somehow, during maturation the question had been forgotten, buried under the layers of time.

Now it was remembered again, the question resurrected.

'Why did you abandon me?'

In that still place, below the furore of my disquiet, this is what I asked God.

Finally, after all these long years, we get to it. 'Why would you let this happen to me?' The answer to this first question came before I'd even finished making the enquiry. The voice was rich in kindness, it was marinated in compassion.

'I didn't abandon you,' It replied.

A beat.

A pause.

A divine vacuum.

Then a question was asked of me: 'Did you abandon you?'

Wow!

Did I abandon me?

Did I abandon me?

Well, did I?

I had to cogitate on this.

Yes, I did.

In psychological terms, I did. Of course. I was eleven years old. The abuse sent me into a cognitive dissonance, and I had no way of coping with the emotional overload. Unable to manage the terror of the situation, something in me, my eleven-year-old developing ego, the embryonic little personality called Geoffrey Thompson, definitely and unequivocally abandoned me. He sank beneath the terror, this scared boy, and fell into a deep sleep that lasted for thirty years. The boy did not wake up again until I was a forty-year-old man, walking around with a wound the size of Birmingham. The child in me was kept in stasis, hidden behind doors of a Freudian defence mechanism, until I was mature enough to wake him from his slumber, and individuate him back into the consciousness of being. Over that frightened boy, a protective carapace had formed. Layers of fleshy armour had grown around him, to protect him until I was old enough and brave enough and wise enough to allow mysterious, glowing beings (during my sound bath experience) to reach into my heart-space and remove the sleeping child to its true home. I abandoned myself too, when, as an adult with free will, I turned to violence for pseudo protection, and courted pornography as a debased and grotesque replacement for love. True protection and pure love is an inside job, it cannot be found in the world of men. Even post Vegas, after my spiritual awakening, after all my earned certainties, even as recently as a week before, hadn't I abandoned myself again, hadn't I abandoned my eternal soul when I exposed it to the corrosiveness of sexual pornography? When I looked back at my life, from the time of the abuse I could see that I had abandoned faith, I had abandoned common sense and decency, I had deliberately broken judicial precedents, forsaken holy laws, family vows had been trashed, I had dishonoured business protocols, forgone societal obligations and my dignity had been lost on more occasions than I cared to recall. At times I had even deserted basic human kindness. I had abandoned myself so often that I cringed at the recollection. My fist shaking at the sky was a juvenile projection. This is basic. How did I ever fall for such a rooky con? I had abandoned myself every day in one debauched way or another, and then blamed the one thing that everyone who is looking for an easy scapegoat blames, God. Even as I was asking the questions, answers were falling into my mind like truth-confetti. I did not take responsibility for my own incarnation, my own journey, even when I knew that I was harming myself, even when I knew that I was harming others, even those I loved. And yet, I still chose to abandon myself and then had the audacity to place the blame at the feet of God.

As for the abuse itself, it was an unfortunate collision of karmic circumstance. You don't need a double first from Oxbridge to understand scientific reciprocity. Every effect has an equal and opposite cause. My unhappy accident was the result of poor decision making by people who used their free will carelessly - society in general, family in particular - and left lambs in the care of a wolf. Nothing more than that. It happens. It was people that placed me in harm's way. You can't blame God for human folly.

'Did you abandon you?'

Yes, I did.

I did, and if I am being brutally honest, I couldn't even guarantee that I wouldn't do it again in the future.

When I first watched *Fragile* on the stage, when I listened to my own dialectic cogitating in a public space looking for clarity, I thought I had found the clear view. I remember thinking to myself, 'Ahhhh, so that's why I don't trust anyone. Everyone I trusted when I was a boy abused my trust.'

Then came a realisation: actually, I don't need to trust anyone. I just need to trust myself. If I can trust myself, I can find equanimity in all things.

Before I was even able to pop the bubbly and celebrate my intellectual breakthrough another question alighted in my head.

'And do you trust yourself?'

Do I trust myself?

Of course I trust myself.

'Absolutely,' I said, with arrogant abandon, 'I absolutely trust myself.'

I was pretty sure I did trust myself, but perhaps I was not certain because the inner silence that followed my answer drew out the poison of doubt.

Could I trust myself?

Could I ever fully, completely, honestly trust myself?

The question was like an iceberg, and my titanic certainty was sunk by it.

I realised that my breakthrough was embryonic, it was another interim truth.

How could I openly admit that I abandoned myself only a week before, and at the same time declare that I could trust myself completely. It was an oxymoron.

Francis of Assisi, even at the point of sainthood said to his followers, 'don't be in too much of a hurry to make me into a saint, I am still capable of producing a child'.

Francis did not trust himself.

He was wise enough to know that, while he wore a body suit, he could never fully trust himself.

Saint Columba, the miracle worker, the saint who brought the dead back to life, was so bereft at his inability to consistently trust his own mind - always abandoning himself, always having to start again - that he called himself 'the beginner man'.

All of the prophets were absolutely sure of one thing: they could not trust themselves. And like Jesus at Gethsemane, they all turned to the only thing that they could trust, the one constant that was beyond question: God.

They could not trust themselves, but they could trust God.

This, I realised, contemplating on the deck of a cruise liner, post-fall, is where the divine covenant becomes proper.

You recognise your own personal untrustworthiness and you refer all things to a higher power.

To know that I can't trust myself is to know everything I need to know.

It is only now, in the writing and re-writing of this book that I fully realise the absolute power of what this very honest and frank dialectic revealed to me: the despicable nature of this anger I was feeling - for God and for all of His creatures – was not mine. The rage and fear that rose in me was an imposter: I was not angry at God, it was an unholy defilement, holed up inside me, a shadow that engaged my attention in a vulnerable moment and pretended it was me, it convinced me that it was me, it hijacked my mind and my sensory body and then dined out like a king on the leaking essence of rage. It was devilishly clever, this Obscurial, it made me think that I was angry at God (and at everyone else), it convinced me that somehow God had not saved me from the abuse, and that this Deity - if it existed at all - was either a wild folly, a shameful betrayer, or it was missing presumed dead, certainly it could not be relied upon. In convincing me of this lie, it closed down my one and only means of healing. It obscured the doorway to emancipation. You are hardly going to call on the help of a god that you don't believe in, or that you are angry at, or that you think might be the cause of all your problems in the first place.

The shadow of ignorance was hiding the doorway to the healing kingdom with smokescreens of unconscious, unqualified perception.

God is the only refuge I need, in fact It is the only refuge I have, and once this is fully realised, once this is accepted as Truth, the shadow is as dead as Python's parrot. It is no more. So of course, the pain-body is going to try and hide God from you, it is going to fight for its very existence to hide Love from you. The moment you fully realise God, you exorcise everything that is not God, and that includes all the ignorant imposters squatting inside you.

I didn't know any of this before, so I was kept in perpetual limbo.

Now, on the ship, my religion broken, doubt rising in me in painful clusters, hot waves of confusion obscuring my clear view, I turned to Abba: 'Please show me things as they are.'

I requested clarity, on that ship, in my suffering, after escaping defilement, and then throwing myself back into the inferno again with one senseless act.

Did you ever make a request that you immediately regretted?

He was not finished with me yet, the God of my conscience.

All of my sin would be paraded past me like a marching band as He showed me things exactly as they really are.

I lay on that ship, on a pool-side-lounger, looking out at an unknown horizon, or in my cabin bed, staring at a foreign ceiling, or on a deckchair witnessing every variation, shape, size, colour and denomination of person waddling around the ship, and I allowed consciousness to enter me like a Redeemer, and I witnessed a legion of befouled components as they were cast out like demons into the herd of pigs. I have to say that the exodus was constant, it was painful, it was frightening, and it lasted for two whole weeks. With my eyes closed, through the third eye I watched as a multitude of old sin, in all of its many guises, left me, like human detritus flushing through a colonic pipe. I sat, and I lay, and I observed in quiet horror as every vacating shadow arose, tried to claim me, tried to scare me, and trick me into emotional engagement in its last ditch attempt at retaining its squat in my being.

I was divinely guarded. I was guided and instructed every step of the way. I could feel immortals coaching me; I could sense the legions of angels falling in behind me like a divine cape, and all around me as a circling halo, and below me as the lamb, my holy foundation stone and above me as the dove of peace - heavenly guards directing the exodus of deviants, the dark legion that had outstayed its welcome within my being. I watched them leave, one by one, as though observing from a high vantage point. Every time a demon broke rank and approached my mind door, it was immediately corralled back into procession by an angelic force. And the same benevolent voice instructed me to, 'just observe. Let everything go. Do not engage'.

This command was spoken to me over and over again for two solid weeks.

Then, in the final days of my cleansing, I suffered a prophetic vision the likes of which I had never seen before. I witnessed the soul, my own soul, disrobed and near naked, a 'seeing' that I have never been able to forget. This rare revelation was proffered to me as a divine gift, but also delivered to me as a stark warning. If ever I felt an inclination towards vice again, in any of its forms, the simple remembering of this vision would be enough to strike it down. By recalling its opposite - envisioning the definite consequence of engagement with vice - I would automatically be able to repel the roaming lion of temptation.

Please forgive the raw nature of what I am about to share with you in the next few paragraphs. To half reveal what I was shown in full, or hint at what I saw so viscerally or to mitigate in any way what was revealed to me would be an offence to the gift I was given: a vision of what we submit the soul to when we debase ourselves, by engaging in personality extremes.

I was wide awake when the vision occurred. Awake but with my eyes closed. The scene projected out in front of me as though I was an omniscient observer, but I was close enough so that not a single detail was lost to me. I saw myself in a room. The door to the room was shut. I was kneeling before a naked baby girl and trying to insert my erect penis into the vagina of the child. The child was looking at me with pleading eyes and screaming in fear and pain as I forced myself about an inch inside her. I watched this from above, not recognising the beastly image of myself below, horror-struck and in mute disbelief that anyone could commit such an indefensible sin. The vision was of a carnal man who did not care for anything other than his own sexual gratification. This man was cruel and heartless and unaffected by the cries of the baby. I wanted to turn away from the vision. I wanted to deny any part of me that would hurt even a fly, let alone a defenceless and innocent child. But I was aware that turning away was not an option. Whilst we can close our physical eyes to the atrocities of the manifest world, we cannot close our spiritual eye, it is forced to see all, whether it wants to or not. As I observed in horror, my heartless doppelganger was disturbed by the sound of someone coming close, someone on the other side of the door, someone who might disturb him in this heinous act. The hellish person that I did not recognise as myself, hurriedly wiped the vagina of the child with a cloth, trying to hide any trace of his actions, believing that if no one saw, no one knew, yet knowing at the same time and with the deepest ache, and from a distant conscience that, to the divine, nothing is hidden.

The vision receded and I opened my eyes, back in the world, back on the deck of the ship, confused, afraid and disorientated. The vision felt so real, so visceral that it attacked every sensibility within me, all at the same time.

What did it mean?

This was not me.

What I saw in the vision was not me, it could never be me, I would never harm a baby, I could never harm a child, it was abhorrent. I had watched porn, yes, and I had an addiction, I did, but my deviance never strayed beyond the usual orgy of adult heterosexual intercourse, so this vision made no sense to me.

Then I was told what it actually meant: it was a parable.

'The child represents your naked, childlike soul,' a voice from the bardo informed me gravely. 'Every time you engage in vice, every time you expose yourself to vice the abuse to the soul is proportionate to what you witnessed in your vision. That is how it feels to the soul.'

What I was being told was true. I was absolutely certain it was true.

The sorrow and shock I felt at receiving this parable have never left me.

'You are in covenant with God,' I was reminded. 'The soul is situated in your heart-space. It is there to serve God, through you. You are its guardian, its carer. You are its first line of defence. Do not willingly allow vice to enter your heart-space, by courting vice. If you choose to engage in vice, you consciously, deliberately and willingly submit your soul to rape. Guard the door to your heart with your very life. If you allow negativity to enter, the defenceless soul will be assailed.'

Everything I did from this moment onwards, every decision I made was inspired by this one yaqeen, the absolute certainty born from divine revelation. Not that I would never again be subjected to moments of temptation. While we are in a body, temptation is to be expected, it is the standard fare of this earthly territory. But when temptation does attack, it can always be defeated by the certainty that I had so painfully been gifted. In this respect I was not given a spiritual vision, I was delivered a divine sword, one that could cut through the anatomy of any temptation darkening my door. If temptation called, all I had to do was contemplate its opposite by calling to mind this image and it would die in its tracks.*

Saint Francis reminded me that temptation was no bad thing. How are debasements to be exposed to the light and claimed if they do not approach, if they are not seen. Temptation is only destructive when we succumb to it. Armed with proof of the defenceless soul and my dharma to protect it was all the purpose I needed to fight the good fight. This was what the Holy Prophet called the Greater Jihad, where we defeat our enemy by observing him without identification, witnessing without engagement. This is *the holy gaze***, and it was a technique that I was determined to master. This was my greatest epiphany so

---

* In esoteric practice this is called *the defence of opposites*.
** Eckhart Tolle's book The Power of Now is a masterclass in this technique.

far. As I write these words, seven years on, the vision, power and certainty are stronger in me now than ever.

After this moment of stark clarity my covenant became clearer and clearer; what I ate changed, how I spoke changed, the nature, level and purpose of my writing and teaching was changed, and my relationships changed, also. In short, I was changed.

I am writing a list here of all the things that were changed, but it would be easier to tell you that *everything* was changed, because everything was. With the noise, the fog, the anger, the rage and the blame associated with the abuse I experienced as a boy now removed, I was gradually able to see true. Like Plato's philosopher, who leaves his cave of shadows to escape *the prisoner's reality**, I was adjusting to a new level of light.

Knowing now the undeniable sensitivity of the soul, I became practiced at protecting it. I kept a border guard of trained attention at the doorway of my heart, allowing in only the things that fed my soul and blocking out everything that did not. I asked myself, as I am instructed to do so by the Torah, "will this food take me Home?" If the answer was in the negative, it did not get past my mind door.

So, I was back on the doors again, only this was no nightclub I was called to protect, this was my living soul.

Back from the cruise I was a new man. As is often the way with the new man, he has a new perspective. Producing *Fragile* at the Belgrade, and the subsequent vision of the soul, opened up incredible vistas of opportunity. I was being called to continue proving myself, but not in the old way. Things had to change. All old ways had to be dismantled and discarded. What was working for me before, would not work for me now, neither would it be effective in the future. I needed new modalities for my upgraded mindset, and this demanded that I strip my house bare to make room.

This grand realisation didn't happen all at once, it wandered into my consciousness gradually. Unique insights that come with an expanded awareness tend not to reveal themselves immediately.

Like a pioneer colonising a new world, delights continue to unveil themselves as you settle and explore the landscape.

---

* Plato's Cave. Plato likens the uneducated masses to prisoners chained in a cave, who mistake the shadows on the wall, cast by a fire behind them, for reality.

I had a very strong inner life now and I had a captain at the helm, a divine CEO who would reveal these next instructions as and when they were needed.

At this time my life was a triptych. I was split three ways, living three disparate lives: the martial artist, the writer, and the spiritual seeker. My personal contact details - email, phone number, address etc. - were in the public domain. I was deliberately accessible to anyone and everyone who wanted to connect with me, and this meant I was corresponding with people from across the globe on a daily basis. I was the martial arts teacher, the writing oracle, and the metaphysical adviser. Lately I had also become an accidental and unlikely agony-aunt for anyone struggling with their human condition. I was talking calls from strangers and answering questions from folk looking for answers, searching for balm or simply wanting to pass an hour with *that bloke who writes the books*. I had been doing this consistently and relentlessly for over twenty years. I was accessible to all, and I can see now that this was an important stage of my own evolution. It forced me to quantify and articulate what I'd been learning myself - there is nothing like teaching others to accentuate and accelerate your own education - it helped me to place my certainties into a metaphoric and parabolic vernacular that people could understand. I can also see that helping all-comers was not only a duty to God, it was a gift to myself. It was for my own personal cleansing, a 'community service' that helped me to atone my many wrongs. It purged the sin that had been residing in me as a living community; this was *the old* that needed to be vacated in order to make room for the new. It was a long and painful process, much of which I have detailed in the pages of this testament. This was soon to stop. The martial arts teacher, the accessible oracle, the wandering guru, they had to go. I was being asked to forswear them all in favour of a solitary endeavour: writing.

More specifically, writing as a solitary method of individual proving.

This direction was to come soon enough, in another powerful epiphany, one that I received when I was invited to workshop a play at the National Theatre Studio, a clear direction that I will detail shortly.

The National invite was soon to arrive on my doorstep, but before that, another message, another inner call to revisit the sexual abuse of my youth.

Fuck!

Fuck, fuck, fuck.

Revisit it?

I'd only just left it five minutes ago.

Fuck!!

Hadn't we just done this?

These were my exact thoughts immediately after the intuitive instruction to combine *Fragile* and *Romans 12:20* (the short film) into a feature film called *Romans*. Before I even had time to draw breath on that request (and say 'fuck' again), I was also invited to do a TED Talk on the same subject, *and* - one more invitation - feature in a forthcoming documentary series about the ego, directed by Guy Ritchie, where I would be called once more to publicly detail my learning. The latter came in an unexpected phone call from Guy, who was making a six-part documentary, featuring such luminaries as Eckhart Tolle, Sam Harris and Deepak Chopra (no pressure then!).

The idea of *going there* yet again, with all these new projects seemed to me like madness if not needless torture. It felt counterintuitive to continue rehashing the same material over and over again. I felt like the sinner Sisyphus, condemned to an eternity of rolling a boulder uphill only to watch it roll back down again. Albert Camus insisted that I must imagine Sisyphus happy in his task and see the struggle itself toward the heights as enough to fill a man's heart.

That's easy for you to say Albert. It's not your shoulder to the rock.

After a short contemplation I understood the logic of my command, even if I did not relish following it. Saint Francis concurred: after kissing the Leper of his fear on the road outside Assisi, he took as large an amount of money as he could raise to the local Leprosy hospital, gathered all the infected patients together, and distributed the coin to them one by one, making sure to kiss each of their hands as the money was given. He said that to win complete victory over his fear, and to free all the essence it was holding, he needed to immediately follow the first attack with a second and a third.

I couldn't argue with that logic.

It concurred with everything I had learned about the greater jihad.

I will talk through the divine commands in order, but please bear in mind that they all unfolded concurrently. This latter detail is important. It was tackling all four simultaneously that led me to a place of personal exhaustion and spiritual vulnerability. My perfect *weakness* would provide the fertile soil for the perfection of my soul. The seismic shift that would occur at its conclusion was a vision that triggered life altering decisions that would reduce my three disparate paths to a single bespoke way.

The writing of my feature film *Romans* was the first command of the four. To say that I wrote this film script would do the greatest disservice to the process. I didn't write it. It was dictated to me internally, and I transcribed it to the page. I sat at my computer and the words came through me. I was working with the Shammasian brothers on this film, as I had with the short version, *Romans 12:20*. I'd promised they could direct it but for this first draft I did not require any notes or suggestions or ideas from them, no input at all, nothing. This script knew what it wanted, all I had to do was open my mind, direct my typing fingers to the keyboard and let it flow.

Before I sat down to write I spoke to my agent Debi. I told her the idea for the feature and asked if she could find a film company that might commission it. When things are in alignment, I have found, the means always present themselves effortlessly.

Debi got me a meeting with a nice producer called James who loved the idea and commissioned it on the spot. This is a rare anomaly in film. Most people in the movie game are not really in the movie game at all, because the film world is largely a game, and generally, fuck-all moves. They are not in the business of making films, they are in the business of nearly making films, or occasionally making films, or never making films at all. Procrastination is the order off the day. Mostly it is jam tomorrow. Executives are double busy looking for guarantees in a world that can offer no such thing. Many more are frantically ticking the myriad boxes that need to be filled before a project gets any kind of funding. And there is a mysterious and invisible hierarchy in the industry that you find yourself trying to negotiate before you can ever reach anyone in a position to make the decision to commission a script. James was not one of these people. He heard my pitch and he said, 'Yes.'

I said, 'Have you got money? Can you pay me?'

Normally producers laugh at this point (manically) and say, 'Money! What is money?'

James simply said, 'I have a small amount of money. But I will pay you.'

I gratefully took his money. I sat and wrote the first draft in five weeks, sent the script to the producers and the directors, *the team*, took notes, made changes and we had a finished script. It was a simple as that. It often is when the project is ordained. They were so impressed with my script that they took it to the amazing casting director Colin Jones and said, 'We want to go 'A' list.'

If *Fragile* and *Romans 12:20* saw me locating my wound and suturing the gape, *Romans* the feature film had me cleaning up any infection left by the original assault. It was also filling in the gaps left by the other two productions. When you approach a subject from multiple genres - short film, stage play, articles, TED Talk, documentary, and feature film - it encourages you to be meticulous in your cleansing. It allows you to eke out any aspects that have not been thoroughly explored and draw out any small anomalies that have not been completely exhausted so that eventually, between the various projects, you end up with a comprehensive exhumation. *Romans 12:20* looked at the displaced violence caused by historical abuse. *Fragile* explored the subsequent cognitive dissonance. Romans concentrated specifically on the second abuse, family denial. This was the film that tied the disparate parts together into an absolute and completed the job.

It would be wise for me at this point to highlight the inherent dangers of poking old ghosts with a pointy-stick and pushing them into the light. Often when you reach the real dregs of a schema, and you reveal the most damaged, obtrusive and defiant elements, they do not want to come out. They will fight you. They fight you tooth and nail to retain their secrecy and maintain their hold. As with all interlopers, if you do not remove the root, you do not remove the weed. The nature of this type of project is divine, I am in no doubt about that. And because it is divine, like the binding-ring of Tolkien, it will draw out the negative in anyone who is associated with it. You have to be aware of this. I had to be aware of this from the very outset, otherwise I too might have been drawn back into dark places.

Romans was a film about the metaphysical power of forgiveness in the face of evil.

In the battle of light against dark, it was courageously taking to the field for light. It had a holy signature. This placed it firmly on the carpet of proximity*.

If you produce a film with divine proximity you will meet resistance. That is a definite. You would be foolish to think otherwise. There are forces in the world and in the atmosphere that do not want a film like this to find an audience, because it reveals spiritual truths that fly in the face of fearful dogma. Ours is a world that trades mostly in the exchange of negative energy. If you think not, pick up any random newspaper, watch any news bulletin, and you will see bad news, wall-to-wall.

They have a popular idiom in news casting: *if it bleeds it leads*. Greedy capitalists (and the adverse forces that work them) get rich on this kind of tabloid commerce. They get fat on the ignorance of the masses, who digest their own faeces because someone has sold it to them as caviar. Even as he turns away or runs away from the horrors before him, even as he screams out for relief, the man of misery that resides in most people is calling out for more.

Revenge porn is the opiate of the masses, but it poisons the constitution. Our film was offering forgiveness as the antidote. It costs nothing. No one makes any money from it, so of course it is not going to be popular with forces that peddle its opposite.

Divine proximity is a powerful force, it will irresistibly draw out the predominant nature in a person who stands on the carpet; goodness if good is at their heart, malevolence if vice is their tipple of choice.

And so it proved to be.

The behaviour of some of those helping to bring *Romans* to the screen, especially as we got closer to production, was nothing short of shameful. These were people who, at the outset, seemed reasonable, nice people, but they became angry, dishonest, deceitful, bullying caricatures of themselves by the time we wrapped. Many of the workers were not paid. Lawsuits were filed. Insults were thrown. Threats of violence were sent by email and phone and across meeting tables, and the loveliest people turned into the most despicable versions of themselves. Each blamed the other when payments were denied, and rationalised their behaviour when their

---

* Al Ghazali called this the carpet of proximity to God. He said that someone who stands close to someone who is on the carpet of proximity is also himself on the carpet of proximity.

behaviour became illegal, unethical or abusive. No need to name names. I am not in the business of revenge; vengeance is not my job. If you have read this far you will already be very aware of my own catalogue of wrongs, so I am in no position to cast stones. I will leave karma to the forces of reciprocity. I am not looking to apportion blame either, only field-report from the front line.

The people who did not meet their own standards know who they are.

Myself and the two directors closed ranks and did our best to stay peripheral to the unfolding debacle. It was not easy. Drama is a tasty treat for those who are asleep, it is a salacious delicacy for those still controlled by their demons.

The moment I felt my own anger and dissonance begin to rise (and it did rise), I physically and proportionately stepped away. Things started to get personal, so I extracted myself completely from the feeding frenzy of drama. It eventually infested the production like a plague.

Like any shadow, I observed but did not engage with it, I witnessed but I did not identify.

Despite our misgivings regarding the project, we managed to bag a Hollywood leading actor for *Romans*. Orlando Bloom starred, and I loved him. He was brilliant, the consummate professional, he was the hardest working actor. I have never met a man who was so thorough. He helped me find areas in the story that I would never have found without him. He was very challenging for others whose mind-guard was not as tight, practiced or aware as it could have been but that is no bad thing, it is often necessary in the learning arc. If the integrity of our guard is not tested, how will we learn to perfect and tighten our defences?

Anyone who can breach our mind door is our teacher.

It's easy to hate people when they secrete themselves through a gap, enter by artifice, or kick down the door by force, but to hate would be to miss the point. Hate never did anything but feed hate. If people get in it is because we let them in, certainly we failed to stop them at the doorway, which amounts to the same thing. And if we let them in, then they are our teacher, and to see them as anything other is to be asleep. The devil, as they say, is God's master swordsman sent to teach us how to perfect our weapons.

And the Shammasian brothers, our directors, what can I say about Paul and Ludwig without quickly running out of superlatives. I love them.

For me they produced a holy masterpiece with *Romans* and although the problems with production and distribution still remain at the writing of this book, the film is out there. It won a best actor award for the amazing Anne Reid at The Edinburgh International Film Festival, and it has had a European, American and Asian release.

At the time of writing this book *Romans* is yet to enjoy a British release. I don't know why that is exactly, all communication has broken down on the production. I don't really care. The film is beautiful, it has soul, it knows its own path and no thing, no power on this earth will stop that.

The offer to deliver a TED Talk came at the same time as we were filming *Romans*, and it came out of the blue. It was a call I did not expect to receive, although it had been a long-time ambition of mine to talk for the TED network. It felt like a good platform, a lofty lectern from which to present my life and my thoughts on fear and forgiveness in a very rich, compact and reduced format. What it would ask of me was different from what the films and the plays and the books had asked, not least because the other mediums offered me a degree of fictionalised protection, some anonymity. With TED I would have to write the words and deliver them without artistic licence, live on stage in front of an audience and it would be filmed and placed on viewing platforms for the whole world to see.

I loved and hated the formats that placed a limitation on me with equal measure. The associated pressure can be unbearable, but it often produces your best work.

With *Bouncer*, my first film, the caveat was that the finished movie (plus credits) needed to be no longer than ten minutes. We had to deliver a story with a beginning, middle and end that delivered impact, without taking it even a few seconds beyond the enforced time constraint. It reminded me of my martial arts philosophy of power via negation. I developed a method called *restriction training*, where exercises in limitation were used to draw out more power from less movement. It would encourage (or force) people to access impact not ordinarily available to them, the hidden power of chi or ki.

TED demanded similar restrictions. They wanted the talks to last no longer than twenty minutes, fifteen was the ideal. They did not want their speakers to ad-lib.

They insisted that we deliver carefully crafted talks that were scrutinised by the TED organisers, learned by rote and then delivered live, preferably without notes. I'd given a thousand speeches before but never one that I'd had to learn by heart. I'd spoken non-stop for two hours without notes to large audiences, but never from a pre-written speech, practiced and learned in advance. I was also encouraged to work in groups with other people, which did not suit me as an author. I prefer to take myself away somewhere and work alone. The organisers felt that working in groups made you accountable, but I didn't need anyone to hold my hand or keep me to account, I was highly self-disciplined, this was a job I could do myself. Nevertheless, it was what they wanted, so I had to see it as a forced-limitation and make the best of it.

I was also forced to write a script that delivered the essence of all I'd learned about fear and forgiveness in the last forty years and fit it into a twenty minute speech. This was very uncomfortable, but it was good for me. Clarifying what I'd learned - the raw essentials - was a great way to reduce what I'd learned down to its absolute nucleus.

Again, this reminded me of working on the club doors of Coventry and the uncompromising restrictions enforced by an environment where tolerances were tight and not meeting them could result in injury or death.

Ted was good for me. I loved the experience but let me tell you the very first mistake I made in my approach.

Pre-talk, I gave the TED experience way too much reverence. I did. I am sure about that. I even described it to someone as like being signed for Man Utd. The reverence made the experience too big, bigger than it actually was. It made it too important. Why was a TED Talk any more important than speaking to people one to one, in person, where I felt no fear at all?

In making TED big in my perception, in making it important in my belief, I placed pressure and expectations on myself that made the whole experience from beginning to end unnecessarily stressful. I was making the point in my talk that fear was a living constant while you occupy a sentient body, but it is still an illusion. I knew this, and yet, because I had entertained an exaggerated perception of the event, the adrenalin flowed and as the talk date drew closer, even an associated email landing in my inbox triggered adrenal dump. I brought all of my training in fear control to bear on this project, and I did the work. I prepared. I did over ninety hours of practice for a twenty minute talk.

I still messed it up on the day.

I messed it up because I'd spent so many years selling myself self-absorbed nonsense about TED. I believed that it was a big deal. I told myself that only the best are invited to talk for TED, and by the time I came to deliver the speech, I couldn't escape my own sales pitch.

Again, I experienced opposition.

Actually, I felt opposition from the very first moment I received the invite. Everything inside me seemed to rebel at the prospect of talking to a worldwide audience about fear and forgiveness. Every negative inner voice was scanning me for signs of insecurity, for hints of uncertainty, offering me ways out of my commitment, telling me that I would fail if I took the gig.

Opposition is a good sign.

I have said this throughout the book.

Strong opposition is a sure sign that you are onto something important. The resisting elements in you will oppose exposure of truth, of course they will, because they will be consumed in the act of revelation.

The level of opposition I felt - mostly in the form of adrenal rush, and inner doubt - encouraged me on. It made me work harder. It encouraged me to be diligent. It helped me to strengthen my eyewall too and prove the guard at my mind door. There is nothing like pressure to force you towards God for balm, and security. I went inwards, every day I went inwards. Eventually, because I was facing so many personal challenges concurrently, I was living inwards more than I was living outwards. I spent all my hours in quiet communion with God. I was in constant prayer.

The problem however was this, by the time I came to speak I knew that the TED Talk was not a big deal. I knew that as a matter of fact. It was just a lovely event, held in a warm and welcoming room in front of a partisan audience. I could have been talking anywhere, I could have been talking in my own front room, but my unconscious had already been sold on the enormous pressure that I had predicted this talk would place me under.

Halfway through my rigorously rehearsed talk, in front of hundreds of people, I dried, I choked, and I lost my way. Murmurs in the audience. People shared furtive glances. Adrenalin. Fear. I'll be judged. I'll be embarrassed. I'll feel ashamed.

'I'm really sorry,' I announced to the audience, 'I've lost my way.'

I looked across to the organisers, 'Do you mind if I start again?'

They did not mind.

I turned back to the audience, and smiled: 'I'm going to start again,' I said.

Roars and cheers and whoops bounced off the walls. People were standing up to will me on. If you get a chance to watch it online, you'll notice that I start my talk to a rousing ovation. Now you know why. Man, those people were kind, they were willing me to succeed. They wanted me to finish my talk; and what a talk. The longest twenty minutes of my entire fucking life. I finished as I started, with a standing ovation. There was no embarrassment, no shame; just another one of my deliveries, filmed for prosperity and out in the world to act as an intercessor.

One of my fellow speakers approached me after the talk.

'How are you feeling?' he asked. He was referring to my stall, searching to see if it had spoiled my experience.

'Well', I said sagely, 'one of my neighbours is suffering with cancer at the moment, he'll probably die in the next few weeks. If this (the choke) is the worst thing that happens to me today, I'm doing alright.'

He smiled.

Context is good.

To capitalise on my choke, I wrote an article and placed it online as a free download.

In it I told everyone all about the talk and my 'dry choke' halfway through. I called the article, 'How I failed my TED Talk'.

Everything the false ego throws at you by way of sabre rattling and scaremongering and posturing is a lie. I have proof.

At the same time as writing and performing the TED Talk, and making Romans (and fighting off friends who had become enemies), I was invited down to London by Guy Ritchie to take part in his documentary series about the ego.

This opportunity came about in a strange and serendipitous manner.

I love these kinds of divine introductions.

I realised later that the meeting with Guy was precipitated some years before when I was training at Neil Adams' full time Judo club. One of the elite players there was a British champion and squad member called James Warren, or Judo Jim (that's how he is listed in my phone contacts). He was one of the teachers who kindly and unofficially gave me private instruction while I was at the club. We became good friends, but after I left the club, after it closed and we all went our separate ways, I lost contact with Jim. Years later I heard though a mutual friend that he was getting involved in film, acting and directing so I reconnected with him, and invited him to some of the film screenings I was holding in the city. Jim is a Londoner, so I thought it might afford me the chance to catch up with him again, and if I could, pay back some of the kindness he had shown to me all those years ago.

As it turned out, Guy Ritchie is a very keen Brazilian jiu-jitsu (BJJ) player and its London headquarters happen to be at the Budokwai (the London headquarters for British Judo) where Jim practised. The two men had become fast friends and training partners, Jim had even played roles in some of Guy's films.

Jim later told me that he was sat with Guy in a London screening room while he was editing his series about the ego and the programme was littered with a pantheon of world renowned psychologists, gurus, religious leaders, self-help and spiritual adepts. But Guy was unhappy; he felt that something in the documentary was missing, but he was not sure exactly what. He realised that there were lots of very credible experts appearing in his programme, but it lacked a street element that would add the necessary sour to balance out the sweet. He needed "a trouble maker" (as he called me) someone with a bit of edge.

Jim had an idea who might fit the brief.

He said to Guy, 'You need Geoff Thompson.'

Guy looked at him curiously, 'Do you know him?'

'I trained with him in Coventry at the Judo.'

Jim sent me a text the same day, but I'd not seen him for some months and he'd sent it from a new number, so my phone didn't register his name when the message landed.

It read: 'Guy wants to talk to you about a programme on the ego. Can I give him your number? Jim.'

I looked at the message, confused, scratching my head: Guy? Jim? Who the F was Guy? Who the flip was Jim? What ego documentary?

I said to Sharon, *who do I know called Jim? Do we know anyone called Guy? I've just had a strange message, from a number I don't recognise, and it makes no sense to me.*

It was a few hours before it finally registered.

'Ah yes, Jim. Judo Jim, he trains with Guy Ritchie.'

I rang Jim. He passed on the message from Guy, asking if I'd be interested in featuring in his documentary. I spoke to Guy and asked if I could look at what they'd shot so far, to see if I had anything to contribute.

The first few episodes of the documentary were sent to me by one of Guy's assistants who told me that Guy had started making it some years before with Madonna, when they were together. When the marriage ended Guy carried on making the documentary as a passion project, investing his own money.

I watched the first three episodes and I thought it was amazing, it was seminal work. Many of my own heroes were already featured in the film, and whilst I was full of admiration for them all, I did agree with Guy; something was missing, an edge, and I knew that I could provide it.

What can be a convoluted subject matter sometimes needs to be translated into the vernacular of the everyday.

I had vast experience in my own life of how destructive the ego could be if it is left to its own devices. I'd damaged many people when my own ego bloated and controlled me like a puppeteer. I was also living proof that evil could be turned to the good, if the false ego was denounced and brought under the control of a higher authority.

There is a big difference between intellectual nouse about the ego, and actual working knowledge of its ways. The former is of little use to anyone if it does not come with the firing pin of practical modality. Information alone is impotent; it won't knock the skin off a rice pudding. If, however, the knowledge comes with a user manual, if it is assimilated, mastered and employed, it can offer life-changing capabilities.

I felt that I could make an empirical contribution, so, I got back in touch and said *yes please* and I thanked Guy for giving me such an esteemed platform.

I was already physically and mentally battered by this time. We were halfway through filming *Romans* and anyone that has ever made a feature film will attest to the fact that making a movie asks everything of you, everything, everything, everything. I arrived at Guy's beautiful home in central London the day after a heavy script session on *Romans*, where Orlando had scrutinised every point in every scene and on every page. What I had naively envisioned as a casual and leisurely read through, where we drank tea and exchanged ideas like bohemians, turned into twelve hours of metaphorical waterboarding. It was painful. I didn't want to be there. I just wanted to go home, and be with my wife, and see my kids, and walk across the green fields near my home and breathe in the free, free air, far away from the smoggy demands being inflicted on me by a whip cracking muse and the actor Orlando Bloom. It was tortuous, not because anyone was unkind, rather it was excruciating because, once again I was on the surgeon's table, and 'artists' were probing my innards with their very sharp editorial tools, looking for signs of residual disease. Orlando wanted to understand the minutia: of the story: of the character he was playing: of his motivation when he was violent: when he was afraid: when he self-abused. Why did he self-abuse? Was he pleasuring himself? Was he punishing himself? Was his a cry for help? Or was he merely possessed by the demon of abuse?

Yes Orlando, for fuck's sake Orlando, yes, yes, yes to all of the above.

Mr Bloom was rigour itself.

I'd only just finished a ninety hour preparation for the TED Talk, plus the two talks I eventually delivered (one botched, one complete), and on top of this, I was still teaching martial arts masterclasses, black belt courses and running the mail order book business with Sharon, and I was about to be offered the chance to work at the National Theatre.

It was close to Christmas by this time and I'd pre-booked a much-needed rest at Center Parcs. I was desperate for a break, but the holiday seemed like the carrot of metaphor: always within reach, ever beyond grasp. I felt overtly nervous the morning I arrived at Guy's house to play my part in his documentary. I was used to feeling nervous, I understood what nerves were. On approaching his door unexpected fears rose up in me, the ghosts of my past: *you are out of your league here; you are out of your depth; these people are heavyweights, they will rip your head off and shit down your neck; they'll see through you like a fucking x-ray; you'll look a fool; Guy is a behemoth of film, he is steeped in the Kabbalah, he was married to Madonna for fuck's sake, she's practically a demigod, he'll eat you alive; Sam Harris is on this film. Sam Harris! He's a Great White in the ocean of intellect, he'll scoff you up like a fish supper and spit out your bones...* and so it went on.

I watched it rise, the fear. I observed but I did not engage. I waited for a break in the bullshit-rhetoric.

'I'm doing it anyway.'

I entered. Guy was welcoming. His people were very kind. I could feel his immense presence from the director's chair, but I knew he wanted to help me present my best game. As soon as I walked into his house I said 'thank you for inviting me'. Then I shared with him that I was feeling nervous. As soon as I said this, I could feel a palpable ease in the room. Probably everyone was nervous, including Guy himself, and one person openly admitting it made everyone feel a little better.

I did my bit on screen. I spoke for two hours. Every opposing fear that had arisen in me was converted into energy and consumed by my delivery. Guy was meticulous in his work. I liked him a lot. I could see that he was born to be in the director's chair. This was a man firmly fixed in his dharma. And he knew exactly what he was looking for and what he wanted, and if I strayed too far from the brief, he quietly brought me back to the point.

Everyone seemed happy with my contribution.

Guy made me tea and jam on toast in his small-house-of-a-kitchen, we shook hands and I headed home.

Another fear overcome; another strong seed planted in fertile ground.*

But I was knackered. I had nothing left. I had no energy. I was dry bones, I was gone. I was spent, spent, spent. I had no capacity for even a single other project until… a spontaneous meeting in London with an actor friend called Nick set off the next buzz of divine direction; an offer that I could not refuse.

---

* At the time of writing, Guy's series on the ego hasn't yet been released.

The National Theatre Studio

Nick is a friend of mine. He was one of the actors who starred in Clubbed. It had been quite a while since I'd seen him, so when I randomly bumped into him outside my favourite café in Leicester square, it felt like a good opportunity for us to catch up. He is a jolly man, *funny bones* as they say, and he always had me laughing until I hurt.

I sat with Nick over a coffee, and we talked, mostly about what each of us had worked on since the last time we met. Our general conversation turned to the subtle, as they tend to do when you spend time with old friends, and we shared our fears and aspirations. Eventually and organically we slipped into the personal, and Nick's damaged past took centre stage. Or to be more specific: how his damaged past had left him impaired to that day. Nick is one of the many walking wounded I have encountered on my travels. Something about what he was saying in the retelling of his abuse, the rhythm, the beat, and the savage honesty of his revelations captured me. His parental abuse as a child had left him with a debilitating eating disorder. He was obese because he just couldn't stop eating. Nick told me that when he was a kid he craved the attention and love of his dad who was cold and emotionally unavailable. Then one day, more by fluke than skill, Nick scored a freak goal for the football team at school and his father, a former professional footballer, was so delighted that he took Nick to the local café, stood him on the table in a room full of hardy builders and said, 'This is my son Nick. He just scored a goal for the school team.' Everyone cheered and clapped. Then his dad shouted to the waitress 'give the lad anything he wants'. Nick tucked into the biggest cooked breakfast of his life.

This only ever happened once.

He never scored another goal for the school team, not one. And his dad never openly showed him affection again. Ever. This led Nick to a lifetime of searching for love through food.

As he spoke, I reached for my bag, looking for a writing pad. I always carry a pad. I write, it's what I do.

'Do you mind if I write some of this down Nick?' I asked, rummaging through my bag.

'No, fill your boots,' he said.

I could not find a pad. Desperate to write down what I was hearing, but not sure why, I approached the café waitress and asked if she had any paper I could use. She tore out about twenty sheets from her order pad and I sat back down. I looked at the note paper that the waitress had kindly given me. At the very top, printed in yellow on every page were the words Food Order.

I smiled at Nick, 'I'm going to write you a play called Food Order.'

I started to write everything my genial friend was saying on the scraps of paper. I filled twenty sheets with notes, quotes and ideas of where I might take the words once I got them home and placed them on a computer.

We shared badinage for a few more hours, him talking and me writing, then we parted ways. Nick promised to stay in touch, and I vowed to write him a play.

And I did try. I really did but… Nick's story was dark and challenging, just as *Fragile* and *Romans* had been. Every time I sat down to write out his notes, the words just would not come. After several failed attempts I decided to put the play on the back burner, which is code in my world for sacking it as a bad job, never looking at it again and blaming that blasted unreliable muse. Even if I did write it, I rationalised, I had no idea where I could put it on. It was such a challenging subject matter that even the theatres who pride themselves on staging 'dangerous' plays would probably not be interested, so I sat on it.

Then, a month or so later, out of the blue, Nick called.

'How's the writing going?'

'It's not,' I told him honestly.

I blamed the muse.

Nick agreed that *she was temperamental and that if she hasn't turned up, she hasn't turned up. What can you do?*

We all blamed the muse when laziness and idleness got in the way of creativity and work.

'Shame though,' he said, 'because my director friend Fi has got a week's slot to develop some work at the National Theatre and she's offered it to us.'

I wrote a rough draft of *Food Order* in a flurry of activity. It took me two days. I wrote it by hand, Sharon typed it out.

A week at the National. Paid. It was like an invitation to tea with the Queen. Every playwright in the country aspires to leave their footprint on the stage at the National

I was not excited just because it was the National. I was excited because God was doffing his hat at me again. Whether the play was eventually staged or not was genuinely of small significance, it was the divine signature that animated me. I was being given a peak into a room that very few writers ever get to see.

And, as it turned out, the divine message I was about to receive was nothing to do with the National Theatre per se. Only that the message needed an elevated platform, from which I could receive it. This Mecca of theatre was on the carpet of proximity. Being there would elevate me and from the peak of my own personal Mount Sinai I'd be able to see and hear the forthcoming communication.

The workshop was booked for a week, and I shared the space with Nick, Fi the director, her musician husband, Kirsten (a seasoned film actor) and Patrick, a veteran of the stage. I was not in charge. I must stipulate that this was not my gig. I was the writer on the team, and, in this case, the boss was definitely Fi.

She is a former elite dancer, and her way of working was both strange and affecting. It was based much more around movement and mood and Shamanic bonding exercises, than it was around learning lines and rehearing scenes. Some of the actors were nervous. They knew at the end of the week that they'd have to perform some of the work before the National Theatre staff, including the Artistic Director Rufus Norris. Not a comfortable ask if you haven't been told what lines to learn or scenes to rehearse. Patrick was a savvy old hack, he'd worked with Fi before, he must have anticipated what would unfold so he quietly learned the first ten pages off book. It was a wise move.

I can't speak for the other artists, but I can say that for me, Fi's eccentric method really worked. It brought out insecurities in me that I was not aware I had. I have a suspicion that the exalted nature of the National, and Fi's crazy shamanic hugging sessions primed me for what I was about to experience.

We were three days into the workshop when I was subjected to the moment of clarity.

Fi had all the actors working on movement exercises that she felt would complement the words in my script and it was a combination of the words, the movements and Patrick's superb acting that triggered the clarity.

He had memorised one of the longer monologues and in this particular scene his character tells the audience about a traumatic and confusing incident from his youth with his violent and depressed mother. In a moving attempt to understand her causeless cruelty, he relates it to a story he'd once heard, about a Jewish prisoner in a World War II Nazi death camp: a callous camp guard chomps on a juicy apple in front of a starving prisoner, whilst restraining a vicious Alsatian on a leash. When he has finished the apple, the guard throws the core onto the floor in front of the prisoner, implicitly and cruelly daring him to pick it up. As soon as the prisoner reaches out to take the core, the guard lets the dog loose and it devours what is left of the apple. The prisoner asks the guard sadly, 'Why?' The guard grins cruelly and replies, 'In this place there is no why'.

Fi had Patrick recite the monologue whilst very slowly, incredibly slowly, moving around the stage. The two other actors followed him, step by step, as though they were his living shadows. When he moved, they moved. When he stopped, they stopped. Almost as soon as Patrick began his recital, I felt the room fall away; he was all that existed, a spotlight in an otherwise black world. His was the only voice I could hear. Even I disappeared into the scene. The sound of Patrick's voice had an acoustic clarity. His eyes moved to the very front of their sockets and stared into the space with autonomy. At moments it was just Patrick's eyes in the room. At other moments it was just his voice, landing in my ears and mine alone; a private performance, just for me. It was incredibly moving. The words did not feel like mine. I was sure I could never have penned such a beautiful soliloquy, words like glowing pearls of sound linked together on a golden necklace of divine rhythm. I was high. I was inspired. I have seen some things in my life, but I have to say that this topped them all; it does not get any better than this. Surely I was not the only person witnessing this elation. I looked over at the director, she was crying.

Then I heard a voice. Not Patrick this time, but another voice, one that often spoke to me when divine commands were delivered.

The voice came from within.

'Get rid of everything now. Just do this.'

That was all it said, and I knew exactly what I was being called to do.

I'd had the most amazing week. You can't imagine how thrilling it is to spend five days travelling back and forth across the Thames each morning and night to spend a day with people in an advanced state of talent, all of them working on words that came from my pen. And in a large room at Festival Hall, the palladium of storytelling, it was like being back at Neil's international judo class again where every player was a British champion, a European medallist, a world number one or an Olympic squad member. How is it possible not to grow when you are planted in such nourishing soil?

At the National, I felt like I was home. I felt that this was me, this was where I was meant to be.

That evening as I walked across London Bridge, I stopped and took in the blaze of

London, shimmering in the night sky, mirrored on the rich baize of the Thames. I rang Sharon, 'We've got to sell everything', I said excitedly, 'I've had a message. We need to get rid of everything so that I can just write.'

She didn't even ask me for detail or explanation, she just said 'ok'.

She knew this was coming I guess, just as much as I knew it was coming. I'd been juggling twenty different balls for as many years, too many to keep in the air at the same time; martial arts, teaching, film-making, theatre, mentoring, the mail order business and book and article writing. Now I was being guided to remove everything but the writing. I was called to make space in my life so that I could sit down with my pen and my pad and dedicate myself to the words that would be directed to me. All other distractions had to go.

I was ready. Sharon was ready. We had both loved the past twenty years of prolific output, but we also knew that our hearts were no longer in much of the work we were doing. It was time to just write and it was intuited that if I emptied my life of everything but the writing, God would fill the vacuum.

This was the right decision, but it was a hard choice to take. It meant letting go of ninety percent of my current income which came from teaching martial arts and selling books and DVDs by mail order. I had three hungry properties, one in London and two in Coventry that needed a mortgage-feed every month. It was a high levy to meet, it demanded a lot of time and energy, and it often meant taking on work that my heart was not fully invested in anymore.

I was divinely instructed to get rid of these distractions and reduce my life to one of basic necessity.

My friend Barry, a mega businessman whom I'd been mentoring for some years, had pretty much underlined this in one of our later sessions, where, as is often the way in personal mentoring, the line between teacher and student becomes blurred and you wonder *who is guiding who here*. 'Why are you still here?' He asked me kindly, but bluntly, 'Why aren't you just writing?' Barry was challenging me to be as brave in my work as I was asking him to be in his own endeavours.

I was assured that if I followed God's command, my needs - roof, supper (a coffee?) means of transport - would be divinely provided.

Needs!

That is the operative word when you agree to a divine covenant. Your needs will be met, but this does not include first class travel on the train, expensive holidays in the Caribbean or ostentatious flings of fancy. He asks that you remove non-essentials from your life as part of the spiritual fast. There will be no divine annuity to cover the things you do not need.

On the divine path, money is a big distraction. I already knew this much. Making money and making art is an oxymoron. At some point, you have to choose which one is more important to you, because they do not make good bedfellows. It's a dichotomy that drives creatives to distraction; trying to maintain artistic integrity whilst at the same time keeping a roof over their heads and putting food on the table. Most artists either just get by or they facilitate their art with whatever work they can find until their art is able to facilitate them. More than a few are seduced by commercialism which is materially sating but creatively vacuous. It is no fun writing another episode of a popular soap when all you really want to do is write the next *Get Carter* or your very own version of *Saturday Night, Sunday Morning*.

When you are financially independent, you can be innovatively free, directed by the muse, not driven by the next pay cheque which provides neither joy nor real pleasure for the artist.

When you have innovative freedom, you can follow your intuition. Today you might be drawn to a spec job, something you create free for a friend; tomorrow it could be a £5K art piece that you'd personally pay to write because you love it so much. Next week it could be a £50m Netflix series where the crew are wiping their arses with banknotes. The point is this: money will not be the deciding factor. You will be directed by the muse and not by Mammon.

Idealistic you might say. Well, yes of course, and why not, heaven on earth is our ground of being, it has been vouchsafed for the human heart.

So, my plan was simple. Get rid of everything. Get rid of everything so that I didn't have to earn money anymore. Or certainly not as much money. This would allow me to write without disruption, distraction or restriction, I'd be free to write only the words I was directed to write, without any of the usual financial considerations.

We had an apartment in Islington that we had bought as a London bolthole which had allowed us to escape our cultural conditioning in Coventry and expand our perceptions.

As much as we loved the apartment, it had to go, everything had to go.

Where prices had serendipitously dropped to enable us to enter the London market five years before, they'd now mysteriously spiked at the very time we were ready to sell. The prices had risen by thirty five percent in five years. This profit left us enough to pay the estate agent, meet the capital gains bill, completely pay off the mortgage on my mum's house and leave enough cashflow in the bank to cover me for the two year sabbatical I was planning to take after the sale had been completed.

Temptations besieged us all along the way. We were advised by a consultant to flip the flat and pretend it was our main residence to save us tens of thousands of pounds in capital gains. But this would mean we'd have to lie which was an affront to my newly situated soul. We paid the tax and gratefully so. We were also tempted, once the funds had landed in our account to keep them there rather than pay off the mortgage on my mum's place. This too was not part of my divine plan, which was to be mortgage free so that I could write without the distraction of having to make money. We looked at the large wad of cash in the account and smiled, and then we transferred it across to pay off her house. The feeling was absolutely freeing.

This enabled me to stop teaching, to stop the mail order business and just sit down and write.

Each time I reduced, another reduction presented itself, then another. After we closed the mail order company, I realised that my three websites had to go too. There was no need for them anymore. They were taking up a lot of our time and resources and - because we'd effectively stopped selling directly to the public - the sites were effectively redundant. The most heart-breaking aspect of this was having to ring my son, who we'd employed to maintain our online presence, and tell him *we don't need you to run the sites for us anymore.* It was one of the hardest phone calls I have ever made. Not only would he miss the monthly income, which supplemented his full-time job in marketing, it would also effectively sever the daily intimacy we both enjoyed. Even though he was upset (he later confessed that he cried after my call) he still encouraged me: 'This is something you were always meant to do,' he said, 'I admire you for doing it.'

His selfless response is a credit to his character.

I closed my Facebook page. I closed my Twitter account. I said to my son, 'How do I close down my social media?' He said, 'I don't know, no-one's ever done it before.'

As it turned out, it was easy enough. If you don't offer a thing your emotional engagement, eventually it must atrophy.

The next phone call was as hard as calling my son and I put it off for weeks. I had to ring my longtime friend and business partner Peter Consterdine at the British Combat Association and tell him that I was stepping down as joint chief instructor. No more association meant no more courses together.

Peter and I had run courses for over twenty years, and we both loved every minute of it. I'd been gradually withdrawing from the association since my Vegas epiphany, but I had never made it official. I just couldn't bring myself to. Peter didn't want me to leave either. We were very tight me and the old fella (as I teasingly called him), I loved him, and I knew that my change in direction would be uncomfortable for us both.

I could hear his sadness on the phone even though he fully supported my decision and wished me well.

No more teaching with my friend Peter Consterdine.

It was a heart dulling day.

I had gotten rid of everything. I had fasted so hard there was a fear I would become socially emaciated.

We had sold hundreds of thousands of books over the years, and taught prolifically, countrywide and beyond, so of course you gather a strong and loyal following. I made a polite and respectful announcement on my sites and on social media (before I closed them down) that I was taking a sabbatical, I would not be contactable for the foreseeable future. I left all my hundreds of motivational video podcasts and articles online free for people to access.

I asked that people respect my wishes to be left alone for a while.

People were generally kind. I was grateful. Some thought I might be depressed. I was not. One or two assumed I must be critically ill or dying (because no-one comes off social media unless they are ill or dying, right?) or that I'd had a breakdown (breakdown, breakthrough, same thing), or simply that I was out of my fucking mind.

Hello! I went out of my fucking mind years ago when I swapped the minimum wage for the life of a buccaneer!

Yes, my friends, that ship sailed a long time ago.

For there to be a new me - and I was patently aware that a new me had risen - of course, I had to let go of all connection with the old me. I changed my email address. I got myself a new phone number. These were very difficult things to do. I felt somehow that I was betraying the past by severing myself from it. But I realised that I was not severing anything that was still living, I was simply cutting away the dead flesh.

I went through my contact numbers and email addresses and thinned them out until all I was left with was a small scattering of vital connections. Some of the people on my contacts list had been there since I was a bouncer and I never heard from most of them anymore. Others were on my list simply because I had been too lazy or too scared (of judgement) to take them off.

Man, I have never felt so free.

So much of the energy I had been consuming on dead things, disconnected names and redundant associations was returned to me so that I could drive it all in one direction and one direction only: God.

I know I said that my one direction was writing. I know I said that, but this had clarified itself now and I knew that the writing was just my living bridge to God. I had a Christ element, and I connected with it through the hand and the ink.

Even though you ask for privacy and even though you announce that you are taking a sabbatical, and you request that people please respect your space, some folk just don't know how to stop *fucking asking*. I received so many messages and calls that were precipitated with, *I know you are taking a sabbatical but: I know you are taking some time out but: I understand you have asked for some privacy but:* which would be followed by requests to send a free book, supply a testimony, proffer personal advice, deliver a course, take a private lesson, meet for a coffee, shoot the breeze, or open a fete. One of the hardest lessons I learned during this sabbatical was how hard it is to say no, and how angry it made me, not at the people asking, but at myself for the inability to say 'sorry, but it's a no from me'. But I had to and I did, and although I know many people associated with my old life did not understand, I didn't mind that they didn't understand.

I had been a people pleaser in one form or another for most of my life, and in order to kill this dead, I had to disregard what others thought of me. I quickly developed a tolerance and a compassion for their inability to understand why I was saying no, no and no again. The ability to accommodate their confusion came by virtue of the fact that I understood their position and didn't judge them for it.

At the time, I had a couple of serious Uchi-deshi (long term students) that I kept with me; people I'd been mentoring for a long period of time. One of them, a superbly successful man of business said to me, 'I don't understand fully what it is you're doing. You are either insane or you are on to something seminal. I want to be around to find out which'.

I was now officially empty. I was a vacuum, ready and open to receive the next level of divine infusion and instruction. It came in droves. Now that I was free to dedicate myself just to writing, I was able to produce at a prolific rate. Not only was I writing, but I was specifically writing works of a spiritual nature. In the following three years I wrote a book called *The Caretaker*, a metaphysical parable about the power of selfless service, a beautiful ninety-eight minute monologue (that I wrote for the actor James Cosmo) that we made into an acclaimed movie (with the Shammasian brothers at the helm). I finessed a script within an inch of its life for a £3million feature film called *Animal Day*. We had a Hollywood lead, the finance was in place, and we are due to start filming imminently. I also wrote an award-winning film called *Three Sacks Full of Hats*, starring Alison Steadman; a musical for the theatre with singer/songwriter Tom Clarke, called *We'll Live and Die in These Towns* (produced in 2019 at the Belgrade Theatre Coventry) and two books: this one, and an esoteric book called *The Divine CEO* (published by Zero Books in July 2020).

The works came naturally; I just sat down and put them to the page. This book and *CEO* came to me so fast that I literally couldn't get them to the paper quickly enough. I wrote the first drafts - 300,000 words in all, 150,000 words for each text - in less than six weeks. The day I finished the handwritten version of this book, the idea for *The Divine CEO* came to me. I said to Sharon, 'I'm going to have the weekend off and start CEO on Monday.' I finished Notes and went for a celebratory walk in my local park. During the next hour, twenty chapter headings for *CEO* downloaded into my head so urgently that I had to write them in emails and send them to myself, before they were lost.

Now that I had dedicated myself to intercessionary writing (writing that acts as a divine intercessor for those who read or watch them) the works came to me unbidden.

For instance, when *The Pyramid Texts* landed in my intuitive inbox, it had no title. It was just a rudimentary tale about an old boxer sending a video message of lament to his estranged son. I realised, after we shot the film that it was much more than that: it was a powerful discourse on fear.

The film was so unusual and unique - one actor, one location, shot in dedicated black and white - that the producers we approached to help us make it, pretty much laughed us out of the room. Even after we got a cinema release, even after James Cosmo won best actor at the Edinburgh International Film Festival and we were nominated for best feature film, one producer still scoffed that 'it's not even a film'.

It so defied categorisation that producers didn't know how to look at it, but the audience acclaim was universal.

After the first public screening I was shown the meaning of the film at a deeper level again. Michael Palin (who called the film *a small masterpiece*) emailed me after watching the film, with an enquiry: '*What **are** Pyramid Texts*'? It was a reasonable question. It was probably confusing to many people because the arc of the film covered the life and losses of a boxing stalwart, what the heck has that got to do with Egypt and pyramids? I found myself meeting Michael's enquiry with an answer that I didn't know myself until the question was asked. This is what I found myself telling him: 'although superficially the film is about love, loss and fear, at the deeper level it is about the human body as a living sarcophagus, where the sins of our past and the trapped souls of our ancestors are suspended in a fleshy bardo. The inspirations and aspirations, the songs and the stories that we put into our body, help those dead ancestors transcend their purgatory, and ascend to the afterlife beyond.'

Before I wrote the film, I'd never even heard of the Pyramid Texts, which is the Egyptian version of the Tibetan Book of the Dead, and offered instruction in negotiating the afterlife. Now I not only knew of them, but I knew how to translate them to the existential world.

The twenty minute short film *Three Sacks Full of Hats* directed by the beautiful Debbie Anzalone, is about the death of my brother Ray (who I mentioned earlier) from alcoholism, and it stars Alison Steadman. The film looks like a piece of art. Again, at first glance you might think that *Three Sacks* is a story about drink, and the caustic family dynamics in and around the excess of drink. To me it was not even a film, it was a prayer to my brother, it was a prayer to my mum and dad. I was using the writing to help them process a death that none of them were strong enough to look at, let alone clean. Carl Jung said that we can never really get away from the fact that we are always going to be dealing with the dead. *Three Sacks* was my way of helping those who could not help themselves to deal with the loss of loved ones. We help our trapped ancestors to ascend when we process their sin through our song. At the time of writing this book the film has already won a bevy of international short film awards,

The musical I wrote was another gift that just fell out of the sky and hit me on the head. It came to me fully formed, and stage-ready. But only because I'd reduced everything else in my life to accommodate it, only because I had created room. I made myself available. I was training in my gym one day, listening to The Enemy's million selling album, *We'll Live and Die in These Towns*, and the idea to write a musical based around the eleven songs fell into my head as easy as a letter through the door. *A complete musical.* I'd never written a musical in my life, but here I was, contacting the artistic director of the Belgrade Theatre, Coventry (Hamish Glen), and asking, 'Do you want to commission me to write a musical, based on the songs of The Enemy?'

Coventry band, Coventry writer, Coventry theatre, how could he say no?

After a twenty minute meeting with Hamish, I was commissioned and the play was on.

And the combinations, the couplings were so profound, so aligned: *The Pyramid Texts* is a boxing film with a subtext about soul individuation. *Three Sacks* is a film about addiction, intertwined with familial cleansing. And *We'll Live and*

Die in These Towns? I was directed to marry this Rock/Punk masterpiece with a contemporary version of Arjuna Pandava's ancient battle with perception in the Vedic classic, The Bhagavad Gita.

I was (I still am) amazed at what was coming out.

But... but, but, but, although the ideas were strong, and the words acclaimed, the money was slow. Man the money was slow. I'd practically stopped earning at this point, all I did was write. The profit from the sale of our London apartment was all but spent, and I had reduced my earnings to a minimum. The faith that enough money to pay the small mortgage remaining on our home and meet our everyday bills was testing for both Sharon and me.

Theatre pays, but not much, it is not lucrative. And film never pays at all until it absolutely has to, unless you put a gun to its head and say *pay you fuckers, pay!* I was not working for the money. I was working for God. And He pays, of course he does, of course, He always delivers. But He is the master of exactitude; what you need (and not what you want, there is a difference) will arrive when you need it, not a moment too soon, not a minute too late. It usually arrives at the eleventh hour, and often from an unexpected source. It does come, but there is no room here for planning or for external security, there is only room for faith. So much of my writing was speculative. I could spend years developing a film only to see it collapse (before anyone gets paid) because the talent pulls out or a financier gets windy or the Chicken Licken sales forecasters think it doesn't tick enough boxes or doesn't have a 'trailer moment' or 'doesn't fit into a genre'.

We had been earning a lot of money for a lot of years and now suddenly we were not earning very much at all.

Listen, I had more money in equity on my two houses than you could shake a stick at, so I was not going to starve anytime soon, but equity (as lovely as it is) is not cash money in your pocket, it is not fluid coin, you can't pull it out of your pocket when you want to buy a Costa coffee or when you need to book a last minute train to London. I couldn't draw down on equity without incurring bigger monthly bills, and this would fly in the face of my instruction to *reduce*. I could sell my home if this was ordained, buy somewhere smaller, use the profit as living capital. I was considering this, but I was not sure if it was a divine instruction, or if I was just being windy, and selling up because it was more comfortable than waiting for God to *show me the money*.

When money is tight, the testing always threatens the same things: *the film money that you've been promised won't come, it's a fantasy: it's a carrot; you will never make money; you'll go broke; it'll be embarrassing; you'll lose your home; no one rates your work that's why they don't pay you; they are patronising you; you are being taken for a mug; you are not good enough to make it as a writer.*

That's pretty much the gist of it.

When all is said and done, the false ego, still hanging around, still looking to dine out on your doubt, uses the same fear tactics again and again and again. But, as I have made mention, the ego lies, fear lies. And anyway, I told myself, I was on top of it. I don't care about money. I know how to make the money shape in a million different ways if I need to, and besides, our feature film *Animal Day* had been given the green light. We would be shooting in a few weeks. I'd receive a large principle photography payment that would guarantee me enough $ to live off for years to come. *Animal Day* was sure fire. We'd worked our nuts off for five years. All of us. We had earned this, we deserved this, it was due us, I'd read the email from our Hollywood producer, 'congratulations boys, you are green lit' - nothing could stop it from going into production. **Boom!**

Our lead actor on *Animal Day* pulled out.

Three weeks before the shoot he pulled out. No explanation, no apology, just a piss-poor email and an impolite au revoir. I wobbled. Doubt, confusion; not doubt at God or confusion with God, but doubt with myself, confusion about my path. Had I read this all wrong? Had I misread the signs? Was this my true path after all or had I been led astray, tempted onto a bleak and soulless path. The money due to us for *Animal Day* was the equivalent of five years pay and it would have kept us going so I could write without any financial constraints. The film, minus its lead actor, collapsed. If it was ever to be made, it would not be for at least another year, if at all. I had lots of other projects with amazing talent attached that promised a lucrative wage but, similarly, they too fell away just as we were about to be paid. When we sold the flat it had left us enough cash to pay the bills for two years without me having to find alternative means of work. Finding the work was not the problem, personal mentoring paid very handsomely. Martial arts courses could earn me a good wedge. The demand was there, the access was easy but… it would be a bank raid, and this was not the vision I had received at the National Theatre, this was not the very clear direction I had been given.

And, if you keep going back, you stop moving forward.

Spiritual kenosis is about self-emptying, not half-emptying or part-emptying or *keeping a bit back, just in case*. It is about creating a vacuum and having faith that the hole you created will be filled. But the money was still not forthcoming and I found myself *in my mind's eye* trying to explain to Sharon that 'it will all work out, all will be well', but I felt like a phoney debtor saying for the umpteenth time, 'the cheque is in the post'.

My main concern was not about the money per se, but the lack of money coming in did trigger a doubt about my whole dharma. I suddenly became susceptible to the inner opponent and the adverse forces. Their spurious arguments were breaking through even though there was little evidence to back their claim. The proof that I had found my true path was all around me in the work I was producing, and the joy that it brought, but the money-doubt hid that from view and I was thrown into a temporary tailspin.

Suddenly I was back in that place again, a spit of rain was a potential flood, a candle flame was a coming inferno, here was better than there and there was better than here and somewhere, anywhere was better than where I was right now.

I felt a hysterical anger rise up in me fuelled by self-pity and childish complaint, 'fuck it. I've done my bit. If You are not going to play your part...'

I stopped myself in the very first spill of vitriol.

Let me tell you, with certainty, that whenever a voice rises in you and suggests that God is not playing His part, you know that it is not the voice of reason or rationality, it is the voice of deviance. When it comes to certainty I am clear beyond question that if there is anyone who does not play his part, it is not God, the accusation cannot be laid at His feet, any more than we can accuse the sun of not shining just because it is temporarily obscured by clouds. God always plays his part. It was just that at this moment, I couldn't clearly discern what part that was or why our film had collapsed and our money lost because of one email.

I fell into a two day melancholy. I asked my mum, 'Am I in the right place mum? Is this where God wants me to be?' My mum suddenly looked very old and sad, she looked as though she might cry. 'Don't you worry son,' she said, 'if you are not in the right place, you'll know soon enough. God will tell you.'

When I went home I meditated. I spoke to God. I asked him, 'Is this where you want me? Am I in the right place? If I'm not, please let me know because I will drop film, I'll drop theatre, I will drop everything if I think for even a second that this is not Your will. All I want to do is serve You.'

I was sincere. I was certain. All I willed was His will.

The answer would come to me a week later.

At this exact time our musical *We'll Live and Die in These Towns* was three months away from being staged. I was actually doing a press conference for it in Coventry when I received the bad news about *Animal Day*. A three day casting was being held in London the next week and the director had kindly asked me to join him.

I was invited to London, but the Belgrade could not afford to put me up in a hotel while I was there. They are a repertory company, they also operate as a charity, so, like all regional theatres, they struggle for funding. I understood this, but I was also aware that the casting sessions would run late into the evening - they always do - so commuting back and forth from Coventry was not tenable. I needed to stay over, but money was very tight, so I did the only thing I could think of with such short notice: I sold a picture that was hanging on my office wall to cover the costs. It was a Lowry print, gifted to me by a gorgeous friend. I hoped and prayed he would understand, that he would not mind. I booked the hotel for four nights and I headed south. I felt embarrassed that I'd had to sell something from my home to buy a hotel bed. I felt a surge of shame rising up in me, I felt like a failure, and that saddened me. I felt cheap. I wandered what my friends might think of my situation, how my family would react knowing that I had no cash-money, how the world at large would judge this outwardly successful man, for having to sell personal items to pay for room and board. I worried too about what my wife thought. I worried about Sharon more than I worried about my own life. She did not understand God in the way I did. Although she backed my every crazy-arse move, even when she didn't understand what this crazy-arse-fool was doing, I knew she quietly feared that my God might be a fraud, or my clarity a trick of the mind. I knew too that she was confused as to why an almighty Omnipotent could not supply a few quid to fund a project that He had apparently ordained. I pondered over all these considerations for about five seconds and then concluded that I did not give too much of a fuck about what any of them thought. I love them all, but I only cared what God thought.

Water the roots, I was told in my prayer, and the whole plant will be sated.

If the previous few weeks had been testing to the point of frustrated despair, the next three days were to contain some of the best moments of my life.

First of all, just to kick it off, I spent three days with the singer/songwriter Tom Clarke. That on its own was worth a kingdom. I'd been listening to Enemy music for over a decade. Their debut album, *We'll live and Die in These Towns* was the soundtrack to thousands of hours spent training in my gym at home. I loved their sound. I adored and admired the cool and abandoned delivery of Tom's songs. He emptied himself on every track, his lyrics were in the pantheon of the song writing gods, and now, here I was sat with my all-time favourite artist (of all time). If I sound like a raving fan it's because I am. I didn't know he was going to be at the casting. At the time he was in the middle of a solo tour so I presumed he might be otherwise engaged. Tom had been hired as musical director on the play, so Hamish felt it important to have him there. I couldn't have been happier.

Tom's presence was the first of my many inspirations.

The second inspiration came from watching Hamish Glen at work. He is a swear-a-second, lumpy Glaswegian, who enjoys a dram, and likes a smoke, and doesn't mind telling you to *fuck off* if you offend his sensibilities. I'd never worked directly with him before, so I was more than pleasantly surprised to find that he was gentle in his work, he was careful and patient and capable of the most subtle, often left of field, genius. I watched the actors blossom under his quiet direction. I learned so much from just being in his company. I discerned a wealth from watching how he measured *not just the performance and performer*, but how the performance and performer might fit into a company, and how that collective aesthetic would work when they occupied a stage together. I observed how he covertly tested the actor's ability to take direction in the audition room, and how it automatically informed him about how well they would take instruction in a rehearsal space. If they were difficult and unresponsive in a fifteen-minute audition, how painful would it be to work with them for eight weeks? And those that came unprepared for the audition were given short thrift, they were automatically crossed off the *potential* list. If you can't prepare for an audition, why would you expect someone to trust you with a professional contract? One or two of the older performers were also curmudgeonly and seemed irritated, even offended, when the director asked for a little expansion on their history, or some detail of their experience or age, as though the performance in the room should be all that mattered. You could be the best performer in the world and not get the job because, frankly, no artist wants to spend any length of time with an uncomfortable energy. You learn from hard experience that it only takes one bad apple to stink out a whole company.

I was also hugely invigorated by my three-day London ritual: waking up in the hotel, next to my girl (Sharon came with me), wandering into Covent Garden for an early breakfast, riding the London Underground across town, finding an independent café close to the rehearsal space, sitting outside with a coffee watching the world catwalk by, a day of inspirational auditions, an early evening hour in a trendy pub, across-the-table discussions about the performance highlights of the day, excitedly collating a call-back list, back on the tube into London central, sharing a simple meal in a West End eatery with Sharon, a Thames-side stroll, digesting and processing the day, talking, talking, talking, celebrating how great it is to be alive, the call of the hotel pillow, lying in bed pondering the gifts that the morrow might bring.

Then there were the auditions themselves, organised by the best girl in theatre land, Debbie O'Brien. She'd arranged three full days, packed from morn-till-night with talent. Every fifteen minutes a new actor performed for us; hopeful talent, inspirational talent, awe-inspiring talent, all aspiring to play a part in our musical.

I had asked God the week before 'am I in the right place?' and every fifteen minutes for three days he replied **yes, yes, yes**.

Perhaps it was just my emotional state at the time - stretched, tested, tired - or maybe it was because I was in my favourite city surrounded by my favourite people doing my favourite things, I don't know, all I know is that, every fifteen minutes for the next three days I knew exactly where God wanted me to be. It was here, telling stories with truth, and exchanging energy with people of the same ilk. I was in the right place, this was my true path, definitely and unequivocally, and if I had to sell my arsehole on EBay in order to facilitate it, I was prepared to do so. The money was secondary. And if there was a lack of money, it was only because I was not exercising the one thing that allows the money-energy to flow: faith.

It's surprising how little money you actually need when you reduce your life to the bare necessities. If you divest yourself of the worthless and cumbersome robes of accumulation, you'd be inspired by how free, how light and how happy you are. It is exhilarating. It is liberating.

All possessions possess us the moment we feel we must have them.

I wrote a bestselling book that became a short film and a stage play and a feature film and a thousand more splendid things from a toilet space in an engineering factory.

Be in no doubt, you need very little to create.

One thing I am very certain of is this: if you are surrounded by luxurious 'ends', finding the means to maintain those ends is often so taxing that it leaves very little of the true artist left.

The joy I felt every time one of these amazing talents auditioned for us is hard to articulate. The very first girl that auditioned (Meg Forgan - she eventually got the part) in the very first fifteen minutes on the very first day of casting wiped me out. She had not even finished acting school yet. She still had two days left before she matriculated into the world of theatre proper, and she had travelled to London from Glasgow to try and win her first role. She was talented, she was cool, she was quirky and beautiful, and her charisma filled the space. My immediate reaction, after she left the room was an astonished, 'fucking hell'.

She was only the first of many.

It went on like this for three solid days. The talents, ranging from eighteen-year-old first-timers, to seventy-year-old veterans, were so raw that they appeared before us as though spiritually naked. That's how it felt to me, and I was overwhelmed. They were completely and utterly abandoned to the song. I felt the strangest connection with each act, a powerful certainty that told me I was privileged, very uniquely honoured to be in a room exchanging energy with these people. Many of them (I was sure) would go on to perform on stages all around the world, telling stories and singing songs that are the narratives of our lives; people live and die on these contemporary parables delivered by the shamans of our day.

I heard an actor say once, thoughtlessly, self-deprecatingly, 'look, what we do is not brain surgery, we are not saving lives here, we're just providing some light entertainment'.

I have not found this to be true.

It is a pretentious conceit recited by artists who are afraid to admit their worth.

If I thought that light entertainment was all we were providing, I wouldn't write another line. It would not be worth the manna in my pen.

Go and sit in the West End of London and watch *Les Miséerables* and tell me afterwards if you think it is just light entertainment. One of my biggest epiphanies came after spending an afternoon in the company of this performance. I went there, if I am being honest, just to research musicals before writing my own. I was prejudiced towards the jazz-hands, break-into-song-at-the-least-provocation type theatrical. I thought I didn't like it. I bought tickets for Les Mis fully expecting my biased views to be vindicated by the time we reached the interval, so I could wander back to my Leicester Square coffee shop, call Sharon and say smugly, 'yeah, just as I thought, I don't like that kind of musical'. I arrogantly imagined that I would write something *like Les Mis, but better* (the arrogance!) more real, something raw and street, a musical for the people, a play where the songs were naturally occurring and you wouldn't be reaching for the sick bag every time some yodeller walked centre stage, stared into the middle distance and sang some trite biscuit tin ballad about the bonny glens of Scotland, or the green, green hills of Loch Morn.

After the last act of Les Mis I was so emotional that I had to practically sprint from the theatre so that I didn't fall apart in the stalls and embarrass foreign tourists. I found myself a corner by the back of the theatre, literally turned my face to the wall so that none of the thousands of passing eyes could see me and I rang Sharon.

'How was it?' she asked.

I opened my mouth but I could not speak.

I never stopped crying for a full ten minutes.

How was it?!

I felt ashamed that this play had been on in London for twenty years and I'd never seen it before because of an unchallenged bias. It was so beautiful and clever and so utterly inspiring that I trembled at the thought of even attempting to write a musical of my own. It was so enthralling and comprehensive and so captivating that I knew in that moment *I absolutely knew* that theatre was potentate in the world of storytelling. It was so visceral that all other forms must surely bow at its feet in reverence. This was the concentrate, and all other genres were mere dilutions by comparison.

Back at the auditions for my own musical, every fifteen minutes for three days I was shown the rich potential I had, we all have, to intercourse at the highest possible level, and exchange energy in its purest form with every other human on the planet. Not just every other human, but every conscious cell in every animate and inanimate thing.

I felt it in concentrate at the auditions and I felt its potential in the world.

This divine intercourse was real, in the sense that it was **real** real. And *intercourse is* the appropriate term because it was a fully immersed, unconditional marriage of energies. Without wanting in any way to reduce this to crudity, I felt as though I was in spiritual intercourse with every person in that room, one at a time, and all at once. It was an intimacy that did not need physical consummation, neither verbal, nor tactile, nor emotional. Here though, I knew that this deiform-intercourse could be shared with anyone, anywhere and at any time. It could be exchanged between complete strangers, platonic friends, long term partners and passionate lovers, or even with a passing acquaintance. It did not need to be announced, only experienced. You could make the exchange with the most aesthetically beautiful man or woman in the world and experience divine intimacy, but equally you could connect with a rough sleeper on Oxford Circus and experience exactly the same level of spiritual union.

I was shown that this is our inheritance; this was the esoteric, it is what was meant by *the Kingdom of Heaven as it is on earth*, it was the Holy Grail of myth and it was available to everyone now, if they wanted it.

All of the nine actors that we fell in love with at the London casting were offered a role in our forthcoming musical, and they all accepted. We had gathered an exceptional company, and for five weeks we shared a rehearsal space at the Belgrade Theatre in Coventry. It proved to be one of the best experiences of my life. Hamish asked me to work with the company for the full rehearsal period, on accents, on script nuances and with anything else that the actors needed clarity on. Every day I got to sit in a room and watch nine brilliant actors work with a bevy of amazing creatives to bring together a two hour show featuring eleven of my favourite rock songs. Every single day in the rehearsal space, I worked with the most beautiful people, and I made lifelong friends. Sitting within touching distance of Tom Clarke as he played my favourite songs acapella was beyond unusual, it was a gift. I was like a private audience of one. Watching the cast - Tom Milner, Andy Burse, Meg Forgan, Adam Sopp, Quinn Patrick, Molly Grace Cutler, Steven Serlin, Julie Mullins and Mark Turnbull – bring to life the characters on my page was so moving that there were tears in rehearsals every day.

God was in the room. I am certain.

When you watch a play unfold, realise how many heads have to be in concert for it to work, witness the stress, the fear and the doubts that the talent has to negotiate before they even take their first step onto the stage proper, behold the hundreds of people on their feet in nightly ovation, lost in the song, rapt by the performance, you realise that this only exists because you placed some words on a page, and it makes you humble to your bones, it spins you dizzy with gratitude, and it leaves you wide-eyed with wonder.

After the final bow, beyond the last curtain call, when the crowds had left and the theatre was dark, I sat alone in the stalls, up in the gods, staring at a three dimensional set that once lived on a two dimensional page, and two things come immediately to mind:

'We had **made** a musical.'

And...

'How the F did we do that!'

Before the casting session in London I had suffered doubt.

It happens.

Even the prophets and the saints occasionally fall.

I asked God for clarity: 'Is this where you want me?'

He answered my prayer with a stilling certainty that abides in me today still. It is with me here, now, in my office in my home in Coventry where I write the word and I live the life. It has not left me. I trust that there will always be moments of doubt. But I also trust that doubt is evanescent, and the mist will be cleared, if I only call for clarity.

NOTES FROM A FACTORY FLOOR

A Memoir

Afterword

This brings me up to date on my journey thus far.

From my first book *Watch My Back* to the present time.

This brings me to now.

The feature film, *Animal Day*, that collapsed has been resurrected and new enthusiasm around it abounds. I trust that it if it is God's will it'll complete its arc, and if it's not God's will I am happy to let it fade away.

Our short film *Three Sacks Full of Hats* is currently enjoying a busy and acclaimed multi-award winning festival life, and spreading seeds of connection internationally. I have just started a new adventure with the film director Jason Connery, who has optioned and will direct another of my features; watch this space. My book *The Divine CEO* has also been contracted and is in the editing process with a lovely publishing house called Zero Books. It will be available in the shops early 2020. And there are many more ideas and projects that are landing at my Heathrow, taxiing down the runway, or taking off to destinations unknown. So many, too many to talk about here.

Perhaps later, in another book, or a film or a play. Or, God willing, maybe you and I will chat in person one day.

So... how did I manoeuvre myself from a shitty bedsit to the hallowed halls of BAFTA, Piccadilly?

How did I matriculate into a reality where class holds no relevance?

And what happened along the way to the snotty comprehensive kid, tethered at the ankle to the ball-and-chain of social mores?

These are my field notes.

Here lie the essential lessons of my pilgrimage so far, the essence of my hero's journey.

I hope you enjoyed the reading and I pray that I have answered some of those questions.

May your God bless you.

Geoff Thompson, December, 2019 Coventry, England.

NOTES FROM A FACTORY FLOOR

A Memoir

NOTES FROM A FACTORY FLOOR

Acknowledgements

A thousand thanks to Matthew and Kerry-Jane and all at Urbane for publishing this book so beautifully, for their patient and skillful and very sensitive editing; and for having faith in me.

Thank you to the creative genius Paul Shammasian for the wonderful cover design, and for directing the promotional films for Notes.

Thank you to my beautiful friends Mike Morris and Andy Clarke for their unending generosity and faith in me, and for kindly funding and making possible all the promotional films for Notes.

Heartfelt gratitude to my wife Sharon for the months she patiently spent in typing this book from the original (sometimes illegible) hand-written note pads.

Thank you to all the people, mentioned in this book or not, who have taken part in the story of my life thus far.

Until the age of thirty Geoff Thompson worked in a plethora of menial jobs, from glass collector to floor sweeper; he even spent a decade working as a nightclub bouncer.

Convinced that there must be more to life than this, he decided to become a professional martial arts instructor (polled by Black Belt magazine USA as the most influential martial artist in the world since Bruce Lee) then followed this by living out his dream of becoming a full time writer. His first book (Watch My Back) made it on to the Sunday Times Best Sellers list and was developed into a BIFFA Nominated feature film for cinema (Clubbed). Geoff went onto to author over forty books, some of which have been translated into 21 languages. He has written many multi-award-winning films (2 BAFTA nominations, one BAFTA win), stage plays (he was invited into the prestigious Royal Court Young Writers Group) and in 2019 saw his first musical, We'll Live and Die in these Towns, staged to acclaim at the Belgrade Theatre Coventry. He has also published hundreds of articles in national magazines and newspapers, including The Times.

Geoff's 3rd feature film for cinema, Romans, stars Orlando Bloom and Anne Reid. It was nominated for Best Feature Film at the Edinburgh International Film Festival and won best Actor (for Anne Reid) at the same event.

Find Geoff on Instagram
#geoff_thompson_official